Additional Praise for *Content Marketing for Nonprofits*

Kivi helps leaders think clearly and strategically about nonprofit communications as a whole, telling the organization's story with a consistent voice and message, and being intentional about the goals of communications and marketing. Kivi's work is applicable to nonprofits of all sizes, urban and rural. Her methods and guidance ~~~~~~~~ straight-forward, and can be readily implemented by an organiza~~~~~~~~~~~~~~~~~~~~.

—**Suzanne Wilcox** ~~~~~~~~~~~~~~~~~~~~~~~~~~~~~ 'rector,
~~~~~~ ation

Marketing has changed. Interrupting people with ad ~~~~~~~~~~~~~~~, or sending direct mail doesn't work like it used to. Now, you have to ~~~~~ people's attention, earn their trust, and be invited into their lives all while competing against countless other entities vying for their attention. Great content matters more now than it ever has before. Kivi has put together a comprehensive guide for those new to marketing as well as seasoned veterans that will help you successfully reach your constituents and future supporters through great content. Pay attention to what Kivi has to say. You'll be a better marketer for it!

—**Frank Barry, director of digital marketing, Blackbaud**

Content marketing is a brand-new world for the nonprofit sector, which traditionally has relied on *target marketing* for communicating with its donors and other supporters and would-be supporters. Brand-new worlds can often be scary, especially if you try to go it alone. In authoring this book, Kivi has offered herself up as your intrepid guide. Whether your organization is young and wiry, or steadfastly entrenched in the "but we've always done it this way" sand trap, she talks—and walks—you through this new and vital approach to nonprofit communications. Her clean writing and authoritative-but-accessible style pull it all together in a way that feels like sipping tea and talking shop with a savvy friend and colleague.

—**Margaret Battistelli Gardner, editor-in-chief, *FundRaising Success* magazine**

Kivi's fabulous book is a must-read for fundraisers! We all know that fundraising has changed. And our donor communications strategies must keep evolving, too. Successful fundraisers have got to master this new art of continued, interesting communications to our donors. We have so many new ways to keep in touch with them—but what to do and how to do it? What to say? Thank goodness for this book because Kivi gives us the answers. She shares a clear blueprint for keeping our donors informed, interested, connected, and most of all—happy with us. If we follow her recipe, then we will be rewarded with the holy grail of fundraising—long-term sustainable gifts and contributions that you can count on year after year. Thank you, Kivi!

—**Gail Perry, author of** *Fired-Up Fundraising: Turn Board Passion into Action*

The web changed the way all of us find, review, use, and share content. This book is a critical piece for all organizations looking to create content that appeals to the community, generates the kind of attention and brand awareness that nonprofits need, and ultimately supports conversion of readers to supporters and donors. Every nonprofit communications, marketing, and online engagement staffer should have this book!

—**Amy Sample Ward, coauthor of** *Social Change Anytime Everywhere*

Content marketing is a jungle full of tigers, snakes, and slimy little creatures that want to suck your blood. Content marketing is also a great tool for making a lot of impact without spending a lot of money. This book will help you navigate and survive the content marketing jungle—successfully.

—**Jeff Brooks, TrueSense Marketing and author of** *The Fundraiser's Guide to Irresistible Communications*

This book is what you've been waiting for! It is filled with a-ha moments and is a smart, fun roadmap to transform your nonprofit communications.

—**Lori L. Jacobwith, master storyteller and founder of the Ignited Online Fundraising Community**

Join Us at
Josseybass.com
▼

JOSSEY-BASS™
An Imprint of
Ⓦ **WILEY**

Register at **www.josseybass.com/email** for more information on our publications, authors, and to receive special offers.

This book includes Professional content that can be accessed from our website when you register at www.josseybass.com/go/leroux using the password **professional.**

Please also visit the author's website for this book at ContentMarketingforNonprofits.com for additional examples, exercises, worksheets, and updates. You can also use this website to pass along your thoughts about the ideas in this book and to connect with other readers.

Content Marketing for Nonprofits

A Communications Map for Engaging Your Community, Becoming a Favorite Cause, and Raising More Money

Kivi Leroux Miller

JB JOSSEY-BASS™

A Wiley Brand

Copyright © 2013 by John Wiley & Sons, Inc. All rights reserved.

Cover design by Michael Cook
Cover image by © Serkorkin/iStockphoto
Published by Jossey-Bass

A Wiley Brand

One Montgomery Street, Suite 1200, San Francisco, CA 94104-4594—www.josseybass.com

No part of this publication may be reproduced, stored in a retrieval system, or transmitted in any form or by any means, electronic, mechanical, photocopying, recording, scanning, or otherwise, except as permitted under Section 107 or 108 of the 1976 United States Copyright Act, without either the prior written permission of the publisher, or authorization through payment of the appropriate per-copy fee to the Copyright Clearance Center, Inc., 222 Rosewood Drive, Danvers, MA 01923, 978-750-8400, fax 978-646-8600, or on the Web at www.copyright.com. Requests to the publisher for permission should be addressed to the Permissions Department, John Wiley & Sons, Inc., 111 River Street, Hoboken, NJ 07030, 201-748-6011, fax 201-748-6008, or online at www.wiley.com/go/permissions.

Limit of Liability/Disclaimer of Warranty: While the publisher and author have used their best efforts in preparing this book, they make no representations or warranties with respect to the accuracy or completeness of the contents of this book and specifically disclaim any implied warranties of merchantability or fitness for a particular purpose. No warranty may be created or extended by sales representatives or written sales materials. The advice and strategies contained herein may not be suitable for your situation. You should consult with a professional where appropriate. Neither the publisher nor author shall be liable for any loss of profit or any other commercial damages, including but not limited to special, incidental, consequential, or other damages. Readers should be aware that Internet websites offered as citations and/or sources for further information may have changed or disappeared between the time this was written and when it is read.

Jossey-Bass books and products are available through most bookstores. To contact Jossey-Bass directly call our Customer Care Department within the U.S. at 800-956-7739, outside the U.S. at 317-572-3986, or fax 317-572-4002.

Wiley also publishes its books in a variety of electronic formats and by print-on-demand. Some material included with standard print versions of this book may not be included in e-books or in print-on-demand. If the version of this book that you purchased references media such as CD or DVD that was not included in your purchase, you may download this material at http://booksupport.wiley.com. For more information about Wiley products, visit www.wiley.com.

Library of Congress Cataloging-in-Publication Data

Leroux Miller, Kivi, 1969–
    Content marketing for nonprofits: a communications map for engaging your community, becoming a favorite cause, and raising more money / Kivi Leroux Miller.—First edition.
        pages   cm.—(The Jossey-Bass nonprofit guidebook series)
    Includes bibliographical references and index.
        ISBN 978-1-118-44402-3 (paper); ISBN 978-1-118-72238-1 (ebk.);
ISBN 978-1-118-72237-4 (ebk.)
        1. Nonprofit organizations—Marketing.   I. Title.
HD62.6.L46 2013
658.8—dc23   2013013519

Printed in the United States of America

FIRST EDITION

PB Printing   10 9 8 7 6 5 4 3 2 1

The Jossey-Bass Nonprofit Guidebook Series

The Jossey-Bass Nonprofit Guidebook Series provides new to experienced nonprofit professionals and volunteers with the essential tools and practical knowledge they need to make a difference in the world. From hands-on workbooks to step-by-step guides on developing a critical skill or learning how to perform an important task or process, our accomplished expert authors provide readers with the information required to be effective in achieving goals, mission, and impact.

Contents

Figures and Tables

Figures

Tables

Foreword

A few years ago, I gave a speech on fundraising at a conference. Midway through the presentation, I mentioned my work at Network for Good to the more than one hundred nonprofit professionals in attendance. This prompted a man in the middle of the room to raise his hand.

"Do you have a question?" I asked.

"I have a Network for Good Donate Now button on my organization's home page," he declared.

I smiled. How lovely to have a fan and client of my organization in the crowd. I thanked him and launched back into my presentation.

But he raised his hand again. So I called on him once more.

"You know that button?" he said. "It doesn't work."

This was certainly not what I wanted to hear. Embarrassed, I apologized. I said to the man—and everyone else in the room—that I was anxious to fix the problem and would get to the bottom of why people could not make donations from his website as soon as I finished my speech.

"I'll call my chief technology officer," I assured him.

Just as I was about to resume speaking, the man waved his hand once more. I wondered if I should pinch myself. The situation was becoming eerily reminiscent of a bad dream. With trepidation, I called on him one last time.

"You don't get it," the man told me. "You can click and make a donation on my website. The problem is, no one clicks on the button."

Ah. This wasn't broken technology. This was broken fundraising.

I have grown to love that man because our exchange makes for a good story, and it captures nonprofits' biggest marketing challenge, which is getting people to care. In addition, his broken button shows both the opportunities and limits of the great technological changes that are roiling our world and our sector. The number of tools and the amount of noise around us grow by the day. We see shiny objects everywhere, and we imagine they might fix our problems and magically enhance our work. Whether they fulfill that promise or not, we tend to attribute our success or failure to the technology.

I hear three schools of thought about technology and the changes unfolding around us. One is wildly optimistic: we are more connected than ever, and this is creating an opportunity to reimagine and revolutionize every industry. Technology has transformed music, publishing, and banking. Philanthropy is next—and when it goes digital, we will unleash the generosity inherent in us all on an unprecedented scale. Another view is wary: our text-messaging, smartphone-wielding selves are losing the ability to focus and reflect deeply. The traditional conversation has changed into mediated connection, leading to our isolation from each other. Small, inconsequential digital actions do little to change our relationships with our causes or the face of marketing and fundraising. The third view is cynical. It's best summed up by a wonderful question posted on Reddit recently: If someone from the 1950s suddenly appeared today, what would be the most difficult thing to explain to him or her about life now? My favorite response was this: I possess a device, in my pocket, that is capable of accessing the entirety of information known to man. I use it to look at pictures of cats and get into arguments with strangers. This school of thought says we're using technology in a way that really makes no difference, and so there is nothing new under the sun when it comes to our work.

So which is right? All of the above. It's up to us which scenario proves true in our situation. That's because the broken button is not about what the technology can or can't do. It's about what we do or don't do. That's the good news and the bad news. You—the very person reading these words right this minute—get to determine whether or not your button or Facebook page or YouTube channel performs—and whether today's technological changes will prove trying or transformative to your cause.

How do you do that? That's the very question this book sets out to answer. It explains the way technology has changed our work. It delves into the way our constituencies expect more of us. And then it describes how to embrace these new realities and turn them to our benefit by focusing on better content that drives deeper engagement.

In other words, this book decodes how you get people to click on your button. It's not by having a higher powered button—it's by having better content around the button and leading to the button.

If I had to sum up why this book matters, I'd say it's because of what it makes possible. It shows how to inject soul into your use of technology so your constituencies enter a world of unleashed generosity—and not just cute pictures of cats.

You can do these things. When you read this book, you learn it's not that hard. And even if it were difficult, you'd have to do it anyway. You have no choice. Your relevance and survival hinges on what you say—and what others say about you. People will click a donate button, "like" a page, or show up in real life to volunteer only when you tell, share, and spread compelling stories (activities also known as content marketing).

So turn the page and read this story on how to make that happen.

Katya Andresen
Author, *Robin Hood Marketing:*
Stealing Corporate Savvy to Sell Just Causes

Preface

I wrote my first book, *The Nonprofit Marketing Guide: High-Impact, Low-Cost Ways to Build Support for Your Good Cause,* because there wasn't a good handbook or survival guide for nonprofit communications directors, especially at smaller organizations. I also knew many nonprofit executive directors doing it all on their own, and I wanted to create something for them too.

My intent in this second book is not to update *The Nonprofit Marketing Guide* but to advance the conversation about what it means to be a good communications director today and how to use one of the biggest marketing trends—content marketing—specifically in the nonprofit sector.

If you are new to nonprofit marketing or work for a very small organization, I suggest you start with the first book and use this one more as a crystal ball for what your future will hold someday. If you've been at nonprofit marketing for awhile or you work for a large or well-funded nonprofit, I hope this book will become a trusted guide that you can turn to for both direction and inspiration. Fundraising professionals, especially those interested in donor retention, will find more content specifically for them in this book than in the first.

What Is Content Marketing?

Content marketing isn't just a new buzzword for the same old communications your nonprofit has always produced. It's a different way of thinking not only about why and how you communicate but, more importantly, about how your program participants, the supporters of your work, and the influencers in your community use, interact with, and in many ways, help you coproduce your communications.

All those communications pieces you've been creating for years—newsletter articles, direct mail letters, press releases, web pages—are content. What's different now is that instead of just pushing that content in front of people, we want to use the content we create to pull them to us, attracting them to our cause, rather than interrupting them with it.

Here's how I define content marketing for nonprofits:

Content marketing for nonprofits is creating and sharing relevant and valuable content that attracts, motivates, engages, and inspires your participants, supporters, and influencers to help you achieve your mission.

If you take an objective look at what many nonprofits share through their communications today, you might conclude that reporting on all of your nonprofit's past activities (the narrative equivalent of summarizing last month's to-do list) while also promoting its upcoming activities (which usually means asking people to do something for you) is what works.

The problem is, it really doesn't. I'm not sure it was ever all that effective, and in today's world, it definitely doesn't cut it. To connect with and engage participants and supporters, you need to do more than summarize your work. You need to put those people front and center in your communications strategy, building relationships with them much like you would with friends, so that you become one of their favorite nonprofits.

It's a Long Trek

Throughout this book I compare content marketing to a long backpacking trip into the backcountry. It's a little wild out there, but you'll be prepared for most of it!

In part 1 you'll get a fuller sense of what this journey involves and the benefits of getting started with content marketing. In part 2 you'll look at the people going on the trek with you and redefine your marketing relationships.

In part 3 you'll plan out the journey with several communications documents, making sure you are ready from start to finish. In part 4 you'll look at making it happen, and how to put one foot in front of the other as you implement your content strategy.

Finally, in part 5, you'll get trail-tested advice on how to use the most popular communications channels and tactics for nonprofits today.

Stop, Think, and Discuss

In the chapters in parts 1 through 4, you'll find lots of boxes with questions that will encourage you to stop, think about, and discuss what you've read and how you can apply it to your nonprofit. Please also stop by ContentMarketingforNon profits.com, where I will be sharing more exercises and worksheets that support the content in this book.

One final heads-up: the chapters in part 1 are stat-heavy. If you are not a numbers person, don't worry—the rest of the book isn't as data dense. Also note that marketing data do shift frequently, so if you need the most up-to-date numbers, check the chapter references for the websites of my sources or visit my website for this book at ContentMarketingforNonprofits.com. Many of the reports I quote are updated annually and sometimes more often.

Let's get started!

June 2013   Kivi Leroux Miller

Acknowledgments

When I set out to write this book, I knew from the start that I wanted it to be a community production. I set a goal of including at least 100 nonprofits in the book in one way or another as positive examples for you to learn from. The official count is 118. Some are examples I have admired from afar, some have provided an anecdote via one of my many surveys, and some have granted me an extensive interview—whatever the method, I offer my most sincere thanks to all who shared information with me. This really is your book.

If part 5 of the book becomes your favorite, and for many it will, you have Nonprofit Marketing Guide's community engagement manager, Kristina Leroux, to thank for it. Kristina did most of the research for these chapters, compiling tips and examples for you to learn from. She also helped me find and fill gaps throughout the book, managed the permissions and graphics, proofread the book several times, and has always been there when I need her, which is just about every day. I love working with my little sister!

I am also very grateful for the generous community of nonprofit marketing and fundraising bloggers, many of whom are quoted directly in the book and who all contributed in their own way by helping me stretch my own thinking. I am especially grateful to Tom Ahern, Katya Andresen, Frank Barry, Jeff Brooks, John Haydon, Beth Kanter, Kerri Karvetski, Gail Perry, and Nancy Schwartz. If you read them—and you should—you will likely recognize their influence on me.

Special thanks also to the fine women who worked behind the scenes on this book, including my editor Alison Hankey, developmental editor Nathinee Chen, and reviewers Katya Andresen, Jocelyn Harmon, and Maddie Grant, whose wisdom guided major changes between the first and final drafts.

Finally, I am blessed with a wonderful husband, Edgar, and two spirited daughters, Ava and Jianna, who only whined for a little while when I said I was writing a second book. As the manuscript grew, so did their self-reliance and patience with their mom.

My gratitude and love to you all.

About the Author

Kivi Leroux Miller is president of Nonprofit Marketing Guide.com and author of *The Nonprofit Marketing Guide: High-Impact, Low-Cost Ways to Build Support for Your Good Cause.*

Through training, coaching, and consulting, Kivi helps small nonprofits and small communications departments at larger organizations make a big impression with smart, savvy marketing and communications. She teaches a weekly webinar series and writes the top-ranked blog on nonprofit communications at Nonprofit Marketing Guide.com. Thousands of nonprofits in all fifty US states, across Canada, and in more than thirty countries have participated in Kivi's online and in-person trainings.

Content Marketing for Nonprofits

Content marketing is a new kind of journey, a trek into the backcountry. While many others have walked this path before you, it is still largely wild and uncharted territory that will require an adventurous spirit as you make your way. You can and should prepare for the journey, but you also need to be flexible enough to adapt to what and whom you encounter along the way.

The chapters in part 1 lay the groundwork for understanding the significance of this new path for your communications plan, why it matters to your long-term success, and how to embrace it by setting some new communications goals.

Chapter 1 reviews some of the major societal shifts under way that will affect your marketing strategy: namely, the explosion in the number of communications channels, the shifts in the ways different generations relate to charities, and growing out of these first two changes, a shift in who's in control of the message. You'll see why communicating in ways that are much more relevant and engaging to your participants and supporters is essential today.

Chapter 2 takes a closer look at the shift from traditional nonprofit communications to nonprofit content marketing and at how you can use this shift to position your nonprofit as a favorite cause. It also reviews the stages nonprofits commonly move through as they evolve their traditional communications plan into a modern content marketing strategy.

Chapter 3 describes setting your content marketing goals and how to measure your progress toward those goals. It looks at understanding the influence of program and fundraising goals on your content marketing strategy, learning what will drive your success, and aligning the kinds of metrics you watch with your goals.

Chapter One
Hearing the Call of the Wild
The Case for Changing Your Communications Approach

> **This chapter is about . . .**
> - Recognizing why the term *target audience* no longer works
> - Understanding the real impact of social media on your communications strategy
> - Communicating with adults in four different generations
> - Reaching your supporters' inner angels instead of their inner bookkeepers

It's a new, wild world out there, and yet many nonprofits are communicating as if they were still living in the '80s or '90s. It's time to throw out your excess baggage, full of illusions that you are fully in control of your communications and outdated notions that you should do the same things as before just because "we've always done it that way." The journey you'll take in this book requires you to be lighter on your feet, so while you'll still carry a big backpack, you need to be smarter about the communications tools you put in it.

Before you start walking down this new path, let me give you a bird's-eye view of the territory you are venturing into.

The End of the Target Audience

Target audience is a common marketing term for the people you are trying to reach with your communications. I've used it regularly since I started working in nonprofit marketing and communications, including in my first book, *The Nonprofit Marketing Guide: High-Impact, Low-Cost Ways to Build Support for Your Good Cause.* But I'm trying to banish it from my lexicon, and I suggest you do the same. This term embodies the old way of looking at nonprofit marketing and communications, an approach that I hope you'll transition away from as you progress through this book.

While the concept of focusing on specific groups of people—via list segmenting, for example—is still very valuable, thinking of this focus as *targeting* is troublesome because it conjures the image of you blasting your content toward the target, rather than an image of you creating content that naturally attracts specific types of people to you. The term *audience* presents a similar problem because it implies people sitting passively and quietly while you present to them.

Today, your goal is engagement with people who care about the same things your organization does. While some people will still sit and silently consume what you produce, the goal for most nonprofit communicators is to get people to take some sort of action in response to that content, even if it is as simple as

---

Engagement means getting people to interact with your organization in ways that build a relationship between them and your organization, so they are more likely to follow through on actions that help you achieve your mission (from advocating for your cause to donating funds to participating in your programs). Engagement is sometimes measured in one-time actions, like sharing a piece of your content with their friends on Facebook, which over time, you hope, will culminate in your organization becoming one of their favorite causes.

Segment Your List to Be More Relevant

Segmenting a list means pulling a smaller subset of groups of names from a mailing list, based on specific criteria. You might sort or segment recent donors from those who haven't given in the last twenty-four months, or you might segment by zip code, by who attended your last event, or by who opened your last e-newsletter. Segmenting allows you to provide customized and relevant content to each segmented group on your mailing list: this means, for example, that you don't remind people to register for an event when your records tell you they have already registered.

"We found that the single most predictive factor in whether someone will open an email from us is whether they have opened one in the past," says Brett Meyer, speaking of his experience as communications director at the Nonprofit Technology Network (NTEN) (personal communication, February 2013). For its various email messages, NTEN will segment based on whether someone

- Has opened two emails in the last 60 days
- Has opened an email in the last 180 days
- Has opened an email in the last year
- Hasn't opened an email in the last year

"We want to keep the email openers engaged, and we want to reengage the others," says Meyer. NTEN messages fairly heavily—two to three times a week—to those who are engaged but sends only the best content or notices about free webinars or new downloads on hot topics to those who are less engaged.

If you haven't opened a message in the first week, NTEN will often send a reminder message. "We have found that people who haven't been very engaged are much more likely to read the content when they get that second reminder message rather than from the first message," says Meyer.

raising a hand and clicking "like" on Facebook or sharing a story they read in your newsletter over coffee with a friend.

For many nonprofits, engaging their community also means actively embracing members of it as not just consumers of content but coproducers of content as well. Communications do not flow in a single, irreversible, targeted direction any longer, but back and forth between a nonprofit and its community members. Oftentimes the community members themselves become the spokespersons for the cause—an idea that still frightens many nonprofit leaders (maybe you?) but that should ultimately excite you because of the potential to reach and connect with so many more people.

So if you don't call those people out there on the receiving end of your communications the *target audience*, then what should you call them?

Participants, Supporters, and Influencers: Your PSIs

I'm not one for making up brand-new words, so I've been using a trio of existing terms instead: *participants, supporters*, and *influencers*, who are collectively your PSIs. I'll use this terminology throughout this book. I think the abbreviation is apropos, because it reminds me of how important it is to keep a car's tires inflated to the right PSI (pressure per square inch in this case). Too much PSI in either case leads to an uncontrolled explosion, and too little leads to terrible performance. There's a PSI sweet spot for your car's tires, and there's a PSI sweet spot for your nonprofit too: the right number of participants, supporters, and influencers to help you accomplish your mission without overtaxing your organization.

When I say *participants*, I am referring to the people your organization serves, as well as those who have actively embraced your mission and are helping you directly to implement your programming, such as volunteers and advocates. When I use *supporters*, I am talking about financial donors, individuals and groups who endorse your work, and volunteers and advocates who help to build your community without directly implementing programs and services. When I use *influencers*, I am talking about people who are typically more disinterested or objective about your particular organization than either supporters or participants, but who can still have a big impact on how others perceive you, such as journalists, elected officials, and some of your professional peers.

There's often some overlap among these groups, especially between participants and supporters and between supporters and influencers, and that's fine. It's less important to categorize someone as a participant, a supporter, or an influencer and more important to view him as part of the community that is making good things happen, rather than as a passive bystander. In addition to referring to these people as your PSIs, I also refer to them collectively as your community. You may call them your network, your family of support, your members, or whatever you like—just try to get away from the term *target audience* as much as possible.

Seismic Shifts Affecting Your Marketing Strategy

What's brought about this shift away from target audience thinking and toward more inclusive community engagement? Just as tectonic plates far underground create lots of little tremors and sometimes shocking jolts at the surface, big and small shifts are rumbling under the foundations of nonprofit marketing and fundraising too.

All your communications should be rooted in the answers to three questions:

1. Who are you communicating with?

2. What is your message to them?

3. How will you deliver that message?

The answers to the who and how questions are being affected by two major societal shifts, in media and in demographics, that are raising great debates among and within nonprofits about how they should approach their marketing and fundraising. Your answer to the question of who you are communicating with needs to take into account the changing demographics of the people who support nonprofits. The growth in communications channels, especially social media, is changing the way you will answer the question about how you will deliver your message.

These two shifts are combining to produce a third powerful shift in who is in control of information and who has the power to share it and discuss it. In other words, you alone no longer decide what's relevant about your work; your participants, supporters, and influencers have a say too. This naturally affects how you will answer the question about the content of your message.

Let's look more closely at these trends.

Media Shifts: More Channels, More Choices, More Power to Decide

If they want to learn more about your organization, participants, supporters, and influencers can go to more sources of information—more channels—than ever before. Some of that information will be created and shared by you, but your PSIs will likely come across content about you created or shared by others too.

> *Communications channels* are the various tools, tactics, and services you use to deliver your message. Common nonprofit channels include direct mail, e-newsletters, Facebook, websites, media relations, and the like.

In 2012, most donors—83 percent—said that prior to making giving decisions, they conducted some level of research, at least occasionally, on nonprofits they were considering for support, according to Penelope Burk (2012) of Cygnus Donor Research. This is up from 65 percent just five years earlier, in part because such research is now so much easier to do. Potential donors do look to third parties, including friends and family (word of mouth), charity rating agencies, and the media, but these sources pale in comparison to the information sources your nonprofit controls: your websites; your publications, like newsletters; and social media.

Moreover, where donors get their information and where they act on it are not necessarily the same. According to Burk (2012), one in three donors who decided to give after visiting a charity website did so offline. Conversely, about a third of donors who were asked by mail to give went online to make the gift.

Social Media Has Changed Everything: Or Has It?

One of my favorite ways to kick off a marketing workshop with a room full of nonprofit executives and staff is to ask this question: "Social media has changed everything about nonprofit marketing and fundraising. True or false?"

The same thing happens every time. About half of the participants will raise their hands for "true," ready to argue that social media has indeed changed everything. The statement is true because social media is about back-and-forth conversations, where previously most communications were one way. People can also start conversations with nonprofits in very public ways. Someone who is excited—or upset—about something happening at your nonprofit doesn't need to spend time finding a specific staff person to call on the phone or trying to convince a reporter to broadcast her feelings to the world. Instead, that person can use Facebook or Twitter to let you, and her friends and family and the rest of the world, know how she feels, right then and there. People do not need your permission to speak out publicly about you and your work, which means that everyone is a potential spokesperson about your organization.

The other half of the participants will put their hands up for "false." While they will concede the points just made by the "changed everything" crowd, they point out that even though the specific tools of communications have changed, the fundamentals of successful nonprofit marketing and fundraising are the same: these basics are still about making personal connections with those individuals who will be good spokespeople for your cause. They point out that having thousands of fans or followers in social media is of no more value than having thousands of people on a print or email list—unless those people are motivated to act on your behalf in some way. How you tap into that human spirit and get people inspired and motivated to act ultimately has little to do with what communications channels you use.

Think of it this way: building your lists of social media fans and followers is like filling a football stadium with people who say, "We like you enough to show up." But only a small percentage of these people will wear the team colors, and an even smaller percentage will paint their faces or bodies, wear goofy hats or costumes, and cheer every play from the sidelines.

Social media offers powerful new tools that may help you fill your stadium more quickly, but it's still up to you to use those tools to build rapport, one by one, with the people who will watch every game or buy the season tickets, identifying themselves as real supporters, ready to donate, advocate, or volunteer for you.

So, as with most trick questions, both possible answers are right. Yet if I were forced to pick an answer myself, I would say that, yes, social media has changed everything, but not for the reason you might expect.

Letting Go of the Illusion of Control

What I rarely hear in these conversations—and what I think is one of the most important lessons I want to share in this book—is how profoundly social media has altered the way nonprofits need to communicate with their communities. It's about much more than just adding another communications channel or two to your to-do list. It's about giving up the illusion of control and being better off for it.

Your brand, your talking points, and your story are no longer yours alone to construct and discuss. Your participants, supporters, and influencers have a very public say now in how others perceive you. Because people know they can speak and be heard quickly and easily now, that ability affects all your communications with them. You may decide to communicate something to a small select group in a private meeting or via a printed and mailed letter. But there's nothing to stop one of those people from talking about it publicly on Facebook, should he decide to do so.

In these same marketing workshops, I often ask another question: "Is this idea that you no longer control the message, and that everyone is a potential spokesperson, terrifying or exciting?" Those who believe it is terrifying picture a number of scenarios in their heads, most of which involve someone saying the wrong thing with headache-inducing if not downright disastrous results. Those who are excited acknowledge that they may occasionally need to address misconceptions spread via less than perfect talking points but also say that the benefits of having more people talking about the nonprofit's work and advocating that their friends and family get involved far outweigh the downside.

Over the last few years I have seen a clear, encouraging shift from more people saying this idea is terrifying to more people saying it's exciting. I suspect that's because more people are accepting what have become the new facts of life for nonprofit communicators.

Stop, Think, and Discuss

- How has social media changed the way your organization approaches communications?
- Is social media just another way to get your message out, or are you using it to build two-way communications?
- Is the idea that everyone is a potential spokesperson scary for your organization? What would it take to increase your comfort level with this idea?

Always On, Always with Us

Mobile technology is further reinforcing these new norms. Just like the 100-calorie snack packs of our favorite foods in the grocery store, we like our information in fast, timely, and convenient chunks too, as we are often reading them on a small screen in the palms of our hands. The first iPhone, which sparked the mobile revolution, was released in 2007, and the pace of change has been incredibly fast.

According to the Pew Internet & American Life Project (Brenner, 2013), as of December 2012, 87 percent of American adults had a cell phone, and 47 percent had a smartphone. More than half, 55 percent, use their mobile phones to access the Internet, with 17 percent going to the Internet mostly through their phones, rather than by using a desktop or laptop computer. And we have these phones with us all the time. Sixty-five percent of US adults sleep with a cell phone beside them at night, and according to Ericsson ConsumerLab (2011), more than a third check the phone for email or social media updates before they even get out of bed in the morning!

Tablet and e-reader ownership is also growing rapidly. According to another Pew survey (Rainie, 2012), in September 2010, just 4 percent of American adults owned tablets. As of January 2013, 26 percent of American adults owned an e-reader and 31 percent owned a tablet computer (Brenner, 2013).

Compare mobile technology as a communications channel to the snail mail box. Mine is at the end of my driveway, and mail comes only once a day and not even every day. Connect with me in a way that's mobile friendly, and you can reach me during most of my waking hours—even in those first groggy-eyed minutes in the morning—every day, no matter where I am.

The nonprofit sector is struggling to keep pace with these changes. According to *2012 State of the Nonprofit Industry*, a report by the fundraising software company Blackbaud (2012), about 30 percent of US nonprofits have enabled their websites and emails for mobile viewing, while about 50 percent of donors in the study reported using their mobile phones to access nonprofit websites and emails.

The Pace Is Fast But It's No Excuse to Fall Behind

If you feel blindsided by these changes, it's understandable. It's all happening very quickly. The online companies and tools that we are coming to rely on for news and information from around the world and around the block are, in most cases, still juveniles. Google was founded in 1998, making it easy to find information, as well as the people and organizations behind that information. In the late 1990s, blogging software also became more readily available, making it easier for individuals to share their own opinions and insights. Then came YouTube in 2005 and Twitter in 2006. Facebook was founded in 2004 and opened to the public in 2006 (it was previously open only to those with certain email addresses from domains such as universities, high schools, and a few major corporations).

These social media sites made it easy for people to not only find information but also to find each other, and to connect and converse about anything and everything, cutting the former middleman—the mass media—out entirely. The way we share information has changed forever and will continue to do so at a relentless pace that is likely to continue for some time. We as a nation are no longer turning to the same handful of TV networks and newspaper wire services that we once did for news. If we all see the same story, it's likely because it went viral on Facebook or YouTube, and then the mainstream media picked it up.

We also expect to find answers to our questions immediately. If we want to know what's happening in some conflict halfway around the world, we expect to easily find the latest updates either on twenty-four-hour cable news or through a few quick searches online. Twitter is the place that many people now go first ("Was that an earthquake? Was that an explosion?") because Twitter users discuss what they are seeing and experiencing as it happens, before news agencies can even draft a story.

Because of this access to real-time information, we've become intolerant of outdated information. If you ask someone what she thinks when she sees outdated information on a nonprofit's website, she doesn't say, "Oh, I bet they're just too busy to update the website." She says, "I guess they've gone out of business." Outdated and irrelevant information is now a sign of your demise—and that's why you can't use the pace of change as an excuse to drag your feet in responding to change.

Your success as a nonprofit depends on your ability to stay in the conversation, week after week, with the members of your community, on their level. Engaging your community requires that you mix and mingle and be seen as one of the community members, rather than as some authority somehow above and removed from everyone else, who decides to speak only on a limited and predetermined schedule. You keep your feet on the floor at the cocktail party, drawing others to you by being interesting or entertaining and by having relevant things to say, rather than by dancing on the bar, yelling, "Look at me!" When you build a community around you, you create opportunities to build rapport with many of its members as individuals. And when they truly become friends to your cause, they will spread the word for you, friendraising and fundraising as they go.

Demographic Shifts: The Four Generations of Your PSIs

Another major shift making the target audience mentality less effective is that we now have a much more demographically diverse society, with four adult generations interacting with nonprofits: Generation Y, Generation X, the Baby Boomers, and the Matures (who are also called the Silent Generation).

Because the Boomers are the largest generation, representing 44 percent of the US population and controlling 70 percent of US disposable income (MarketingCharts, 2012), it's often helpful to split that generation in half, into younger Boomers and older Boomers, to better understand them. There are some significant cultural and economic differences between younger and older Boomers, as younger Boomers are now typically in their peak earning years, while older Boomers are approaching retirement age.

Because younger Boomers are still very much active in the workplace, they have adopted technology as a necessity for staying relevant at work and staying in touch with family and friends. Older Boomers are more likely to have a case of *senioritis*—as they approach retirement and age sixty-five (the cultural definition of a senior citizen)—they may feel less urgency to stay current. Therefore, they may see new technology such as social media as irrelevant to their needs and experiences (Wolfe, 2012).

Demographers will argue about the exact edges of the four generations, but they generally fall into the groups shown in table 1.1.

TABLE 1.1 Generations by Birth Year		
Generation	**Birth years**	**Age in 2013**
Matures, or Silent Generation	1945 and earlier	68 and older
Baby Boomers	1946–1964	49–67
Older Boomers	1946–1955	58–67
Younger Boomers	1956–1964	49–57
Generation X	1965–1980	33–48
Generation Y	1981–1991	22–32

In terms of sheer size, Generation Y (Gen Y) is almost as big as the Baby Boomer generation, and Generation X is about two-thirds the size of the Boomer generation or Gen Y. However, that doesn't take immigration into account, and by some estimates, immigrants are bringing Generation X up to parity with Gen Y and the Boomers.

How Each Generation Views Philanthropy

Lumping millions of people into categories always creates stereotypes. But for purposes of understanding some of the macro shifts that are taking place, I have boiled down into just one word how each of the four generations approaches philanthropy (table 1.2).

Matures are more likely than others to give out of a sense of responsibility and *duty*. That's what good people do. Giving back is important. Giving to charity is what's right.

Boomers are more likely to give because it fits with their personal sense of *identity*, who they are. They want to make a difference and believe that they are change makers, and they see themselves as having a role to play with the charities they support.

TABLE 1.2 **How Each Generation Relates to Nonprofits**		
Generation	**Age in 2013**	**One word describing how they relate to nonprofits**
Matures, or Silent Generation	68 and older	Duty
Baby Boomers	49–67	Identity
Generation X	33–48	Entrepreneurial
Generation Y	22–32	Community

Generation Xers are more likely to give when they can see a problem being solved. In other words, they are *entrepreneurial* about their philanthropy. It's less personal and more about getting things done.

Generation Yers are more likely to give when they feel they are part of a *community* of change. They see themselves as connected global citizens and are confident that together they can correct injustices of the past and make the world a better place.

Of course there is some overlap. Generation Yers share a sense of civic duty with the Matures, are politically savvy like the Boomers, and value work-life balance as Gen Xers do. And these group trends will apply unevenly or not at all to many individuals (you can certainly find twenty-year-olds who have more in common with their own great-grandmas than with their college roommates).

But it's undeniable that the way people approach philanthropy is changing. Take a look again at just the four relationship words, in age group order:

Duty

Identity

Entrepreneurial

Community

What kinds of change or progression do you see in these words? How does this progression affect your nonprofit's communications?

Here's one way to look at the changes. When people are giving primarily out of a sense of duty, then at some level, it really doesn't matter how good your communications to them are. If you can present a need reasonably well, these people will feel that sense of duty to respond to that need.

I've heard many a fundraiser with thirty years of experience or more talk about how much easier it used to be to raise money. Now those same fundraisers talk about how much more competition there is, both from other charities and for people's attention. They also talk about how donors' expectations have changed.

That the rise of *donor-centered fundraising* over the last decade is no coincidence becomes apparent when you look at the second word in the list: *identity*. Boomers in particular respond to communications that are about them and their role in solving a problem. Donors also say, in numerous surveys, that they want to hear about results and success stories from the charities they support, which sounds like *entrepreneurial* thinking. And largely thanks to social media, donors can feel they are part of many different *communities* with whom they can share their various passions, including the causes they believe in and the charities that they support.

Suddenly, those way-we've-always-done-it communications aren't enough anymore. That doesn't mean you need to drop everything you've always done and replace it with something new. But it does mean you need to take a hard look at what you are doing now, adjust what's worth keeping, get rid of what's not, and add in what's missing.

Donor-centered fundraising is a phrase coined by Penelope Burk in her 2003 book by the same name, *Donor Centered Fundraising: How to Hold on to Your Donors and Raise Much More Money*. She defines it as an approach to raising money and interacting with donors that acknowledges what donors really need and puts those needs first.

Stop, Think, and Discuss

Take one of your major programs or services. How would you describe it to reach a *duty* donor in contrast to an *identity* donor? How about an *entrepreneurial* donor in contrast to a *community* donor?

Let's say you wanted your newsletter to reflect all four donor descriptions (duty, identity, entrepreneurial, and community). How does your current newsletter match up, and what changes would you make to better reflect these four concepts?

How Media and Demographic Shifts Affect Communications Choices

How much do these media and generational differences really matter to your organization? If your nonprofit has limited marketing and fundraising energy and resources, how quickly do you need to respond?

The nature of your nonprofit's work, the size and age of your organization, and the demographics of your particular community will determine just how these media and generational dynamics come into play. You may not be forced to make the decision about whether to focus on those under or over fifty-five, or your mission may make that choice more clear.

If your nonprofit is a larger, older organization with a well-established direct mail fundraising operation, its perspective will be quite different from that of a younger nonprofit that's always operated primarily online. If your nonprofit advocates for early childhood education and its program participants are families with young children, the ways in which it will communicate with those participants will likely be different from the approaches taken by organizations like land trusts, whose participants are mostly family matriarchs and patriarchs who own large parcels of land they want to protect from development.

But communications choices are not always this clear, and the debate can get complicated, fast.

Reaching out to new people is infinitely easier now because of the wide variety of online tools available to nonprofit marketers, including email and social media. It's true that the younger a person is, the more likely he is to prefer online communications, but all generations use the Internet. The year 2012 marked the first time when more than half of US adults sixty-five and over (54 percent) reported using the Internet. Of these older Internet users, 48 percent reported using email daily, and 18 percent reported using social media daily (Pew Internet & American Life Project, 2012).

What's more, 69 percent of donors of all ages now say they prefer electronic communications, according to the *2012 Cygnus Donor Survey* (Burk, 2012). For many of these donors, email and social media are simply more comfortable and convenient, but some of those who are less comfortable with online communications still say they prefer that charities use them because online materials are more cost efficient than print materials.

All of this might lead you to conclude that the trend is toward online communications and print is a thing of the past. But I think the statistics actually point to a more complex outcome. What I believe you should take from the information in this chapter is that the trend is toward multichannel communications. You can't drop print communications, but print alone is not enough anymore either. (And yes, this does seem to imply more work for you, since you have more communications channels to feed now, but I'll talk in future chapters about how it doesn't really have to mean more work.)

> *Multichannel marketing*, or *integrated marketing*, means that you are sharing the same content, message, or call to action by means of several different communications channels (for example, printed information, online materials, and in-person events) in order to reach all of your PSIs in the way they prefer.

When we look at how people are choosing to donate to charities, we see an interesting, but not surprising, dynamic: Baby Boomers are the transition generation, falling between those who prefer to give through traditional direct mail and those who prefer to give online. The *2011 donorCentrics Internet and Multichannel Giving Benchmarking Report* (Flannery and Harris, 2011) found that, in 2010, Gen Yers, Gen Xers, and younger Boomers were more likely to make a first gift to a charity online, while older Boomers and Matures were more likely to use direct mail (figure 1.1).

FIGURE 1.1
Distribution of New Donors by Age in Two Origin Channels: 2010 Medians

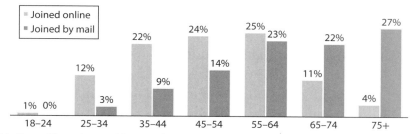

Medians will not always add to exactly 100% across each channel.

Source: Helen Flannery and Rob Harris, *2011 donorCentrics Internet and Multichannel Giving Benchmarking Report*, 2011, www.blackbaud.com/targetananalytics/multi-channel-report.

So, if you wanted to take your best shot at raising money from new Boomer donors to your organization, you'd need a strategy that was part direct mail and part online. It's important to remember that the overwhelming majority of individual fundraising is still done through snail mail. This same report points out that the typical organization studied received more than three-quarters of its total gifts through direct mail and only 10 percent of its gifts online. Direct mail acquisition is also responsible for three-quarters of all new donors.

Why You Need to Respond to These Shifts

If donor retention rates are any indication, nonprofits are failing to adequately respond to the shifts described here and are not delivering what their supporters are looking for. Various national surveys calculate a donor attrition rate of between 60 and 65 percent—and getting worse (Association of Fundraising Professionals and The Urban Institute, 2012; Burk, 2012). That means for every one hundred people who give you a first-time gift, only thirty-five to forty give a second gift, with the numbers trending in the wrong direction.

Nonprofits may capture people's attention, but then they fail to keep it. They fail to remain relevant. I believe this trend is directly related to the target audience mentality and everything connected with it that's now so outdated. As nonprofit communicators we are simply failing to connect with our communities in ways that are relevant to them today and that would keep them engaged in the good work. That lack of connection exists largely because what nonprofits think is important is not what donors feel is important.

The things that motivate donors and that they say they want from nonprofits have little to do with the detailed grind of the day-to-day work of a nonprofit organization. Yet that daily output is what many nonprofits emphasize in their communications, producing a narrative built on their to-do lists and transactions. To be relevant to donors, you need to connect on a more relational level. The level at which donors get and stay involved depends on how they feel about their altruism and, to varying degrees, also on how effective they feel that altruism is and on how much they trust and like your organization—regardless of their generation. Given these different donor interests, communicating to donors in a relevant manner raises what I call the inner angel–inner bookkeeper problem.

The Inner Angel–Inner Bookkeeper Problem

When you write your communications, are you speaking to your supporters' inner angels or to their inner bookkeepers?

The inner angel is the part of your nonprofit's supporter who decides to give you a donation or to volunteer with you because you have touched the supporter in some way, and that angel wants to touch you back. Angels are all heart, and they are in charge of decision making. You need to keep the angel on your side.

The inner bookkeeper is the part of your supporter that needs a receipt for the donation for taxes or the directions to your event or some other logistical or factual information. Bookkeepers are all head. We like to think our bookkeepers are in charge most of the time, but they really aren't. You can certainly annoy a person's inner bookkeeper if you don't supply the data (like that tax receipt) when the bookkeeper really needs it, but the truth is, if the person's angel is on your side, it doesn't really matter whether the bookkeeper is irritated or not.

It's hard, if not impossible, to speak to both equally at the same time.

For example, I argue that a good thank-you letter should be much less a receipt for the bookkeeper and much more a greeting card (or even a love letter) to the angel. Make the body of the letter all about the angel, and put the receipt info, including that awful IRS disclaimer language when it's needed, at the very bottom, maybe in italics or in a smaller typeface, after any PS, and fully apart from the letter.

Using a content marketing approach in your communications—one that produces relevant and valuable communications—gets you much closer to the inner angel and much closer to becoming a favorite organization of your participants, supporters, and influencers. We keep our favorite things close and don't let go of them easily.

Stop, Think, and Discuss

Take a look at the donor communications you sent out over the last month or two. What percentage spoke to your donors' inner angels and what percentage spoke to their inner bookkeepers?

What would your communications look like if you spent 80 percent of your time speaking to your donors' angels and 20 percent speaking to their bookkeepers?

Why It Matters: Your PSIs Decide Relevance, Not You

What you and the others who work in your organization believe should be communicated does matter. But what your participants, supporters, and influencers want to hear matters too, and that needs to carry much more weight than it currently does in many nonprofit organizations.

One-way, traditional nonprofit communications aren't enough anymore. They don't provide the relevance and engagement that many people now expect. Can you listen to your participants, supporters, and influencers and learn what they really want from their relationships with your cause and your nonprofit? Can you shift your communications to respond to their values and needs, to build more of a two-way relationship, one in which your nonprofit is clearly relevant in their lives? A content marketing strategy will help you do that.

Chapter Two
Understanding This Trek
How Content Marketing Is Different

This chapter is about . . .

- Reaching your goals by attracting, rather than interrupting, people with your communications

- Recognizing the power of becoming a favorite cause

- Understanding your nonprofit's marketing maturity level

Have you ever seen Yosemite Falls—the tallest waterfall in North America? It's one of my favorite places in the world.

Maybe you've seen a picture of it. Or maybe you drove by on a quick swing through Yosemite Valley. Or perhaps you parked the car and took the flat and easy, mile-long walk to the base of Lower Yosemite Fall. Maybe you even did the strenuous, daylong climb up 2,700 vertical feet to the top of Upper Yosemite Fall, on a rugged trail constructed between 1873 and 1877. I've done the full hike twice, and it's worth it!

The differences in viewing Yosemite Falls in these four ways are like the differences between the traditional nonprofit communications of old and today's more relevant, engaging nonprofit content marketing. If you are sending out a newsletter without really understanding who is on your mailing list, you are doing a drive-by. At least get out of the car, walk closer, and feel the mist on your face—that's how you start to engage with your environment. Invest the time and energy in the climb—and in your content marketing strategy—and you'll really understand the power.

The Theory of Change for Nonprofit Content Marketing

The *theory of change* is a popular strategic planning model in the nonprofit world. It graphically lays out all the building blocks required to get from where you are now to where you want to be, so that your tactics are clearly connected to your larger goals. Let's look at what a theory of change could look like for nonprofit content marketing (figure 2.1) and then compare it to traditional nonprofit communications.

You can also reverse the order of the change path and put it into words as a series of "so that" statements.

- You understand the wants and needs of your participants, supporters, and influencers (PSIs), and your communications evoke the personality and promises you want to be known for, so that

- Your content marketing strategy is relevant and valuable to your PSIs, so that

- New and current PSIs are engaging with you and strengthening their relationships with you all the time, so that

- You are one of their favorite organizations, and you can rely on your PSIs to help when you ask, so that

- You have the community support you need to achieve your mission.

As you can see, this process starts with what your participants, supporters, and influencers want and need from you, and how you in turn want to be perceived in your relationship with them so as to keep them engaged. This is Marketing 101: understand the interests and needs of the people you are communicating with so that you can craft messages and calls to action that are relevant to them.

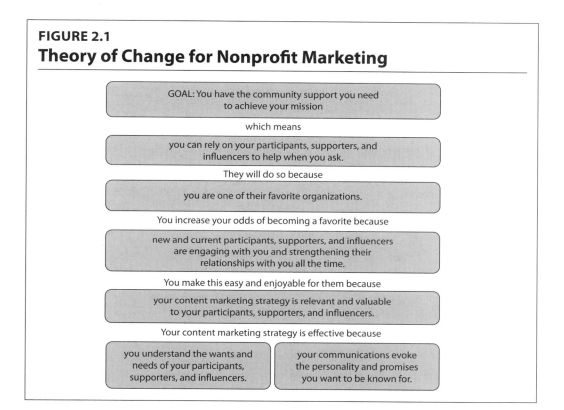

FIGURE 2.1

Theory of Change for Nonprofit Marketing

GOAL: You have the community support you need
to achieve your mission

which means

you can rely on your participants, supporters, and
influencers to help when you ask.

They will do so because

you are one of their favorite organizations.

You increase your odds of becoming a favorite because

new and current participants, supporters, and influencers
are engaging with you and strengthening their
relationships with you all the time.

You make this easy and enjoyable for them because

your content marketing strategy is relevant and valuable
to your participants, supporters, and influencers.

Your content marketing strategy is effective because

you understand the wants and
needs of your participants,
supporters, and influencers.

your communications evoke
the personality and promises
you want to be known for.

How to Stop Interrupting and Start Attracting

Creating and sharing communications that are truly relevant and valuable to
people outside the organization will require a major transformation in many nonprofits. This kind of transformation is consistent with what's happening beyond
the nonprofit sector, in the larger world of for-profit marketing too.

It's the difference between *interruption* or *outbound* marketing tactics that
scream, "Look at me! Help me!" and *attraction* or *permission* or *inbound* marketing tactics that say, "Do you care about this? If so, let's talk. We do too." It's less
calling out and more holding natural, open conversations.

With old-style interruption marketing, you push out a lot of information,
hoping that it reaches the right people. This is also called *spray and pray*. Much of
what we consider traditional nonprofit marketing—newsletters, press releases,
event advertising—is outbound marketing.

With inbound marketing, in contrast, you create content that people want, they identify themselves as being interested in your topics, and they actively ask you to communicate with them, because they want more or they are at least open to having those conversations.

How the Nonprofit Technology Network (NTEN) approaches getting new visitors to its website to sign up for its newsletter is a good example. It used to be that NTEN asked people to sign up for the newsletter first. "We were really asking people to do that on faith," says Brett Meyer, NTEN's former communications director. Now, it's much more likely that new people will sign up for a free webinar or a free download before getting on the newsletter list. "We offer the content first, and then the way to stay in touch second," says Meyer (personal communication, February 2013). NTEN used to have its newsletter sign-up box in the upper-right-hand corner of the site's pages, but now you'll find it at the bottom of articles, so if you like what you've just read, you can sign up for more.

The key is to create relevant and valuable content and to share it, so that when people are actively searching for resources on your topic, they find you. You become known as a great source of information on your topic, so that others see you as the expert and refer their friends and family to you. You create such good stuff that people can't help but talk about it, can't help but share it, and everyone notices that. People come to you via searches or because they see others they already know and trust talking about you on Facebook or on Twitter or on YouTube.

If you are interested in getting mainstream media attention—guess what? Inbound marketing works with reporters too! They use Google searches and social media just like everyone else to find story leads and expert sources.

Outbound marketing tries to push your messages in front of people, often interrupting their focus on something else. Advertising, particularly in the form of television commercials, is a classic example of outbound marketing.

Inbound marketing tries to attract people to your messages. A website article found when someone is searching on a particular topic is a classic example of inbound marketing. This is especially true if that article includes a way for the reader to connect further with the organization that published it (for example, by subscribing to an e-newsletter).

You then share your interesting content and start those conversations on topics you and your participants and supporters care about in many different places, which leads to what's called *multichannel marketing* or *integrated marketing*. No single communications channel is enough anymore. In our 24/7 media environment, the reality is that nonprofits need to use multiple forms of communication—or multiple channels—to effectively reach existing and potential participants and supporters. But you can't just spread messages throughout all available channels willy-nilly. You need to coordinate and integrate your messaging. Knowing which channels to use and coordinating the ways your messages go out across them is also part of your content marketing strategy.

Finally, you may have heard the term *brand journalism,* and the approach it describes will likely be a big part of your content strategy too. Because no one single story or ad will fully explain what an organization is all about, nonprofits can function as brand journalists and tell lots of stories over time that, taken altogether, convey the organization's interests and values. Brand journalists tell stories about what's happening within an organization and about the people being served, and they take us behind the scenes so that we better understand what's at stake and the role we might play in that larger story.

Brand journalism involves applying some of the concepts of journalism, such as objectivity, research and reporting, timeliness, and storytelling, to the communications of an organization. This approach can also be used to weave the stories of a nonprofit's staff, board, participants, supporters, and influencers together to create a more complete view of the organization's work.

If your organization has already adopted a *donor-centered* approach to its fundraising communications, then you will see content marketing as a logical extension. You will apply this new focus to all of your communications with all your participants, supporters, and influencers, not just your donor stewardship pieces and not just communications to recruit new donors.

While you'll see an emphasis on integrated or multichannel marketing when I'm talking about implementation of a content marketing strategy, don't be misled into thinking that's all there is to it. Using multiple communications channels well is important, but that channel mix will work for your nonprofit only if you are also creating and sharing high-quality content that your community finds relevant and engaging and that leads people to want to help you achieve your mission.

How Inbound and Outbound Communications Work Together

Can traditional (outbound) communications work together with content marketing (inbound) communications? Yes!

Creating content that attracts people to you doesn't mean that advertising or traditional direct mail can't or won't work for you as well. There are pros and cons to both inbound and outbound marketing strategies.

While content marketing will produce better community engagement, it also requires that you create more content and invest more time in conversations with your community than you would when using outbound marketing tactics. When you are relying on search engine optimization, for example, it can take months before you start to see significant results, whereas outbound advertising can produce results more quickly. But such advertising is more expensive and short-lived than content-based search engine optimization. If your strategy depends on word-of-mouth sharing, people are much more likely to share good content than they are to share advertising or PR messages.

Remember, content marketing isn't an all or nothing strategy. It can be paired with or used alongside traditional outbound marketing channels.

Communications at VolunteerMatch before and after Content Marketing

When Robert Rosenthal joined VolunteerMatch in 2006 as manager of communications and marketing, growing awareness of a nonprofit's work was mostly about mainstream public relations, and it had been that way at VolunteerMatch for several years. "VolunteerMatch was hot stuff in 2001," says Rosenthal. "Oprah had talked about us, and it brought down our server. President Bush talked about us post 9/11. So we had already had our PR supernova. By the time I got there in 2006," he recalls, "it wasn't clear where we should go next" (personal communication, February 2013).

In addition to PR, most of the other communications work focused on VolunteerMatch's main product—its database that matches volunteers with nonprofits who need them—and how individuals, nonprofits, and businesses could use it. "But there wasn't much content on the website that described or analyzed the field that we were working in," says Rosenthal.

So he started thinking about ways that VolunteerMatch could create content that would attract and serve two very different parts of the VolunteerMatch community: nonprofits who are listing volunteer opportunities in the database and corporations who pay to use VolunteerMatch's software platform to manage their own employee volunteering programs as part of their corporate social responsibility (CSR) programs.

He started with the nonprofit side. "Before, we didn't have any education or training about working with volunteers on our site. All we had were some website help files on how to use our database and update your account," says Rosenthal. Today, after implementing a content marketing approach, the VolunteerMatch Learning Center houses dozens of free webinars on the practices of volunteer engagement, such as recruitment, screening, orientation, and recognition of volunteers. "We had 50,000 nonprofits on our list and they all had similar needs. But if they wanted to get better at their jobs, they often had to pay an army of consultants to get answers and help," says Rosenthal.

It didn't happen overnight. In fact, it took about two years to secure the grant funding, get the curriculum developed, and set up the system to deliver the training. "This was a big shift for us, and it took a lot of conversation and buy-in, in addition to actually creating all the content," says Rosenthal. The learning center launched in early 2009. "Today, it's a robust minisite at learn.volunteermatch.org, and we serve between 5,000 and 10,000 nonprofit professionals there a year."

The strategy on the corporate side was approached a bit differently. "We had a tradition of doing conference calls with our corporate clients, but not a tradition of using content as a lead generator to attract potential new clients," says Rosenthal. "We looked at what it was costing us to acquire new leads and realized that there was tremendous potential to educate and inform companies while growing our revenue at the same time."

Rather than developing a curriculum as it had for the nonprofits, VolunteerMatch tapped into its community to provide guest speakers to lead the conference calls. Topics have included such subjects as effective branding strategies for volunteer programs, how to communicate program success as part of overall CSR, and measurement and assessment of volunteer campaigns. "We are connecting experts in corporate sustainability and social responsibility with experts in volunteerism. While volunteering is a small part of the bigger CSR picture compared to topics like shareholder transparency and greening the supply chain, it's still important," says Rosenthal. Because VolunteerMatch relied on outside experts to deliver content, and because this activity was seen as a clear lead generator, getting this side of the content marketing program up and running took only about six months.

VolunteerMatch is now implementing two distinct content marketing strategies for the two parts of its community, and the two strategies are implemented by different staff as well. "We do keep them segregated, because they have different goals and a different language. Mingling the nonprofit and corporate messages confuses everyone," says Rosenthal. The names of the two related blogs say it all: the blog for nonprofits is called *Engaging Volunteers*, and the blog for corporations is called *Volunteering Is CSR*. Keeping them separate allows VolunteerMatch to focus the messaging for each group. "Otherwise the content would get watered down, or it would be all over the place, and hard for members of each group to find what's there for them," says Rosenthal.

As for Rosenthal's job now, he spends very little time pitching to the media and much more time thinking about content that will delight and inform people. "And reporters still call," he says.

Nonprofit Communications with and without a Content Strategy

For a summary of the first part of this chapter, take a look at table 2.1, which displays some of the benefits of using a content marketing strategy to drive your communications plan, rather than a traditional, organization-focused strategy.

TABLE 2.1
Nonprofit Communications with and without a Content Marketing Strategy

Without a content strategy	With a content strategy
You publish a random collection of articles and other content.	Each piece you create fits into the larger story you are telling.
You focus on your organization's goals, like fundraising, increasing participation rates, and reporting on activities.	You focus on supporters' and participants' goals, like having fun, being a better person, and beating the bad guys.
You write about your expert staff.	You share your expertise.
The first (*I*, *our*) or third person (*the nonprofit*, *it*) dominates your writing.	The second person (*you*, *your*) dominates your writing.
You feel like a salesperson as you write.	You feel like a journalist as you write.
You make your readers feel suspicious and annoyed.	You make your readers feel smarter and happier.
Readers may think of you as an intruder or someone who interrupts all the time.	Readers are likely to think of you as an invited guest who seems to know just what they wanted and what to say.
Your website, newsletter, and social channels are all managed separately.	You tailor and repurpose content for different channels, but the core message remains the same.
Marketing, fundraising, and program staff talk to each other only when they need something from someone.	Marketing, fundraising, and program staff work together constantly.
You leave people hanging.	You suggest next steps or opportunities.
You make it all up as you go.	Your work is planned, but with built-in flexibility to adjust as needed.
Your communications are unpredictable.	Your communications are consistent, like a promise made and kept.
You create long, tedious to-do lists.	You create results.

Stop, Think, and Discuss

Looking at table 2.1, ask yourself whether your nonprofit's current communications are best described by the left-hand column or the right-hand column?

What easy changes could you make so that more of your communications would have the characteristics in the right-hand column? What changes would take longer to implement?

Focusing Less on Channels and More on Reactions

Another way to think about the shift from traditional nonprofit communications to nonprofit content marketing is that it moves the emphasis off the specific communications channels used (such as a newsletter or website) and puts it on the people who are using the content provided through those channels (for example, when donors read stories and see pictures in a newsletter and on your website that show the changes taking place because of their support, they become a communications focus). This may seem like a subtle difference, but in the hustle and bustle of overworked and underfunded nonprofits, it's vitally important to understand and embrace it.

Furthermore, you want to focus on what you believe your PSIs' reactions to your content will be. How will a particular article or campaign make them feel about your organization? Do you expect them to trust you more, or feel a sense of kinship? Will they feel inspired and compelled to learn or to do more? Does the content help build the relationship between people and your organization to the point where they would consider your nonprofit one of their favorite causes?

Kevin Schulman, founder of and partner in the donor relationship and experience company, DonorVoice, says nonprofits are too focused on specific communications and fundraising activities, which, he says, get talked about as if they were actual strategy (personal communication, November 2012). "It's a false choice," says Schulman, "to think you have to pick sides in debates about which channels to use to reach which people" (for example, how much to invest in direct mail versus online communications in order to reach a certain demographic). "Nonprofits need to nail their core positioning and their brand in a way that really resonates and that differentiates [them]—it is a sea of sameness right now," says Schulman. "If this becomes the focus and the litmus test for decision making, does this content and message fit our positioning regardless of channel or form?—these questions of channel get relegated to tactics where they belong," he continues. Remember, people are crossing back and forth between communications channels all the time. "Yes, you should pay attention to tactical best practices, but what really matters is how donors think and feel about the nonprofit. That's what causes giving, not the communications channel."

The conclusion of the report *The Next Generation of American Giving* (Bhagat, Loeb, and Rovner, 2010) says it well: "[Nothing] is as important as the content you produce. There is not a single tactic or giving channel that is nearly as important as the quality of your message and your ability to inspire, arouse and engage the hearts and minds of your donors. Especially their hearts."

A *brand* is the personality of your organization, or what you want it to be known for, or how you want it to be perceived by participants, supporters, and influencers. Your nonprofit's brand includes its visual identity, like its logo and colors palette, but also includes its voice, style, and tone and the topics that it communicates about. You'll explore your brand further in chapter 5.

Example: Remaking a Newsletter Using Content Marketing

The typical nonprofit newsletter is very much an outbound marketing communications channel. It's full of announcements and summaries of recent staff work that the nonprofit desperately wants its PSIs to know about, and yet there is little incentive for them to actually read it. Their main reaction to it may be so what and who cares?

But that doesn't mean newsletters are no good. Far from it. You just need to transform your newsletter into something that's much more focused on the reader and less about you and the organization. That's what the Nonprofit Technology Network has done over the last few years.

Brett Meyer was the communications director at NTEN for six years. When he first started at the organization, the monthly newsletter was written primarily by staff, with occasional guest articles. NTEN would publish four or five articles all at once on its website, and then send out teasers for the articles in an e-newsletter, in the hope that readers would click over to the website for the full article. "In 2010, we noticed that our web traffic from the newsletters was going down, so we needed to do something different," says Meyer.

NTEN decided to shift to a much more robust guest author model in which it recruits ten to fifteen people from within its community to write an article each month. Then NTEN publishes one or two of these articles on its blog each day for the first two to three weeks of the month—and watches what happens. Which articles get the most views? Which get shared the most? What kinds of comments do they generate? The articles' popularity as blog posts is what determines whether they will be included in the e-newsletter that goes out toward the end of the month.

"We've gamified our newsletter content for the authors," adds Meyer. If an author really wants his article to get out via the e-newsletter—which goes to many more people than would see the content on the blog alone—he has an incentive to share it with his own networks, driving additional visitors to the NTEN website. "While some authors really don't care about the extra visibility, some are excited about the challenge," says Meyer, "and they will actively promote the article they wrote for NTEN with their own social media and email lists so they can increase the popularity of the article in NTEN's eyes."

NTEN now knows which articles are likely to be most interesting to those on the newsletter email list before they are sent out, based on what has essentially been an informal focus group in social media. While the decision on which handful of articles goes into the e-newsletter is not based solely on popularity, it does weigh heavily on the decision.

This approach has multiple benefits:

- NTEN staff don't have to write all the content.
- Authors in NTEN's network get excited about contributing.

- NTEN gets more content than it needs for the newsletter, so it can just use the best of it.

- "Best of" is determined largely by NTEN's community itself.

- NTEN can provide a broader selection of content to its community in its newsletter and on its website than it could if it produced the content with staff alone.

- The less popular content that appears only on the blog still helps NTEN by broadening its search engine optimization.

In addition to developing and prioritizing the content this way, NTEN also dynamically generates the newsletter content that goes out to members based primarily on each member's job category. Therefore members of NTEN who are communications directors do not get exactly the same newsletter content as members who are IT directors.

The Power of Becoming a Favorite Nonprofit

DonorVoice (2011) argues that measuring a supporter's attitude about your non-profit is the single best way to measure her likelihood of supporting you in the future—more so than such popular techniques as looking at how recently or how frequently she gives to your organization. "This might feel fuzzy and abstract, but what constitutes a relationship can be managed and measured," says Schulman. DonorVoice has developed what it calls the Donor Commitment Score, which is determined by answers to just three questions, scored on a scale from 0 (strongly disagree) to 10 (strongly agree). These three questions were identified through a rigorous, iterative process that started with more than 100 items.

1. I am a committed [*organization name*] donor.

2. I feel a sense of loyalty to [*organization name*].

3. [*Organization name*] is my favorite charitable organization.

Schulman recommends that nonprofits catalogue all their activities, across all departments, that can affect the strength of the relationship with a donor. This includes not just the obvious communications and fundraising activities but also how program staff interact with program participants and supporters, how frontline office staff answer the phone or greet office guests, how customer service issues are handled, and more. "What we find in working with our clients is that it's like an archeology exercise to identify all of these activities, but they add up to a de facto donor retention budget that's not being managed as such," says Schulman. If they were managed like a budget, it would be easier to see what is positively affecting relationships and what is not.

For example, with one nonprofit client, he discovered that it had decided to scale back the size of a newsletter because it thought this communication cost too much to produce, only to find out through a relationship analysis that the newsletter was vital in maintaining donor connections. With another client, however, he discovered that the newsletter did little or nothing to strengthen the relationship.

We know that donors who feel committed and loyal to a favorite charity do much more for that organization than for others. According to the *Nonprofit Donor Engagement Benchmark Study* (Charity Dynamics and the Nonprofit Technology Network, 2012), most people (78 percent) who give to charity support more than one organization. But it's that single favorite charity that wins big.

This study found that while supporters will often donate to multiple charities in a given year, they are likely to become more engaged with a single organization—their favorite charity. Donors in this study gave two-thirds of their annual charitable donations to that one favorite charity. They were more likely not only to send money but also to become champions of that cause.

Stop, Think, and Discuss

When you look at the time you and others in your nonprofit spend discussing communications, how much of that time is spent on coordinating the production of the content and how much on identifying the kinds of reactions you hope the content will elicit?

Is your organization producing content that you believe will make it a favorite? How could it produce more of that kind of content?

Finding Your Nonprofit's Marketing Maturity Level

A content marketing strategy, well planned and well executed, can make your nonprofit a favorite charity. But first, you may need to overcome some institutional, cultural, or historical barriers within your organization. We all grow and change as people and as professionals, and so do our organizations. Let's look at three stages of nonprofit marketing maturity and how they may affect your organization's ability to embrace content marketing. This is not primarily about the set of communications tools you use but rather about the attitudes and approaches to marketing and communications within your organization. To give you a sense of what it feels like to work at organizations in each stage, the description of each stage begins with comments shared with me via the survey I conducted for the *2013 Nonprofit Communications Trends Report* (Leroux Miller, 2013).

Stage 1: Doing

Survey Comments from Stage 1 Nonprofits

"It's so hard to keep up with the speed at which new forms of communication appear and disappear. There are so many ways to communicate and I don't have the time or resources to do them all."

"People here are stuck in their comfort zones. It's the same old, same old. We'll do what we did last year, because it's what we did the year before."

"There is a stigma attached to marketing here. The board and management want people to know about us, but they won't work on a marketing plan or give me anything to work with. They think it should just happen without investing time or money."

"Our executive director is sabotaging efforts to involve other staff, board, and volunteers in influencing the 'voice' of our organization by insisting that all communications come through her."

"We are in the 'throw everything at the wall and see what sticks' mode. No one seems to know what to say 'no' to here."

Nonprofits in the just-doing-it stage are focused almost exclusively on tactics, like getting out the newsletter and updating the website or Facebook.

Communications work is often parceled out among program staff and the executive director. But at some point, staff members tire of doing what feels like extra work, and the nonprofit then hires a communications coordinator or director.

All the communications to-dos are dumped on the new person, who is quickly buried in tactical implementation.

You'll find both communications and program staff in stage 1 nonprofits constantly brainstorming and hand-wringing about what they will put in the next edition of the newsletter—or being flippant about it because they don't think it really matters. These conversations feel random and disconnected from month to month because there is no real strategic focus or messaging.

When asked to identify specifically whom they are trying to communicate with, they'll usually respond with "the general public" or "everyone." The goal is to "get the word out," which to them means getting updates about their work out the door. The approach to using the various communications channels is one size fits all, with text frequently copied and pasted between channels with few changes. Content will often swing wildly from jargon-filled, passionless updates to fake enthusiasm for some event, with lots of exclamation points.

The success of the communications program is judged by the quantity of communications, whether those communications talk about what's most important from the staff's perspective, and what insiders think of the communications ("Our board loves our newsletter!"). Decisions to make changes to the current approach are often simply decisions to mimic what other nonprofits are doing or "what's hot right now," without much strategic reasoning behind them.

This lopsided view of the role of communications in the organization places more emphasis on the internal needs of the nonprofit than on the needs of participants or supporters. Therefore, should the organization fall into a financial crisis, the communications program is the first to be cut. The communications person was really there to make life easier for the program staff, so in tough times what's seen as a luxury is cut back and the workload is shifted back onto the program staff or the executive director.

Frankly, it's hard for a nonprofit to implement content marketing while it's in stage 1. There simply isn't enough strategic thinking taking place. But if you are in this stage, that doesn't mean you shouldn't try! You might start small, by focusing on one distinct group of people you'd like to improve your relationship with through higher-quality and more engaging content. Given the lack of organizational support, it will be best to start small and choose something that you have some control over (even if that's because of benign neglect by management).

Of course, if you think your organization is ready for a major overhaul, go for it! This window of opportunity can open when new leadership is brought on board. But it won't open overnight. Be prepared to explain over and over (and over) why you are doing things differently now, to prevent others from backsliding into old habits. Internal training and communications will be as important as, if not more important than, external communications at first.

Stage 2: Questioning

Survey Comments from Stage 2 Nonprofits

"We are struggling to understand who our online community really is, and trying to align our messaging across all of our communications platforms."

"It's a challenge to create an open environment where staff are comfortable and confident in engaging and contributing to social media."

"We are trying to figure out how to meet our community where they are. I'm having a hard time communicating the urgency of needing to create new communications that appeal to younger and more tech-savvy prospects and program participants to my Baby Boomer board."

"We are working on ways to measure what we are doing so we can get smarter about our communications strategy. I think there is some nearsightedness within leadership that the immediate fundraising target is more important than long-term engagement."

"We have a lot of lofty goals, and I worry about getting the rest of the organization on board. They are all very busy, but I need their help to be successful with my communications plan. I need to articulate very clearly how they can help me and why they should."

In the second stage, which I call *questioning*, nonprofits discover that good marketing is about much more than just pushing out content through various communications channels. Instead, it's about understanding the people you want to reach so that you can discuss your work in ways that are relevant and valuable to them.

Nonprofits in stage 2 begin to realize that they need to ask and answer important questions about whom they are communicating with (that is, their participants and supporters) and what they should say to these people (that is, the messaging about the value that the organization can provide to its participants and supporters) before jumping into tactical decisions about which communications channels to use. They acknowledge that the spray and pray mentality doesn't work, and they start to think about how to segment the general public into more specific groups.

Discussing these questions often leads to more formal communications planning, which can range from simple editorial calendars to full strategic marketing plans. As stage 2 nonprofits discuss what it will take to get the right message to the right people, they start to explore the budget implications of these decisions and begin writing communications into proposals for program funding.

Program, fundraising, and communications staff consult more often with each other but still often work in silos without much real collaboration. While other staff and managers acknowledge that a communications plan is essential, they don't see this work as part of their own jobs.

Communications become more valued but are still not fully integrated into either strategic planning for the organization or day-to-day executive decision making. Success is still measured mostly by keeping track of the quantity of communications, rather than attempting to measure the impact of those communications.

The communications materials themselves will start to look more professional or sophisticated, at least on the surface. The staff's approaches to their work will also become more efficient, as they think further ahead, repurpose content, and coach program staff about better ways to communicate about their work.

While these nonprofits are asking more of the right questions, they still aren't ready to be fully responsive to their participants and supporters, nor to include them much in the content creation process. While staff will grasp in theory how important it is to really understand who these people on the mailing list are and what motivates them to care about the cause, the nonprofit won't invest much effort in researching the answers.

Most of you reading this book will be in organizations at stage 2. Shifting more consciously toward content marketing is a good approach for stage 2 organizations because it will provide some structure and direction for the questioning and planning that's already taking place.

Stage 3: Integrating

Survey Comments from Stage 3 Nonprofits

"We are much more focused on engagement now, so I need to learn what moves the engagement needle in different channels. I know that depends on quality content and understanding my audiences. But I'm concerned about our capacity to produce the content required to continually drive that engagement."

"I'm excited about continuing our donor-centered communications and being able to show that that is more effective than talking about ourselves all the time."

"I'm learning all the time in an environment that allows a certain amount of risk taking. I love helping those connected to our organization tell their stories, and to give people the words and stories they need to talk about us to others."

"The leadership in our organization is receptive to trying different things and giving staff more authority in driving the marketing/communications approaches and content."

"I am excited about the interconnectivity of different communications media—ours, those of key partners, members and the public at large. We are crowdsourcing more engaging content."

"We've developed engagement goals around most if not all of our communications channels. I feel growing engagement will help with many other goals, like donor retention, program involvement, event participation, etc. I am excited to see what we can achieve with this new focus."

In the third, most mature stage of nonprofit content marketing, the organization has more fully integrated its approach to marketing and communications in numerous ways.

First and foremost, its marketing is very supporter and participant centered, so that knowledge of what these people outside the organization think, want, and need is constantly brought back inside and folded into program, marketing, and fundraising decisions. The communications staff are tasked with listening to and understanding this community as much as they are with communicating out to them. The staff become not just the mouth of the organization but the eyes and ears too.

Communications are seen as an essential part of program and fundraising success, and the effort is relatively well staffed and resourced. Communications, program, and fundraising staff collaborate on projects or campaigns where each staff member or group brings specialized skills and expertise but all staffers see themselves as jointly responsible for the outcomes.

Communications work is judged, at least in part, on the extent to which it helps the nonprofit meet short-term program or fundraising goals. But communications are also recognized and valued for their contribution to the long-term success of the organization: for example, by building brand recognition, increasing the size of mailing lists and engaged communities online that might be asked to support the organization more directly at a later time, and strengthening relationships within the community.

At the tactical level, messaging becomes much more relevant and targeted, as contact lists are segmented and communications are customized by channel. While different people may be responsible for different communications channels, these individuals regularly consult with each other to ensure that the overall messaging coming out of the organization is consistent, regardless of where a participant or supporter may see it. While staff do plan their work by mapping out editorial calendars, they remain nimble so that they can quickly merge breaking news and last-minute program changes into planned material.

The organization's management recognizes that communications practices are changing faster than at any other time in history, and staff are given permission to experiment and to fail as they try new ways to connect with supporters and participants. Learning is valued more than always having the right answer.

Nonprofits in stage 3 are likely already taking a content marketing approach, whether they call it that or not. If your organization is in this stage, some sections of this book will feel basic or obvious, reassuring you that you are on the right track, while others will help you identify and fill any gaps in your content marketing strategy.

Stop, Think, and Discuss

In which stage is your nonprofit now? Do others on your staff agree or disagree with your assessment?

What would it take for your nonprofit to move to the next stage?

Why It Matters: Favorite Organizations Win

I suppose it would be nice if participants, supporters, and influencers fully researched every nonprofit before they interacted with it, made objective comparisons, and always selected the "right" nonprofit. But that's not how the world works, and it never will. We are human, after all, not computers interested in data crunching alone.

How people feel matters. Their hearts (or guts) overrule their heads all the time. That means you have to connect—really connect—on that human level in order to get their attention. To keep that attention, you must try to become one of their favorite organizations. Working on an important cause and doing a good job isn't enough. You have to engage your participants, supporters, and influencers so that they personally feel invested in that good and important work too.

Chapter Three
Planting Your Flag at the Destination
Setting Content Marketing Goals and Measuring Progress

This chapter is about . . .

- Deciding on goals for your content marketing strategy
- Understanding the tension between fundraising and community- or brand-building goals
- Figuring out how you'll measure your progress along the way

---

We all know that life is about the journey and not the destination. The moments I remember most from my various backpacking and hiking trips are the events and conversations that happened on the trail or at campsites along the way—not reaching the destination itself.

But that doesn't mean that we shouldn't set goals. The excitement of reaching the mountain's summit or finding the perfect swimming hole under a majestic waterfall is what gets you moving in the first place. Setting content marketing goals is what helps you redirect your marketing toward engagement and becoming a favorite nonprofit. Just like on the trail, you will constantly adjust as you go. But to motivate yourself and encourage others to join you, you need some clarity about where you are heading and why. You need to pick your destination on the map and plant your flag there, so that you can keep walking toward it as you implement your plan.

This sounds simple enough, but I believe setting content marketing goals in the nonprofit sector is much more complicated than in the business world. In business the ultimate goal is nearly always making a sale. But in the nonprofit world, we are seeking many different legitimate and worthwhile outcomes.

We may want people to participate in the programs and services we offer, many of which are free to them, and they may need some convincing before they'll participate. Or conversely, we may be overwhelmed with people who use our services, and therefore we need to communicate who qualifies for help, while also providing self-help or alternatives for those who don't qualify. We may want people to change behaviors in their own lives, or to advocate for policy changes that affect everyone. We may want people to give their time as volunteers or their money as donors. We may want them to open doors or put in a good word for us. In many cases, we'll want the same person to do many of these things. It's like the relationship setting on Facebook: it's complicated.

Why Are You Communicating in the First Place?

To make content marketing goal setting less complicated, think about where your communications staff sit in the organization now. To whom do you report? Some nonprofit communicators serve the fundraising department. Some serve the program departments. Some are completely separate from both these areas. Some lead the decision making about how the nonprofit communicates with the outside world, and some follow the lead set by program or fundraising staff. Some act as internal marketing or PR agencies that offer strong advice but ultimately do not make final decisions.

Based on my polls during webinars, conversations with nonprofit marketing staff, and more formal surveys, I estimate that about 25 percent of nonprofit communicators work directly on development goals and feel responsible for raising money during the current year.

Another 25 percent of nonprofit communicators do not have any real fundraising responsibilities. There is either a separate fundraising staff, or the organization is funded primarily via grants or fees for services, which means fundraising from individuals is minimal. In these cases the communications work is more about recruiting program participants or volunteers rather than donors (about 10 percent of nonprofit communicators are in this category), or more about broadly engaging the community, including influencers like public officials and the media (about 15 percent of nonprofit communicators). While this engagement can certainly create a fundraising friendly environment, these communicators do not feel responsible for specific fundraising outcomes. Figure 3.1 summarizes these findings.

For the first half of nonprofit communicators—those who are either clearly responsible for fundraising or not responsible—goal setting is fairly straightforward. It's the other half of nonprofit communicators, those who say they are responsible for program, fundraising, *and* marketing goals, who have more

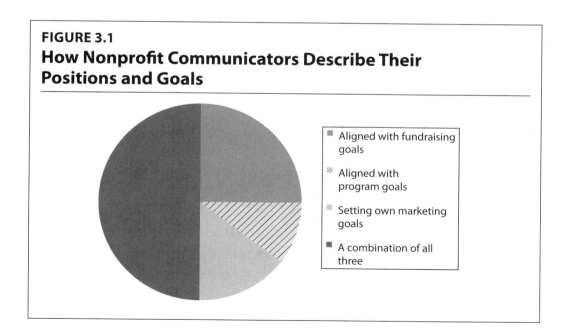

FIGURE 3.1
How Nonprofit Communicators Describe Their Positions and Goals

- Aligned with fundraising goals
- Aligned with program goals
- Setting own marketing goals
- A combination of all three

difficulty prioritizing and setting goals. These communicators are the ones I worry most about, because their jobs are much more likely to be poorly defined, which means success is poorly defined, and therefore they are much more likely to burn out and hate their jobs. We need all the creative, dedicated people we can get in this work, so I don't want that to happen!

If you find yourself in this situation, I suggest you start by talking about the importance of short-term fundraising in your job. It's not that having fundraising goals as a communications director is a good thing or a bad thing. It's just that the extent of the overlap needs to be clear to everyone up front. Short-term fundraising goals may have a big impact on the tactical choices you make about whom you are trying to reach, your message to them, and the communications tools you use. And you are only human, so you can only do so much.

Starting Your Goals Discussion: The Relative Importance of Short-Term Fundraising

Many of the tactical workshops I teach are filled with a mix of fundraisers, marketers, and program staff and managers. As we discuss using a variety of different communications channels, I'll start to hear lots of "yes, but . . ."

"Yes, but not everyone uses Facebook."

"Yes, but we don't have email addresses."

"Yes, but direct mail is too expensive, too slow, and too formal."

At first, on the surface, these debates sound as though they are about which communications channels should receive the most attention. But then, after people dig a little deeper, they quickly turn into conversations about the media and demographics shifts I reviewed in chapter 1. Whom are we really trying to reach, and what communications channels work best for them? What's the ultimate call to action? From there, the conversation invariably turns into this debate: what's more important—getting fundraising results now or building an engaged community of supporters? While this may seem like a simple question, as I noted earlier, I suspect that about half of nonprofit communicators are struggling to find the right balance.

How do these debates play out?

Marketing staff will often suggest that their organizations should invest in reaching out to the younger generations (let's say younger Boomers, Gen Xers, and Gen Yers, or roughly those under fifty-five years of age). Don't others in this organization realize that we have to broaden our base of supporters and build their engagement in the organization in order to survive long term, say the marketing directors?

Fundraising staff will argue that their organizations should focus on the people who give the most, that is, the older generations (the older Boomers and the Matures, or those over fifty-five). Don't others in this organization realize that older donors provide nearly all of our fundraising revenue, say the development directors?

Program staff may fall into either of the previous two camps, depending on what they think they need more of for their own success: people to participate in their program work or people to donate money to support it.

These two camps will look at each other askance and whisper about how the other group just doesn't get it.

My ten-year-old is very bright and gets the answers to her math homework right more often than not, but she sometimes gets marked down for not showing her work, that is, how she arrived at those answers. I attribute the battles between nonprofit marketing staff and fundraising staff about communications strategies to the same problem: not taking the time to share with each other the details behind those closely held points of view, so they can jointly make the right decisions for their organizations.

Let me "show the work" for both of these positions.

Why Fundraisers Tend to Focus on Reaching the Older Generations

First, let's look at why fundraisers would insist on focusing on people over fifty-five. It's simple: their primary goal is to raise money today, and we know that the average amount of money individuals donate to charity increases with age.

According to the report *Donor Perspectives: An Investigation into What Drives Your Donors to Give* (Blackbaud, 2012), on average, US donors over the age of sixty-five gave nearly twice as much as donors aged twenty-five to thirty-four, and more than three times as much as donors aged eighteen to twenty-four (figure 3.2). Generation Y individuals just don't have anywhere close to the same kind of giving power right now as their grandparents do.

According to this same report, however, individual donors who are members of Generation X or younger Boomers (that is, combined, those aged thirty-five to fifty-four) do give roughly the same amount as their older friends and family. So why not focus equal energy there?

While individuals in these groups will often have the same capacity to give as those in older groups, fewer of them actually *do* give. They often still have children at home and other expenses and preferences that limit their philanthropy. Conversely, those over fifty-five have more disposable income and are entering a stage of life where they are more inclined to share their wealth

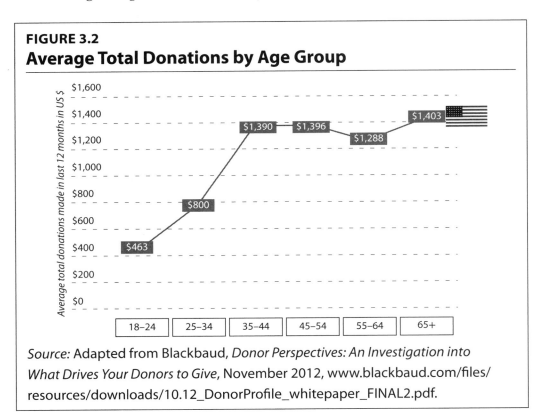

FIGURE 3.2
Average Total Donations by Age Group

Source: Adapted from Blackbaud, *Donor Perspectives: An Investigation into What Drives Your Donors to Give*, November 2012, www.blackbaud.com/files/resources/downloads/10.12_DonorProfile_whitepaper_FINAL2.pdf.

with others. It's the fact that the percentages of donors across the generations are quite different, rather than individuals' likely capacity to give, that makes focusing on those over fifty-five, and especially over sixty-five, so much more lucrative for fundraisers.

This is also why long-time fundraisers will quickly dismiss the idea that they should spend time trying to raise money from Generation Y. It's not because there aren't people in their twenties who can and do give; it's because compared to members of older generations, there are a lot fewer of them who actually do give, and their gifts are much smaller.

Of course this will all change as these younger generations age, but it's going to be awhile, as revealed by figure 3.3, which shows the number of US

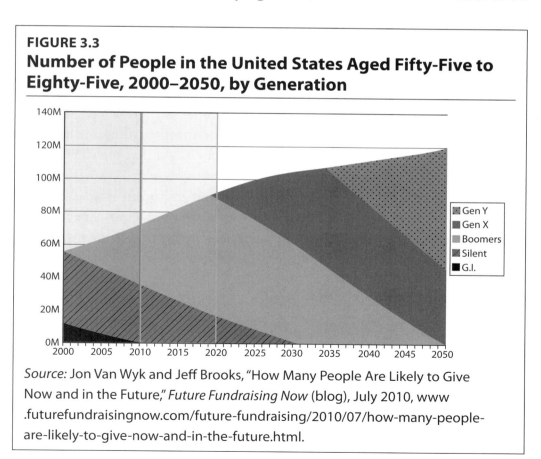

FIGURE 3.3
Number of People in the United States Aged Fifty-Five to Eighty-Five, 2000–2050, by Generation

Source: Jon Van Wyk and Jeff Brooks, "How Many People Are Likely to Give Now and in the Future," *Future Fundraising Now* (blog), July 2010, www .futurefundraisingnow.com/future-fundraising/2010/07/how-many-people-are-likely-to-give-now-and-in-the-future.html.

adults between the ages of fifty-five and eighty-five, divided by generations. Draw a vertical line upward from any year, and you can see which generations will be in what Jeff Brooks of True Sense Marketing, and author of the *Future Fundraising Now* blog, calls the "prime donor age group" at that time. As of 2010, the Boomers had edged out the Matures, or the Silent Generation, as the largest generation in the prime donor age group. These two generations will continue to dominate until 2019, when Boomers will peak at 79 percent of donors in the prime age group.

In 2020, Generation X will hit age fifty-five and enter the prime donor age group. At this point, both the Matures and the Boomer groups will decrease, but Gen X won't overtake the Boomer generation in size until 2033. The Boomers don't exit as a generation until 2050, when those in Gen Y will dominate. Remember, these are not necessarily donors, but rather that part of the population most likely to donate (aged fifty-five to eighty-five) grouped by generation.

Here's a somewhat different take on the value of fundraising from different generations. A 2010 report called *The Next Generation of American Giving* (Bhagat, Loeb, and Rovner, 2010) found, as we know, that total annual charitable contributions grow with age. But this report concluded that the difference is driven primarily by the number of charities contributed to, rather than by differences in gift size. This suggests that if your nonprofit is successful in attracting younger donors, it can be quite profitable for your organization, especially considering their lifetime potential as donors and how responsive they are to lower-cost, online communications compared to more expensive direct mail.

This report went a step further by coupling average giving data (excluding major gifts—an important distinction) with the size of the donor population in each generational group to compare their relative attractiveness. This chart in figure 3.4 shows that Boomers and Gen Xers represent much larger donor pools than the Matures, who in this analysis represent just 28 percent of contributions, with Boomers responsible for 40 percent of giving, and Generations X and Y combined responsible for 32 percent of giving.

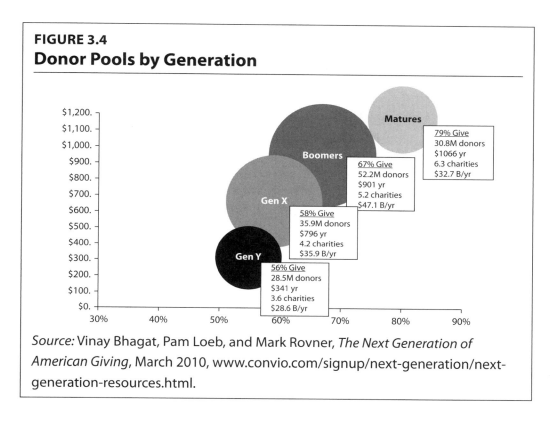

FIGURE 3.4
Donor Pools by Generation

Source: Vinay Bhagat, Pam Loeb, and Mark Rovner, *The Next Generation of American Giving*, March 2010, www.convio.com/signup/next-generation/next-generation-resources.html.

Why Marketers Tend to Focus on Reaching the Younger Generations

Now let's take a look at the reasons why many marketing staff are particularly interested in reaching people under fifty-five. Marketers' goals are different from fundraisers' goals. Rather than focusing on short-term fundraising results, they take both a broader and a longer-term view of success. They are more interested in building and engaging a community of participants and supporters. Whereas fundraisers live by the revenue generated now, marketers are more interested in the long-term value of their community, which they measure according to metrics like size of the various contact lists (direct mail, email, and social media) and the level of engagement with those on the lists. Donations today are just one of many metrics that interest marketers.

Let me show the work for this point of view, with community engagement of people under fifty-five as the primary goal. Is making people feel connected to the cause or engaged with a nonprofit worth anything? Without a doubt, yes, it is.

Just as age defines the prime donor group, it also affects what else people are willing to do for the charities they support. The US Bureau of Labor Statistics (2011) reports that 66 percent of volunteers are under age fifty-five, while just 34 percent are fifty-five or older—a flip-flop from what we see with donors. The volunteer rate tends to be higher in teen years than in early adulthood, when the volunteering rate is typically at its second lowest point after very old age. In the middle to late twenties, volunteering rates begin to pick up again, growing until they reach a peak around the time of middle age. After middle age, volunteering rates begin to drop again as age increases (figure 3.5).

According to the *Nonprofit Donor Engagement Benchmark Study* (Charity Dynamics and Nonprofit Technology Network, 2012), people aged thirty to sixty-nine were all highly willing to donate to their favorite charities. But when we look at other

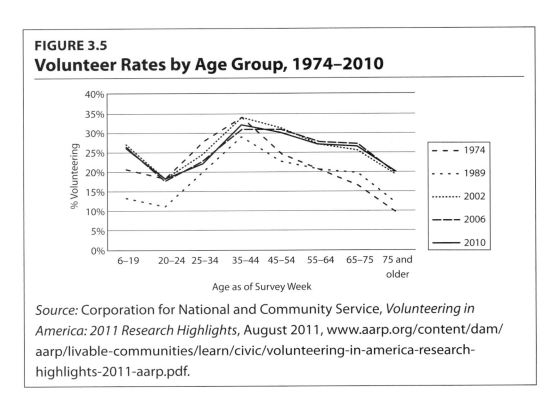

FIGURE 3.5
Volunteer Rates by Age Group, 1974–2010

Source: Corporation for National and Community Service, *Volunteering in America: 2011 Research Highlights*, August 2011, www.aarp.org/content/dam/aarp/livable-communities/learn/civic/volunteering-in-america-research-highlights-2011-aarp.pdf.

activities, we see that people under fifty are much more willing to fundraise on behalf of their favorite charity. Those under forty are more likely to volunteer, to participate in fundraising events like 5K runs or galas, and to sign a petition or pledge.

While a $5 donation from a twenty- or thirty-year-old may not seem like much today, what's more important in the eyes of nonprofit marketers is that the person is now potentially available as a volunteer, advocate, peer fundraiser, event attendee, or other kind of program participant, supporter, or influencer. If it's a good match, and the nonprofit can keep the person engaged, perhaps that $5 donation will grow into something much more significant as that person ages. One study found that online campaigns can double the giving response rates when connecting a fundraising ask with an advocacy initiative, and that advocates are seven times more likely than nonadvocates to give financially (Daigneault, Davis, and Sybrant, 2011).

But even if the donation doesn't materialize, there is still value in other forms of engagement today. Let's use the term *altruism*—unselfish regard for or devotion to the welfare of others—to describe the relationship between a person and the nonprofit she supports, whether that's through donating, volunteering, or advocating for the cause.

We know that altruism spreads through networks, creating a ripple effect. Research by James Fowler at the University of California, San Diego, and Nicholas Christakis of the Harvard Medical School has demonstrated that altruism can spread by three degrees—from person to person to person to person. "Each person in a network," they concluded, "can influence dozens or even hundreds of people, some of whom he or she does not know and has not met" (Fowler and Christakis, 2010).

There's serious power—human and financial—behind the network effect. That's the thinking behind language like this from a fundraising email sent by Barack Obama's campaign in 2011: "We measure our success not in dollars but in people—in the number of everyday Americans who've chosen to give whatever they can afford because they know we've got more work to do" (Salant, 2011). The Obama campaign also solicited small contributions through a variety of contests, such as offering a chance to attend Obama's fiftieth birthday party to anyone who recruited fifty donors or fifty supporters.

In this case, engaging smaller-dollar donors also meant acquiring voters and signing up volunteers to knock on doors and make phone calls, getting both friends and strangers to contribute to the campaign and to go to the polls. Whether a nonprofit's call to action is "vote" or "advocate" or something entirely different, the network effect is the same: people participate in the work of the nonprofit, cooperating with the organization to achieve its mission, and that altruism spreads to others, further building support for the cause.

How does all of this play out then in the communications goals nonprofits are setting?

For my *2013 Nonprofit Communications Trends Report* (Leroux Miller, 2013), I asked nonprofits to identify their three most important goals for their communications strategies, choosing from a list of twelve options, not including "other" (figure 3.6). Acquiring new donors (57 percent), engaging our community

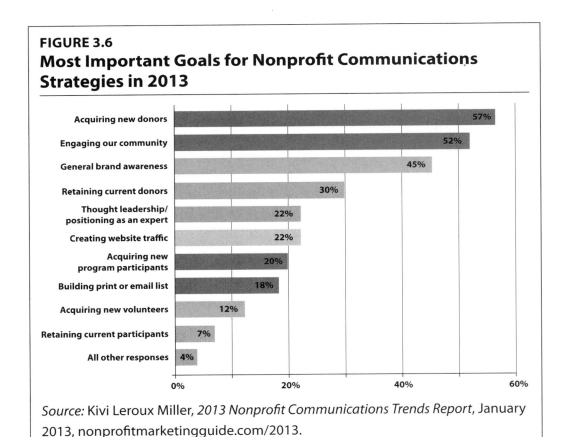

FIGURE 3.6
Most Important Goals for Nonprofit Communications Strategies in 2013

Source: Kivi Leroux Miller, *2013 Nonprofit Communications Trends Report*, January 2013, nonprofitmarketingguide.com/2013.

(52 percent), and general brand awareness (45 percent) were the clear, stand-out answers.

Communicators at larger organizations (those with organizational budgets over $1 million) were more likely than smaller organizations to focus on donors (88 percent prioritized donor acquisition and/or retention). For smaller organizations (those with organizational budgets under $1 million), that goal dropped to 77 percent. Conversely, smaller organizations were more likely than larger organizations to focus on acquiring program participants (22 percent versus 17 percent) and volunteers (17 percent versus 8 percent).

The 1,535 nonprofits who participated in the survey selected more than eighty different trios of top goals, further reinforcing how varied the jobs of nonprofit communicators are. The most popular combination represented barely 7 percent of nonprofits (see table 3.1).

TABLE 3.1
Most Popular Goal Combinations for Nonprofit Communicators in 2013

Top three goals	% of communicators using this goal combination
Donor acquisition, donor retention, community engagement	7
Donor acquisition, community engagement, brand awareness	6
Donor acquisition, donor retention, brand awareness	5
Community engagement, brand awareness, thought leadership	4

Note: For additional information on the various ways these goals overlap, you can see several Venn diagrams created from the survey data at npmg.us/venngoals.

Source: Data from Kivi Leroux Miller, *2013 Nonprofit Communications Trends Report,* January 2013, nonprofitmarketingguide.com/2013.

Fundraising Communicators versus Community- or Brand-Building Communicators

What I found most interesting were the differences between the survey participants whose communications strategies were focused on both acquiring new donors and retaining current donors (I'll call them the *fundraising communicators*) and the participants who were focused on engaging our community, general brand awareness, and thought leadership/positioning as an expert (I'll call them the *community or brand builders*).

Compared to the fundraising communicators, the community or brand builders were more likely to have written plans and to work for larger organizations (60 percent of the respondents in this category had organizational budgets over $1 million). They were more likely to identify media relations and PR, blogging, and social media as very important tools. They were also more likely to say that phone calls/phone banks and paid advertising were their least important tools. They planned to email more frequently and were much more likely to rely on and experiment with social media.

The types of content community or brand builders were spending most of their time on revealed a content marketing approach to communications. These respondents were much more likely to be spending their time producing blog posts, webinars or other training content, Twitter updates, infographics, and research reports or white papers than those with fundraising goals were. They were also more likely to identify lack of time to produce quality content, producing enough content, producing engaging content, and difficulty integrating communications channels as their biggest challenges.

Conversely, the fundraising communicators were much more likely to identify both print marketing and email marketing as very important communications tools, along with phone calls/phone banks and in-person events. They were likely to send direct mail more often and to take a more conservative approach to social media. For example, they were more likely to say they were experimenting with sites like Twitter and YouTube, sites that have been more fully adopted already by community or brand builders.

Fundraising communicators were also much more likely to spend their time on print and email fundraising appeals and print and email newsletter articles.

They were somewhat more likely to say that the budget for direct expenses, lack of clear strategy, and lack of knowledge or training needed to produce content were big challenges.

When I see two nonprofit marketing professionals arguing with each other, I now ask about their roles in their organizations and how important short-term fundraising goals are to their own success. And when I advise nonprofit communicators about their content strategies, I ask them how important short-term fundraising is to their definition of success.

Stop, Think, and Discuss

To what extent are your communications staff responsible for short-term fundraising? What is the appropriate level of overlap, if any, between fundraising goals and community- or brand-building goals in your organization?

Aligning Your Goals with What Defines Success

Once you've clarified the extent to which fundraising is a part of your responsibilities as a nonprofit communicator, you can move on to selecting some goals and planting your flag at your content marketing destination.

Setting Fundraising Goals

If your work is very closely aligned with your organization's fundraising, development, or advancement department, then your objectives will be closely aligned with traditional fundraising goals.

Your goals may be some variation or combination of

- Acquiring new donors
- Retaining current donors
- Increasing levels of giving, either how often or how much
- Securing funding for new programs
- Encouraging peer-to-peer or social media fundraising

I also recommend that you and your staff talk about the difference between donor acquisition and donor retention as priorities. In the *2013 Nonprofit*

Communications Trends Report, I found that according to what nonprofits say they plan to do in 2013, acquisition beats retention as a goal by two to one (figure 3.7). I also found that larger organizations were more likely than smaller ones to strike a more even balance between these two goals, probably because bigger organizations tend to have more development and communications staff who can think more strategically about these questions. Larger organizations don't usually have quite the same crisis-survival mentality that smaller nonprofits do, which leads those smaller organizations to focus more on acquisition.

FIGURE 3.7
Ranking Acquisition versus Retention among the Top Three Goals

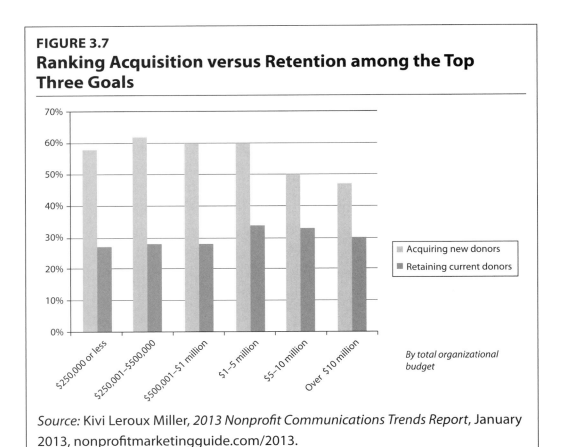

By total organizational budget

Source: Kivi Leroux Miller, *2013 Nonprofit Communications Trends Report*, January 2013, nonprofitmarketingguide.com/2013.

This donor acquisition focus is in stark contrast, however, to what you will read in most fundraising blogs and other trade press, where experts are strongly urging more focus on donor retention. I encourage you and your nonprofit to listen to that advice and to place more emphasis on donor retention than the *2013 Nonprofit Communications Trends Report* suggests nonprofits are currently doing.

Setting Program Goals

If your work is more closely aligned with the program side of your nonprofit, your goals should be more aligned with program results than with fundraising.

Your goals may be some variation or combination of

- Getting more program participants or volunteers
- Diversifying program participants or volunteers (by age, skills, geography, or some other factor)
- Getting people to register for or attend events
- Collecting and analyzing feedback from program participants or supporters
- Educating people on specific issues

In either case, if your work is closely aligned with the work of another part of your organization, you shouldn't be setting your own goals and deciding on your own how you will measure your success. These conversations must be held in concert with the staff with whom you are aligned.

Setting Community- or Brand-Building Goals

If you operate somewhat independently in your organization, or if you work across the entire organization, you may be interested in a different set of goals—ones that both directly and indirectly help fundraising and program staff. For example:

- Engaging participants and supporters
- Increasing website traffic, including search engine optimization
- Building direct mail, email, and social media lists
- Improving awareness or perceptions of the organization
- Positioning the organization as a thought leader or expert
- Getting reporters to view your organization as a reliable source

Stop, Think, and Discuss

What goals make sense for your organization? Where are you planting your flag for your content marketing strategy?

But Isn't It All the Same Thing as Engagement?

You may be thinking that you can take all these goals and roll them into one, calling it *engagement*. After all, a reporter writing a story, a donor making a gift, and a participant attending a workshop are all interacting with the nonprofit—and therefore engaging with it, right? Yes and no.

It's important to keep your calls to action in mind. What are the specific things you want your participants, supporters, and influencers to do, and more important, when do you want them to do these things? How urgent is it that they follow through on what you are asking of them? The more urgency, the more specific your goals have to be.

It's also important to build both pragmatism and accountability into your goal setting. All the goals discussed in this chapter (and listed in figure 3.6) are worthy, but it's nearly impossible for a small communications department to reach all of them at once. If you overreach in setting your goals and everyone knows it, it's likely that staff won't feel accountable for achieving those goals. Or if they do feel accountable, they are likely to end up thinking of themselves as failures, no matter how hard they worked. Goals that stretch people are fine. Goals that are more likely to break people are not.

That's why it's so important to be clear about your goals before you develop your specific content marketing strategy. I suggest that you pick no more than three goals as your priorities for any given year.

Measuring Content Marketing Progress: Are We There Yet?

All the companies that you use for online marketing produce data for you on how people are interacting with your content, from Google Analytics to Facebook Insights to your email open and click-through rates. There are plenty of data out there to view, but it's not always so easy to make sense of them. Just having a number available to you doesn't make that number meaningful. Many nonprofits end up collecting lots of interesting but ultimately useless data because the numbers don't help the organization make decisions. Instead, you should collect data that help you determine what's working and what's not during your journey toward your goals, so that you can do more of what's working and less of what isn't.

Measuring Exposure versus Engagement

Let's go back to the stadium analogy I used in chapter 1 for a moment. The number of people who are in the stadium is akin to the size of your mailing and social media lists: that is, the number of people who are exposed to your communications. However, the number of true fans in the stadium is quite different from the total number, and there is a range of behaviors even among these fans, from wearing the team colors to buying season tickets to wearing face paint and standing up and screaming for the whole game. That's the level of engagement. You need to look at the combination of these two measures. While engagement is ultimately more important, you won't have anyone to build that rapport with if you aren't introducing yourself to new people and starting those conversations by building your lists.

There are important distinctions between measuring impressions (how many people saw something) and measuring impact (what those people did after seeing it). It's the difference between measuring coverage (how many media outlets, big and small, covered your story) and measuring the conversation it created (again, what people did after seeing the coverage). You need to measure both. Don't stop with measuring exposure; pair that measurement with engagement.

Stop, Think, and Discuss

What do you measure now? Are those measurements helping you to understand exposure or engagement?

Five Ways to Measure Marketing

Before I talk about what your specific objectives should be, let's look at several ways to gather information that you can use to measure your progress along the way. I recommend using some combination of the following five techniques as ways to gather the data. Your combination will depend on your goals and specific objectives.

1. Regular Surveying or Polling of People Who Matter, Including Your PSIs

Build regular surveying into your workflow. It shouldn't be the kind of thing that comes up randomly in conversation, as in, "Oh geez, we haven't asked anybody what they think in awhile. Maybe we should do a survey." Really structure this into your work plan.

Perhaps you can do surveys after you deliver specific types of programming. Or you can poll your blog and email newsletter readers regularly. Ask questions all the time. Always be thinking, how can we learn more about our participants, our supporters, and our influencers?

Jennifer Charney, the communications manager at Save the Redwoods League, has been surveying readers about the league's publications since 2009 (Charney, 2012). These publications include an annual report, two biannual print newsletters, a calendar, and a monthly e-newsletter. While the league knew the best results would come from hiring a survey expert, it just didn't have the budget.

Charney decided to conduct the surveys herself, believing that some feedback was better than nothing. Through various surveys she has been able to determine favorite newsletter features and story topics, with the added bonus of receiving testimonials that the nonprofit can publish in promotions.

For example, one survey was printed on a postage-paid postcard, and 2,000 were mailed with the organization's annual redwoods wall calendar, which is produced as a thank-you to major donors. The postcard offered donors a chance to win a branded water bottle or tote bag if they answered the eleven multiple-choice and open-ended questions. On this survey, Charney asked donors

- Whether they used the calendar, and how
- What they liked and disliked about it, and what they'd like to see in future calendars

- Whether they learned about the organization's work from it (the calendar features accomplishments)

- Whether Save the Redwoods League should continue publishing it

This survey had a 10 percent response rate, and the results showed that practically all respondents used and liked the calendar as it was, and they wanted the organization to continue producing it. Other revelations:

- Recipients wrote reminders on the calendar, even in these days of Outlook calendars and smartphones. "Writing on the paper calendar makes sense because our members are older," says Charney, "and that's what they're accustomed to. But we assumed they used the calendar primarily as a decoration."

- They wanted to receive the calendar in October, not November.

- The date numbers and the hole for hanging were too small.

- They wanted more variety in the photos.

The postcard survey also asked people whether they visited the Save the Redwoods League website. Most respondents said they did not because they didn't have access to a computer or didn't know how to use one.

With this feedback, Charney changed subsequent calendars and other publications. The calendar continues to be a donor favorite.

A similar printed survey about the league's *Bulletin* newsletter garnered 600 responses. About 98 percent of the respondents said they read the newsletter, and the great majority of their comments were positive. Results also revealed people's favorite parts of the newsletter and suggestions for improvement.

These and other surveys give Save the Redwoods League a baseline against which it can measure future results, and are a way to show management what is working and what isn't working with publication content.

2. Periodic Informal Focus Groups with PSIs and Staff

Perhaps a few times a year, conduct some informal focus groups where you gather people together in person for a discussion. For example, maybe you will find that you have several different categories of people coming to an event, so you could decide to ask them to come an hour earlier or stay an hour later for a focus group. Lead the group through a conversation with some open-ended questions. You're not steering the conversation as much as gently guiding it.

Informal focus groups work best when there is a common denominator that ties everyone in the room together. Maybe you could do a focus group with participants who are new to your organization. Or you could invite people who have been participating over the last six months. Maybe you could talk to supporters who are over sixty-five. When the group has a unifying criterion, you'll be able to do more with the resulting conversation, because it represents a particular, defined group.

3. Monitor Online Mentions and Listen to Representatives of Important Groups, Including Your PSIs

You should set up some kind of automated mention monitoring or listening system. You set up searches on keywords or phrases and save them, so that new reports are sent to you automatically.

The success of your system is very dependent on keywords. You need to know ahead of time what you are listening for. What are the mentions that you care about? What vocabulary are your participants using when they're talking about your programs and services online or when they're searching? They may be choosing words very different from the ones you use professionally. Keep this in mind as you structure your keyword list and monitoring.

4. Watch for Trends in Your Online Analytics for Your Website, Email, and Social Media

What are your website analytics, like Google Analytics, telling you? What's happening with your email? All your online communications tools have built-in metrics. Again, they give you more data than you need, and often don't give you the information you really want until you've done a lot of data crunching.

Which website analytics you pay most attention to depends on your goals, but common numbers to track include the following:

Unique visitors versus return visitors. Unique visitors constitute one measure of the size of your reach. Return visitors can be a measure of engagement: for example, they like your content so they come back for more.

Time on site, pages per visit, and bounce rate. These measures tell you how long or how deeply people are using your website.

Referrers. This measure tells you where your site visitors are coming from. For example, is your organization's activity on social media sites driving traffic to certain pages on your website?

Conversion rates. This measure tells you how many people are following through on calls to action on your website.

The same points apply to email metrics. Pick the numbers that help you measure progress of various kinds toward your goals. Here are some email metrics that are frequently tracked to determine whether they are increasing (or not):

List growth. The overall size of your list.

Open rates. The percentage of people who open your emails.

Click-through rates. The percentage of people who click over to your website.

Conversion rates. The specific emails that lead to completion of certain activities on your website.

What's getting clicked. The topics that are most popular.

In social media, you might track

Engagement. The number or percentage of people who like, share, or comment on your content.

Sentiment. The attitudes expressed by people who are interacting with your content.

5. Network and Compare Notes with Your Peers

Talk with others about what they are doing as another way to see how your organization is stacking up. You may want to talk to peers who have the same job title as you do or who work for organizations like yours. Check in with them regularly to see how the sands are shifting over time. You'll pick up intelligence about what's happening in your field or in your community that will allow you to make adjustments much more quickly than if you waited to discover it on your own. Nonprofits are in a rather chaotic state with the growth of communications and marketing. Getting out of your little bubble and seeing what other people see can be a very important way to measure your organization's progress over time.

Do You Want Your Strategy to Be Data Informed?

I highly recommend that you read *Measuring the Networked Nonprofit: Using Data to Change the World* (2012), by Beth Kanter and Katie Paine, for a much more complete discussion of how you can use data, particularly from online communications, to inform your decision making, including your content marketing strategy.

Stop, Think, and Discuss

Here's a way to make measurement a little more fun: put your intuition about what your measurements are into a pretend time capsule (writing it down somewhere and not looking at it for a few weeks or months), and then track the data and see what actually happened. How good was your intuition? How have you changed your mind based on what you've seen in the data?

Setting SMART Objectives

You have your broad content marketing goals. You have some sense of the ways that you could collect data as you work toward those goals. But how, exactly, will you know when you are approaching them? Start by adding more specific objectives to your goals. I think of objectives as the dots that connect larger goals and the data I can track.

SMART is a mnemonic that helps you set objectives. Talk to ten different management consultants, and they'll give you ten different lists of the words the letters stand for, but here's the general idea.

S: Specific

You want objectives that include specific details, such as who, what, when, and where. If your goal is "acquiring new donors" you could make that more specific by saying you want more donors to support a specific program, or you want more donors from a certain geographical area or demographic group.

M: Measurable

Whenever possible, it's good to include a numerical objective. How much or how many? How will you know when you are done? "Increasing our email list by 20 percent over this time last year" is more specific and measurable than "building our email list" or "reaching more people." It also makes it clear that you are comparing this year to last year at the same time, instead of 20 percent growth month to month or 20 percent growth from the time you started your email newsletter.

A: Attainable

Is each objective challenging but still achievable? This idea connects your objectives directly to the resources available, including time, talent, and treasure. Whether or not something is attainable is completely dependent on the amount of time you have to give to it, the amount of talent and skill you have available to you or your staff or via your consultants, and amount of money in the budget to make it happen.

Sometimes it's hard to know whether something is attainable or not, especially when you are starting something new. You can look for best practices and benchmarks in the nonprofit sector as a whole or within your field. Or you can benchmark against your peers or against organizations you look up to. If you are duplicating something another organization has done somewhere else, it's worth having a conversation with people in that organization about what their start-up process was like and what kind of growth they saw in the early parts of the program.

Ultimately, it's most important to benchmark your organization against itself. Make progress, plain and simple. Trust your own judgment for what feels attainable to you, and agree to stop and readjust the goals and objectives once you get some experience with implementation.

R: Relevant

So what and who cares? You need to measure the things that really matter most to the success of your organization. Just being able to measure something doesn't make it relevant. While Google Analytics will let you measure hundreds of details about your website and how people are using it, only a handful of those metrics will likely be relevant as you make decisions about your website content and how that site should be integrated with other communications channels. As you set objectives, make sure you can explain why they are important to the overall success of your organization.

Another way to think about relevancy involves your ability to convert raw data points into trends over time. Can you make sense of data in ways that produce clear trends that you or others in your organization are then able to act on? If your organization is unlikely to change its behavior in response to a trend going up or down, then your ability to see that trend is irrelevant.

T: Timebound

Set a deadline. Break down annual goals into quarterly or monthly goals, either by dividing equally or adjusting within quarters based on your expectations. I'm sure all your organization's board members are tired of hearing you or staff explain that the income goal is divided equally across twelve months, when you and they know the organization will earn 70 percent of its income in the fourth quarter. Instead of talking about how it just looks as though the organization is horribly behind for the first three quarters, manually adjust the goals by quarter. For example, if the annual goal is $100,000, you don't have to set a $25,000 goal per quarter. Instead, you could set a $10,000 goal for each of the first three quarters—adding up to $30,000—and close with a $70,000 goal for the fourth quarter.

It's also important to measure regularly and search for the meaning of those measures as you go along, so that you can adjust along the way. You may see that you are making progress, but much more slowly than you had hoped because a task is more time consuming that you thought. At that point you can make a decision to devote more staff time to the task in order to achieve the original objective, or you can revise the objective downward to make it attainable with the allotted amount of staff time.

> ## Stop, Think, and Discuss
>
> If you could track only a handful of metrics, what might they be?
>
> Could you agree to track just three numbers for three months to see what you learn, and then readjust, perhaps adding some new metrics then?

Why It Matters: Goals Get You Moving

If you define your ultimate success as becoming a favorite, and building relationships that get you to that point, you can approach how you measure your progress in many different ways. What's most important is that you don't get lost in the numbers themselves. Lift up your head, take a deep breath, and think: what do these numbers really mean, and what can we do more or less of to improve them next time?

Regardless of how well your organization matches up with national survey results or what stage of development the organization is in or what role you feel you are playing in it, the bottom line is the same: move forward toward the flag you have planted at your destination. The world of communications is changing around us so fast that if you stay still you will be left behind. Don't fall into the oblivion of sticking with old-style nonprofit communications. Set some goals, however small, and move forward.

Just like solo hiking, content marketing on your own can be done. But it requires much more preparation, focus, dedication, resourcefulness, sheer will, and good luck to pull it off safely and successfully. I recommend you travel with a group and be welcoming and friendly to all whom you meet along the way. That's the approach I will ask you to take in part 2 of this book, as you redefine your marketing relationships.

Chapter 4 is about all those new friends you hope to meet along the way: your participants, supporters, and influencers. You'll get to know them a little better, try to understand why they are out on the trail themselves, and see if you can find ways to encourage them to hike along with you, rather than staying in their own tents the whole time or taking a path that splits away from yours.

Chapter 5 explores what is often called your *brand* or *personality*—how you want to be known and remembered by others you meet along the way. You'll learn how your decisions about your communications style, tone, and voice can blend with the goals you set earlier to drive your content marketing decisions.

In Chapter 6, you'll give close attention to those in your organization who are taking this trek with you. Whether you are part of a formal communications team or not, it's time to start thinking of those around you—other communications, fundraising, and program staff; board members; dedicated and skilled volunteers—as part of your team. You'll look at the roles you can play in leading, training, supporting, and encouraging your team along the trail.

Chapter Four
Making Friends on the Trail
What Supporters, Participants, and Influencers Want from You

> **This chapter is about . . .**
> - Understanding why people are inclined to help nonprofits
> - Recognizing what motivates people to give, donate, volunteer, and advocate
> - Learning ways to structure your relationships

Keeping your head down on the trail and staying in your tent the whole time won't make you many friends. Instead, you need to smile, wave, and invite others to share the view and the warmth of your campfire. You want to be the kind of person others will want to smile and wave back at, and maybe even share some s'mores with. You can start by trying to better understand the people that your nonprofit is most likely communicating with, including what's relevant and valuable to them. You can learn more about what motivates participants, supporters, and influencers to get and stay involved with, to trust, and to love nonprofits, especially your nonprofit.

Why People Give, Volunteer, and Advocate

Why do people support charities? It's quite simple: it gets them high. The Greater Good Science Center (2013), at the University of California, Berkeley, has compiled the research that proves it. Researchers have found time and again that people report significant boosts in their personal happiness after doing kind deeds for others. Some studies suggest that giving to others makes adults happier than spending money on themselves and that this is true even among children at a certain age. This is not just an emotional reaction; it's biological too. Giving to charity activates the regions of the brain associated with pleasure, social connection, and trust and most likely triggers the release of endorphins in the brain, producing what's called the *helper's high*.

And it's not just giving money that does this. Volunteering produces the helper's high too (Greater Good Science Center, 2013). People who volunteer also report fewer aches and pains and less depression than those who don't. Older people who volunteer or regularly help friends have a significantly lower chance of dying than those who don't. Medical researcher Stephen Post concluded that altruism can even improve the health of people with chronic illnesses like HIV infection and multiple sclerosis—the effect of doing good for others is that profound. High-quality service-learning programs that add real-world community service to classroom learning have been shown to improve academic performance and make students feel more connected.

It's this sense of connection that's so important to achieving many of the societal changes that nonprofits are working so hard for. When we help others, it brings us together. Both the helper and the person receiving the help feel closer to each other. "Being kind and generous leads you to perceive others more positively and more charitably," says psychologist Sonja Lyubomirsky (2008) in her book *The How of Happiness*, and this "fosters a heightened sense of interdependence and cooperation in your social community."

Steve Daigneault, vice president of eCampaigns at M + R Strategic Services, a nonprofit campaign strategy firm, believes that people give to charity for one of four reasons, starting with the pursuit of happiness (Leroux Miller, 2012a; personal communication, February 2013). Each of the four reasons in the following list includes an example of fundraising language you might use to tap into that motivation:

1. To feel happy

   "You'll not only fund our work—you'll know you changed a life."

2. To feel important

   "Give today to become a member and get insider info and updates."

3. To feel like part of a success story

   "We saved the savannah elephant. We can save the Asian elephant too."

4. Because everyone's doing it

   "From Martha L., a grandmother in Tennessee, to Jim T., a construction worker in Florida, Americans everywhere have already committed to our fight."

Donors' sense of identity and their role in supporting organizations—as I discussed in chapter 1—is increasingly important to getting and keeping donors' attention. Jen Shang, a philanthropic psychologist, observes that "the psychological transformation from paying attention to giving money is the process of integrating that cause from the external world into one's most inner sense of who they are" (Wallis, 2012). And who are your donors, or who do they aspire to be?

Shang's research uncovered nine adjectives that she says Americans use to define a moral person:

- Kind
- Caring
- Compassionate
- Helpful
- Friendly
- Fair

- Hard-working

- Generous

- Honest

She also notes that the adjectives *strong*, *responsible*, and *loyal* do well with men. Shang suggests that nonprofits use these words more often in their communications, including fundraising appeals, to help donors see that supporting such organizations is one way to show that they are good individuals.

Being involved with a nonprofit is not just about the donor but also about the donor's network of family and friends. The *Nonprofit Donor Engagement Benchmark Study* (Charity Dynamics and Nonprofit Technology Network, 2012) asked donors why they were involved with their favorite charity and received these responses:

- I believe in the charity's cause (65 percent).

- I want to help make change happen (30 percent).

- I have friends and family who support this cause (20 percent).

- I know someone who has received services from this organization in the past (19 percent).

- The charity asked for my help (18 percent).

Finally, research conducted by Ogilvy Public Relations Worldwide and The Center for Social Impact Communication at Georgetown University (2011) has revealed that other people are highly influential in how supporters get involved with causes. Fifty-seven percent of US adults in the study said they were motivated to get involved with causes because these causes were important to them personally or to someone they knew. Fifty percent said they were involved because the cause had a direct impact on them personally or on someone they knew (figure 4.1).

Stop, Think, and Discuss

Have you asked your participants and supporters why they got involved with your cause? How do you think their answers would line up with this research?

FIGURE 4.1

What Motivates People to Get Involved in a Social Issue or Cause?

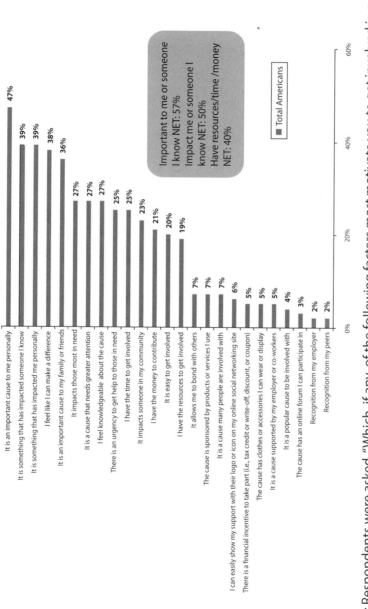

Note: Respondents were asked, "Which, if any, of the following factors most motivate you to get involved in a social issue or cause? (Select all that apply)."

Source: Ogilvy Public Relations Worldwide and The Center for Social Impact Communication at Georgetown University, *Dynamics of Cause Engagement,* November 2011, *www.slideshare.net/georgetowncsic/dynamics-of-cause-engagement-final-report.*

What Supporters Want from You

Let's look at what supporters say when they are asked directly about what they want from nonprofits.

Cygnus Applied Research has heard three consistent messages from donors over and over via several national studies since 1998 (Burk, 2012). Donors like

- Receiving prompt and meaningful acknowledgment whenever they make a gift

- Having their gifts assigned to a specific purpose that is narrower in scope than the whole organization

- Receiving a report that describes and offers data on what was accomplished with the gift (usually when combined with the gifts of other donors), before being asked for another contribution

DonorVoice (2011), through its research on thirty-two possible indicators, has developed a list of seven key indicators, each of which shows a statistically measurable link between how donors feel about the organization (that is, their commitment level) and their behavior. As donors' ratings of a charity's performance on these seven indicators go up, so does donor commitment and financial performance:

- Thanking you for your support in a timely manner

- Providing you with a feeling that your involvement is appreciated

- Providing you with a feeling of being part of an important cause

- Providing opportunities to make your views known (for example, soliciting your opinion on where the charity should focus its effort; making it easy to make suggestions)

- Effectively trying to achieve its mission

- Sending information that shows who is being helped

- Knowing what to expect from the organization each time you interact with it

It's also interesting to see what didn't rank as highly with donors in this research. For example, even though personalized thank-yous were important, timeliness trumped personalization. Kevin Schulman, founder of DonorVoice, says, "Our work suggests that within a couple of days is the target for turn-around. If getting thank-you notes personalized is impacting timeliness, and that process can't be streamlined, then choose timeliness" (personal communication, November 2012).

Based on more recent and longitudinal research into donor commitment, Schulman further argues that a real competitive advantage for a charity can come from breaking the cycle of what has become an increasingly efficient but less impactful and effective acknowledgment process. The quickly delivered thank-you note has become expected and commoditized and no longer contributes sufficiently to the second key indicator and relationship driver: creating the feeling in donors that their involvement is appreciated.

Schulman also identified a few activities that don't seem to affect donor commitment as much as the key indicators do:

The frequency of requests for donations. "Frequency in and of itself is not the issue and not a maker or breaker of relationships."

Tax benefits. "This simply does not matter to relationship building and greater commitment."

Efficiency in how donations are spent. "There is a lot of hand-wringing by would-be watchdogs and plenty of pie charts showing overhead, but we, and others, continue to find it simply does not matter. This isn't to suggest that some isolated PR nightmare for a given charity discovered to be spending very little on programs is not a death knell, just that the cost of fundraising and other efficiency ratios are not on the collective radar of donors."

Stop, Think, and Discuss

How do your communications stack up against this research?

How timely are your communications?

How often do you explain to donors what has been accomplished with their support?

Let's take a closer look at how these donor desires might specifically play out on your website or your home page. A few studies have asked donors what they want to see on a charity website.

The 2012 Cygnus Donor Survey (Burk, 2012) found that

- Forty-nine percent of donors say they visit the website to read news about the organization or learn about its activities.

- Thirty-six percent say they visit the site to make a gift online.

- Thirty-five percent say they visit specifically to learn about what the non-profit has accomplished.

- Twenty-three percent say they visit to learn what the nonprofit intends to do with donations.

This study also found that younger donors are considerably more likely than older ones to visit nonprofit websites to register for an event or to learn more about volunteer options.

A study report called *Money for Good II* (Hope Consulting and GuideStar, 2011) found that only a third of individual donors researched organizations before giving. However, people who advise donors on giving (for example, professional wealth managers and accountants) and foundation funders researched almost every donation they made.

When organizational funders and individuals do look for information about your nonprofit before giving, here's what they want to see:

- Its financial information (how it gets its money and how it spends it)

- Its impact (what difference it is making)

- Its legitimacy (its status, reputation, and credibility)

- Its mission (what it is trying to accomplish)

What Volunteers Want from You

Volunteers are much more likely to stay engaged when they can see that their effort makes a difference, they feel appreciated, and they feel good about the time they spend volunteering. It's important that you are constantly reinforcing the message that their work really does help and that, with the support of other volunteers and advocates, it adds up to something much larger.

Susan J. Ellis, president of Energize, Inc., a training, consulting, and publishing firm that specializes in volunteerism, says that today's volunteers come in many forms, including students fulfilling community service requirements, corporate employees on flextime projects, families volunteering together, and participants in all-volunteer civic groups. "Today's volunteers are likely to want a short-term assignment: something with a clear beginning, middle and end," says Ellis (2000, n.d.). "But if that works out, the volunteer is just as likely to then say: 'What can I do next?'"

Ellis recommends that nonprofits talk about volunteer involvement on their home pages, with a big button to click for more information about volunteering. On the volunteers page of the site, she recommends that you include an overview introducing volunteers at your organization: what they do, who they are, and how they are chosen. For each point, she suggests offering the choice to "learn more." Further clicking might show

- Volunteer position descriptions for openings available now
- A wish list of skills or schedules needed
- Photos of volunteers at work (showing their diversity of age, race, and gender)
- Data on volunteer achievements
- Personal testimonials from volunteers in certain assignments
- Specific ideas for students
- Specific ideas for groups or teams

You should also go where people are looking for fun things to do with their friends and timely ways to help during a crisis: Facebook. Consider this story shared in *Unleashing Innovation: Using Everyday Technology to Improve Nonprofit Services*, by MAP for Nonprofits (2012):

> As one of Minnesota's eight volunteer centers, Community Thread connects people with volunteer opportunities, provides volunteer support to other nonprofits and sponsors large scale opportunities

to volunteer. Executive Director Valerie Jones said the organization wanted to find a way to reach a new and larger audience, and the organization's strategic planning process had identified marketing as a priority.

A staff member began experimenting with using Facebook to reach out about events and opportunities. "We hired a young person," Jones said, "and one day, she said, 'Can I try this?' I told her to go for it. Once we got a response, we started getting more conscientious about what we were posting."

Jones quickly realized she'd found a means not just to promote the organization and its events, but to recruit and engage volunteers, and bought into the social media effort. The organization's social media presence became like a snowball gathering mass.

In 2011, when the nearby St. Croix River flooded, Community Thread served as the volunteer manager for relief efforts and used its Facebook page to spread the word, recruiting roughly 1,500 volunteers for flood relief efforts.

"That emergency created a lot of public awareness," Jones said. "Facebook was an immediate channel to keep people up-to-date."

She estimated that the organization's other programs recruited about 200 volunteers using social media in 2011, as well. In addition to posting links and invitations to events and to volunteer, staff began taking photos at events and posting them with quotes from participants.

"We use a lot of photos—we're kind of obnoxious with our camera," she said. "We've had great luck using photos and pictures to tell our story." That led to an attempt to create videos, beginning with one celebrating the organization's annual Spring Into Service event.

"The only cost for social media is staff time," Jones said—from two to four hours a week spread out over five days. "Let's see, now we do Facebook, Twitter and a YouTube channel, and we guest blog for the local Patch (community news website). It became clear to us that we could use messaging there to engage people for volunteering."

So far, she has not yet begun using any analytical tools to measure results and is tracking only the number of volunteers, though she said there are other signs that point to the success of the effort: "We get people who call and say, Hey, I saw this on Facebook, how do I sign up?" she said. "We also get some walk-in traffic from people who say they saw this on their friend's Facebook page, and they want to participate. And it's increased a number of backdoor things—local businesses will say, 'We heard about you, are you new?' Well, no, we've been here for 43 years. The only thing we've changed is the social media."

If you want to learn more about the volunteer scene in your state, VolunteeringInAmerica.gov is another great resource. You can drill down into statistics by state or large city, broken down by age, gender, type of volunteering done, factors affecting volunteerism in the area, and more.

What Advocates Want from You

Advocates are often motivated to work with you because of their personal experiences or because they have capacities as professionals in your field. It's important to equip them with the information and advice they need to be effective advocates, while also giving them very clear calls to action and directions so they know what to do.

The American Diabetes Association knows that there are many different levels of advocacy, so it has structured the "Advocate" section of its website accordingly. The main page includes headings like "Advocate at School," "Advocate at Work," and "Advocate for Public Accommodations," recognizing that many advocates are inspired to become involved by situations in their own lives and are motivated by those personal experiences to take action locally. This page also includes a link that says, "If you are already a Super Advocate, go here." The linking page focuses on government affairs and lobbying at the state and federal level.

The American Diabetes Association (2012) also publishes the Advocates in Action Calendar, which lists month-by-month advocacy tactics for both leaders and grassroots advocates, tactics that are carefully timed with legislative or other events on the calendar. The association hopes that this calendar will result in a more coordinated focus on particular actions across the country, maximizing the association's impact nationally and ensuring that local and state groups have the resources and support they need to effectively engage additional advocates.

The fact that a person is a subject matter expert doesn't mean he is ready or willing to use that expertise to advocate for your cause. "We know there is a big difference between our staff, who regularly traverse Capitol Hill, and our members, who may never have called their Congressional representative," says Samantha Lee, communications, media, and marketing coordinator for the National WIC Association (personal communication, November 2012). The members of the association are nonprofit and government agencies that serve mothers and young children through the Special Supplemental Nutrition Program for Women, Infants and Children (WIC).

"We strive to create content that helps staff at every level see the big picture of how WIC helps our nation, and give them ways to personalize and communicate it," says Lee. "We know our members are devoted to improving the health of our nation's families, and we try to motivate them to parlay that passion into educating others about WIC's importance, especially policymakers."

Lee says it's important for her organization to help guide members through the advocacy process: "We know we can't just arm them with statistics; we need to cover the political basics first. People are intimidated by the idea of talking to members of Congress, and we have to remind them that representatives are people too—people there to represent them."

She also knows that the association's members are busy, so she tries to convey information by email and on the association's website concisely, and to make asks from the association simple and easy. The website provides resources on the latest WIC policy information, state profiles with WIC data, numerous fact sheets, and an area that allows members to easily send form letters or personalized emails to their congressional representatives. "That encourages people who want to be involved, but think they're too busy," explains Lee. "In addition to having limited time, our members often aren't sure what policymakers want to hear. We provide fact sheets to help our members develop talking points, along with how-tos on communicating with policymakers, like how to schedule an appointment, what to expect when there, etc."

The association also presents advocacy training webinars and hosts an annual leadership conference in Washington, DC. Members learn about current WIC policy and budgeting in depth, engage in role-playing exercises about meeting with members of Congress, and then travel in groups to scheduled meetings on Capitol Hill. "A recent short movie we produced shows before and after experiences of [association] members who visited Congress for the first time. We use this as a tool to show all members that they shouldn't be intimidated, and that anyone can be an advocate!" says Lee.

What Influencers Want from You

Influencers are quite different from participants and supporters, and you don't necessarily need them to think of you as a personal favorite (although that doesn't hurt). Instead, it's more important to be considered trustworthy and available to help when called upon. But just as with any other group, you also have to consider their interests and motivations when creating a communications strategy to reach them.

Working with Elected Officials

That's the take-home message in a report called *The Advocacy Gap: Research for Better Advocacy* (Eglin and Hankin, 2012). There is really no such thing as communicating with Congress. Instead, you have to think of this activity as communicating with 535 members of Congress, all human beings with their own idiosyncrasies and ways of doing business. Each member of Congress really cares only about what his or her constituents think, so asking people nationwide to send messages may just drown out the district voices (for the US House) or state voices (for the US Senate) that members of Congress do want to hear. Members of Congress are bound by process, so they can do something only when there is a specific bill in play. Asking them to generally support your issue is not as helpful as asking them to vote a certain way on a certain bill. Stories from within the district or state matter more than talking points. Some members of Congress say they go through constituent communications looking for real stories that they can use in their own speeches and communications.

Sometimes, it requires good old-fashioned politicking to get those in a position of influence to pay attention to your organization. Hoong Yee Lee Krakauer, executive director of the Queens Council on the Arts, says she visits every politician in the borough of Queens, New York, to let him or her know how funding emerging immigrant artists in the borough will help the residents view that politician as a trusted supporter of cultural communities in Queens. "The key to gaining support from legislators is to find common ground and common goals," she says (personal communication, February 2013).

For the Queens Council on the Arts, those goals are diversity and trust that transcends borders.

"My request to all of them is for them to join me and their colleagues in being a trusted part of these cultural communities," says Krakauer. "For every legislator, I clip a list of every artist we fund on top of our request letter. Being in Queens, the most diverse county in the galaxy, every list of artists is a snapshot of demography in motion, mixed marriage, biracial, immigrant and multi-ethnic influences."

Here's her process:

1. She starts with the most senior members of the council. They will often have seniority and accumulated funds at their discretion.

2. She invites them to consider being the lead on her request and to suggest the person who should be her next ask, so she can build a committee of champions for the request.

3. She includes a highly publicized event, marketed throughout diverse communities, where legislators can be publicly thanked and acknowledged for their support.

As Krakauer says, "The fact that these communities are the home of the elusive immigrant vote doesn't hurt. I just make it easy for them to do the math."

Working with the Media

Margaret Lillard worked for the Associated Press for nearly twenty years before becoming the communications director for the Conservation Trust for North Carolina and then the associate director for communications at the Duke University Energy Initiative. She says that understanding the workflow of reporters is essential to getting their attention today. For example, do you know what time the copy you hear being read over the radio on your morning commute is actually written? Often, the night before. AP reporters are also pulling together news for Monday morning on Friday night. "If I am going to release something to our supporters on Monday morning, for example, I will send the press release out on Friday so that it might appear in the news Monday morning," says Lillard (personal communication, January 2012).

You will also greatly increase your odds of getting coverage if you help reporters fill dead space in their schedules. The week between Christmas and New Year's is usually very slow, for example, yet news organizations like the AP are under contractual obligations to supply a certain amount of content to the other news organizations they serve.

That worked to the advantage of many local land trusts that Lillard was advising, because those nonprofits tend to close many real estate deals in the last few days of the year. "Several small land trusts issued press releases a day or two after Christmas that were used by the AP and then appeared in many regional newspapers," says Lillard. "The AP also produces the 'across the USA' news from each of the fifty states for *USA Today*, and we've seen even very small volunteer organizations get into that section because their timing was right."

Jennifer Doron, director of marketing and communications at the Ohio Environmental Council (OEC), says the way her organization handles press releases has changed over the last few years (personal communication, February 2013). The OEC used to post the press releases as pdfs, but now each has its own web page. Doron says she can better optimize each web page for search engine traffic and can direct followers on social media to a specific link.

The way the OEC interacts with the press through social media has also changed. Instead of having one main Twitter account, the OEC has created separate accounts, based on the different aspects of the organization's work. Each account has its own persona.

Doron explains: "For instance, our lobbyist, who is very well known through the statehouse halls and with reporters, tweets first-person accounts and opinions of what is going on in the legislature. On the other hand, our law center director tweets about legal matters in a bit more matter-of-fact tone. Our water team takes turns between staff members tweeting about water news, events, and policy issues."

Now that the OEC has focused its communications more narrowly, based on issues, each of the accounts is followed and regularly retweeted or mentioned by particular reporters and bloggers who are influential in their respective fields. Those reporters and bloggers do not need to sift through the organization's entire Twitter feed trying to find something relevant for their readers.

My first book, *The Nonprofit Marketing Guide: High-Impact, Low-Cost Ways to Build Support for Your Good Cause* (Leroux Miller, 2010), contains a chapter called "Become an Expert Source for the Media and Decision Makers." In it, I describe the five qualities that people are looking for in an expert:

1. **Be accessible**. Can people reach you when they need to? This is more important than being the smartest person or even having the best quotes.

2. **Be cooperative**. Answer the questions people ask; provide brief but substantive answers. You have to say something really meaningful to be quoted, while also keeping it short.

3. **Own a well-understood niche**. What is your particular expertise or perspective on the issues? You want to be specific, without focusing too narrowly.

4. **Build a solid track record**. The more often you are quoted, the more likely it is that other reporters will call you, because they've seen you work with their colleagues.

5. **Be trustworthy**. Be nothing more than you are, honestly and with transparency. If you don't know something, say so, rather than trying to make up an answer.

Reaching Overlooked Program Participants

Organizations in which participants and supporters are often one and the same (from humane societies to museums) do make substantial investments in recruiting participants. But for many nonprofits, finding new program participants is far from a problem: it's not uncommon for social service organizations to have waiting lists. Some organizations rely exclusively on other nonprofits or government agencies for referrals. In both cases, marketing to attract new program participants isn't a top priority. In fact, my 2013 *Nonprofit Communications Trends Report* (Leroux Miller, 2013) noted that only 20 percent of nonprofit communicators included acquiring new program participants in their top three priorities.

But here is another case where old assumptions about the world of nonprofit communications may not work anymore. Take homeless people, for example. Should agencies that provide support to that clientele treat them as website users? I suspect many people would say, "Well, homeless people don't have computers." Or they might concede, "Well, I guess they could go to the library and use a public computer."

But look at what Mark Horvath of Invisible People and We Are Visible says: "Homeless people are not really thought of as consumers, which is sad! With tablets now getting affordable, a tablet + wifi gives great access" (Leroux Miller, 2012b). Forget the computer with wired Internet access. Heck, forget the mobile phone with the monthly data package. Horvath is talking about people who can get and stay connected online with a one-time technology purchase (or donated device) and free wifi.

It's estimated that about 44 percent of homeless people have jobs, and others get disability or other government support, and therefore can make some choices as consumers (National Coalition for the Homeless, 2009). Another recent study found that homeless teens consider having a smartphone as important as having food (University of Southern California, 2011).

Now, of course, these findings do not apply to all homeless people, not even a majority. But in today's fragmented media environment, it's hard to say that any particular communications channel is a slam dunk for a majority of any particular group. It's now a multichannel, multiscreen world, which means you need to provide multiple options so individuals can pick the best ways to communicate with you, given their particular preferences and circumstances.

How Your Needs and Theirs Come Together

You have an idea of what your organization needs from potential and current participants, supporters, and influencers. You've also looked at some of their likely interests, needs, and values. Now how do you bring these two together and add some structure to these relationships?

The Ladder of Engagement

One way to describe the relationship between supporters and nonprofits is to use the *ladder of engagement*. The idea is that you ask the biggest group of people you are in contact with to take the easiest step. A smaller group within that first group will be willing to move up the ladder to the next slightly harder step, and so forth, until you have a much smaller but highly engaged group of people at the top of the ladder. This is akin to the *sales funnel*, where you put all your leads into the wide top, and they filter down, until those who will buy come out at the narrow bottom.

Groundwire, a nonprofit that helped other social and environmental non-profits with community organizing and engagement strategies, developed the Groundwire *engagement pyramid* (figure 4.2), which employs the same concept as the ladder.

As Groundwire describes it, at the bottom of the engagement pyramid, communications and relationships are technology-centric and more automated; at the top they are more personal and labor intensive. Using technology like websites, email, and social media can help you manage interactions with lots of people at once. To get beyond the middle of the engagement pyramid requires more personal attention and relationship building. While communications technology still plays an important role, there is no substitute for the human touch.

If you can clearly see how a ladder (or pyramid) of engagement can work for your organization, start with the six levels that Groundwire describes, and customize them for your participants or supporters.

FIGURE 4.2
Engagement Pyramid

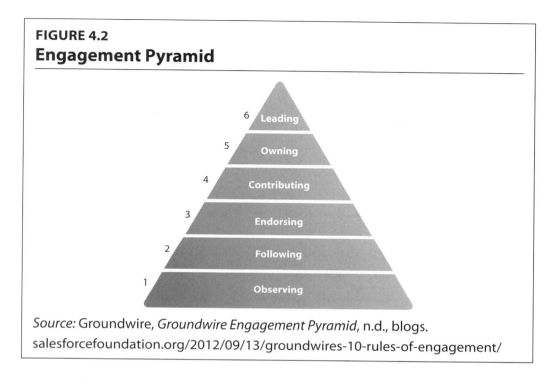

Source: Groundwire, *Groundwire Engagement Pyramid*, n.d., blogs. salesforcefoundation.org/2012/09/13/groundwires-10-rules-of-engagement/

The Engagement Vortex: Better Than the Ladder?

In their article "The Permanent Disruption of Social Media," Julie Dixon and Denise Keyes (2013) argue that the ladder of engagement doesn't really work anymore because it doesn't accurately reflect the ways that people interact with nonprofits. Examining research conducted in late 2010 by Ogilvy Public Relations Worldwide and the Center for Social Impact Communication at Georgetown University, Dixon and Keyes concluded that "a person's engagement with an organization is generally more continuous—and messy"—than a ladder model can accommodate. That's because people enter at different levels or even multiple levels of engagement, and they don't necessarily travel in one direction or another from there.

For example, in a typical ladder of engagement, a nonprofit will place connecting via social media on a bottom rung, with donating money on a much higher rung. But Dixon and Keyes's work and other studies have shown that people consider donating money to be one of the easiest entry points, and that they often connect on social media only after donating money. In other words, they appear to slide down the traditional ladder, an image that carries many negative connotations. That is, they've already done what most nonprofits expected to have to build them up to: giving money.

"Instead," say Dixon and Keyes (2013), "we need a model that allows people to enter into a relationship with a nonprofit and to be engaged at multiple levels." They prefer a more circular model they call the *vortex*, where both communications from the nonprofit and peer influence from others circle around the individual continuously. Their engagement and their ability to influence others are measured by the width of the vortex around them. The study's authors also refer to this as a *surround sound* experience.

Whether you find the vortex metaphor useful or not, Dixon and Keyes suggest that any new model should incorporate these characteristics:

- Allows a donor to be engaged at different entry points and to move easily between them during the life cycle of engagement

- Has no fixed end point for a donor's engagement

- Allows the donor-engagement footprint to expand or contract in ways that are unique to and driven by the individual donor

- Places the donor's needs—not the organization's—at the center of the engagement

- Accounts for the influence of other people on the strength of the donor-organization relationship

At Least Know Your Theory of Change

If you find that drawing a ladder, pyramid, or vortex accurately conveys the way you want others to engage with your organization, great. If you don't, that's OK too.

I do recommend, however, that you take some time to map out a theory of change.

A theory of change is a way to connect the specific actions you are taking with the larger societal change you hope to bring about. A theory of change is often shown graphically as a *pathway of change*, demonstrating a logical, doable, and measurable series of steps, one leading to another, until the change comes to fruition. Start by identifying your goals and the assumptions behind them, then map backward to identify all the outcomes or interventions needed to get to those goals. You will also develop indicators to measure progress along the way (Theory of Change Community, 2013).

You may recall that I shared a theory of change for nonprofit content marketing in chapter 2. Let's look also at the theory of change behind one huge communications success: *Kony 2012*, the short film created by Invisible Children that reached 100 million views within six days of its March 5, 2012, release, a speed record at the time (it's no longer the record holder). A Pew poll found that 58 percent of US adults aged eighteen to twenty-nine said they had heard about the video ("Kony 2012 in Numbers," 2012).

Critics have said that Invisible Children dropped the ball by focusing on moving young people to pressure the US government to act, and that Invisible Children should have spent its money in the countries where Joseph Kony operates, rather than on making a video to show to young people in the United States. But, as Raven Brooks (2012) points out, Invisible Children was able to defend itself against that charge (at least in part), because it had a plausible theory of change, which was narrated in the video itself, starting around minute 21 of the thirty-minute video:

> In order for Kony to be arrested this year, the Ugandan military has to find him. In order to find him, they need the technology and training to track him in the vast jungle. That's where the American advisers come in. But in order for the American advisers to be there, the U.S. government has to deploy them. They've done that, but if the government doesn't believe that people care about arresting Kony, the mission will be canceled. In order for the people to care, they have to know. And they will only know if Kony's name is everywhere.
>
> This is the dream. Kony arrested for all the world to see, and the abducted children returned home. But nobody knows who he is. . . . He's not famous. He's invisible. Joseph Kony's invisible. Here is how we're going to make him visible. MAKE HIM FAMOUS.

Stop, Think, and Discuss

What is your organization's theory of change, and how does your communications strategy fit into it?

Leaving Content Cairns for People at Different Stages

No matter the process that people move through in their relationships with your organization, it is important to remember that different people will be in different stages. Rather than expecting them to bushwhack their way through all your content, leave them some clues to follow.

That's what backpackers do for each other. In places where the trail is hard to follow, backpackers will leave stacks of rocks, called *cairns*, to indicate where the trail is. Think about the stages that your supporters go through as you build rapport with them over time and determine how you can add some cairns to your communications that will help them find where they belong.

To see how this might work, let's focus on one communications channel, your website, and group your website visitors into three categories:

- **Newcomers**: people who know nothing or very little about you.
- **Friends**: people who like your organization or cause. You might be a favorite some day.
- **Fans**: people who love your organization or cause. You are their favorite!

What kind of content does your website need for each of these groups?

Newcomers: People Who Know Nothing about You

When someone who knows nothing about your organization lands on your website, what's the first thing you want her to see?

It's not your mission statement. Trust me.

What you want her to see is the answer to her question.

When a stranger lands on your website, odds are she is searching for the answer to a specific question about something going on in her life right now. Maybe it's a problem she wants to solve, or something she heard from a friend or saw on TV that piqued her interest. She went searching, and Google or another website with a link to yours pointed that stranger to you, thinking that you might have the answer.

What three questions are strangers who land on your site most likely to have? For some nonprofits, the answers are obvious. If you run an animal shelter, one question will be, "What animals are available for adoption?" If you run a Meals on Wheels program, one question will be, "How can a senior get food delivered?" If your organization addresses a particular disease, one question will be, "What is the treatment?"

The best way to build rapport with strangers is not to babble on about yourself; it's to be a Good Samaritan who answers their questions. These questions are almost always about your programs, and rarely about donating, volunteering, or otherwise helping you out.

Devote space on your home page or within your navigation to answering the three big questions most likely to bring strangers to your site. You might also consider using these tactics.

The Welcome Series

What if every new subscriber to your email newsletter received a set of three *welcome* emails before he received the first edition of your newsletter? You could use these three emails to talk about what your organization does and whom it serves, how other people are getting involved, and some particularly interesting events or work coming up soon. The new subscriber will then be more up to speed when he receives the regular e-newsletter.

Jennifer Doron of the Ohio Environmental Council says her organization has introduced a series of welcome emails sent out after someone signs up for its email list or action alerts through its website or Facebook page or at an event. It sends one email a week for the next three weeks. The first is a simple "Welcome to the OEC" email thanking the person for signing up, giving him a few bullets of information about the organization, and inviting him to explore the website. Other than a standard "Donate" button in the email header, there is no ask in this email. The second email, sent a week after the first, is a story about how the organization has helped someone or achieved something—with the support of "people like you." The third email, one more week later, asks him to become a member.

Doron says the open rates for this email series are consistently 12 percent higher than the open rate for the OEC's regular email newsletter.

The New Donor Series

Once you get a new donor, you don't want to let that person go. Help ensure the second gift by sending that new donor a special series of emails that emphasizes your gratitude and talks about the results of your work. Before you ask again, make her feel that she is part of the family and that her investment in you was a great decision.

Start Here Buttons

To help newcomers find what they need as quickly and easily as possible, consider adding "Start Here" buttons or tabs to your website navigation. You can organize these by visitor type: for example, "Parents, Start Here"; or by experience level, "Entry-Level? Start Here"; or by any other category that will make sense to your website visitors.

Friends: People Who Like Your Organization

Friends know you, at least a little bit. They may have an incomplete picture of you, but the one they do have is favorable. What do they want to see on your website?

No, it's still not your mission statement.

Tell your friends some good stories.

Stories are the quickest and most memorable way to explain what it is you do, how you do it, for whom, and why. You want these friends to understand all this.

Tell stories about people like them, so they can see that they belong. If you are trying to get more young families to participate in your program, tell a story about (you guessed it) a young family already in your program. Tell stories that appeal to their inner angels. Show them how they—through being your friends—can look out for someone else or change someone's life for the better, even if only in a small way.

Tell stories with a sense of adventure or wonder. Appeal to that inner child that's looking for a break from the day-to-day responsibilities of adulthood.

Help them learn more about what you do, but not through long statements of need or bulleted lists of programs and services. Images tell stories too—often better than words—so don't forget photographs and video as you create your website content. Connect with your friends through good storytelling, and some of them will grow into big fans.

Fans: People Who Love Your Organization

Fans are people who know your nonprofit well, and they love it. They are ready and willing to help—as long as you make it easy for them. What do they need from your website?

Anyone for the mission statement? Anyone? Of course not!

Give your fans clear calls to action so they know exactly what they can do to help or support you—which means not asking for them for "help" or "support." That's too vague. Be specific. Ask them to donate $50 toward a specific campaign. Ask them to volunteer for an hour. Ask them to retweet your event invitation to their followers.

Empower them to help you on their own time and in their own ways. Give them downloads and checklists they can use at home, at work, or in their community to advance your cause in their own small way (it will feel big to them). Give them pass-along content like short videos and sample email text that they can share with their friends.

Give your fans the personal touch by encouraging them to connect with you in lots of different ways. When they mention you on Twitter, comment on a Facebook update, or reply to your email newsletter, respond with a thanks or some other kind of encouragement.

Integrate your real-time communications channels into your website, for example, by using Twitter or Facebook widgets or RSS feeds that bring the live conversation to your site. When they can see that ongoing conversation, it reinforces for your website visitors that you are here and now with your fans.

Stop, Think, and Discuss

Do you have website content for newcomers, friends, and fans? Are there content cairns on your website that will help people see where they should start and go next?

Why It Matters: They Are Your Partners, Not Your Audience

It's easy for nonprofit marketers and fundraisers to get caught up in the numbers games and to see the relationships they have with participants, supporters, and influencers as nothing more than the names on a list, hours volunteered, or donations in the bank. As you develop your content marketing strategy, stay true to the relationships—to the journey. Always remember why people are there on the trail with you. It's not solely for your benefit. It's because they want to get something out of the experience too.

Chapter Five
Deciding on Your Trail Name
The Voice and Style You Want to Be Known For

This chapter is about . . .

- Picking a content personality or voice that you want your nonprofit to be known for

- Customizing that voice with different tones and styles for different purposes

- Creating content that helps others recognize your nonprofit

---

On trails that take several weeks or months to traverse, like the Appalachian Trail or the Pacific Crest Trail, it's common for hikers to go by trail names. Sometimes people make a name up for themselves, and at other times a name is given to them by other hikers. Sometimes the name is funny or colorful or mysterious, but the name itself or the story behind it always provides insights into the person's personality or his experiences on the trail.

What do you want your nonprofit to be known for? When discussing content marketing goals with nonprofits, I often ask this question during the discussion about goals. If, as I believe, content marketing is as much about the relationships that you are trying to build as the communications themselves, then you need to understand the part you are playing in each relationship. This conversation about personality and voice is also part of defining your nonprofit's brand.

Picking Your Content Personality or Voice

Think of your voice as the perspective from which you speak. It's the core relationship that you have, or want to establish, with the people on the receiving end of your communications. My voice with my children is as their mother, and that voice comes with a variety of unshakable characteristics. For example, I'm known as the "sheriff" to my kids, compared to their dad, who lets them get away with much more than I do. But my relationships with my husband and with our friends are not those of a mother or a sheriff, so my voice with them is different.

Your nonprofit may have different voices for participants, for supporters, and for influencers in your work. Here's another way to think about this: how do you want your organization to be perceived?

Here are four content personalities or voices commonly used by nonprofits that you can use as a starting point for discussions within your organization.

Be a Helpful Friend

This is a great approach if you provide services to either individual clients or members. It involves sharing information and other communications with an overall style and tone that is down to earth and friendly, even casual, with spot-on, pragmatic advice. Be a good listener who is responsive to what you hear. Use your content as a way to build personal relationships and a sense of kinship or community. If you want people to participate in your nonprofit's training programs, for example, you should create content that positions the organization as a knowledgeable source that can explain things well without talking down to people.

Amanda Welliver, communications coordinator with Community Neighborhood Housing Services (CNHS) in Saint Paul, Minnesota, is taking this approach on Facebook, Twitter, and Pinterest (personal communication, August 2012). CNHS promotes community development through education and affordable housing programs, including home-buying and home improvement loans. But rather than focusing on that alone, Welliver talks about common issues and concerns for homebuyers. "I tend to post links to helpful information like home repair and maintenance tips and budgeting ideas," says Welliver. "I try to link the advice to current events. Rainy day? I'll post about why it's important to have clean gutters." This content represents the majority of what she posts, with about a quarter of the posts being more directly about the organization and its activities, including programs like homebuyer education classes and credit counseling.

Nal'ibali is a national, reading for enjoyment initiative with the goal of making children and adults in South Africa passionate about telling and reading stories. Its theory of change goes something like this: If Nal'ibali is able to capture the power of stories—both oral and written and in more than one language—children and adults with enjoy reading and sharing those stories. That in turn will lead to more children and adults who will be literate in the multiple languages used in South Africa. "Enjoying books and stories enables children to experience the power of reading and so helps stimulate the desire to read independently. This is as important for literacy development as skills like sounding out, forming letters and learning to spell," says Esther Etkin, campaign manager with PRAESA of Cape Town, South Africa, one of the organizations that initiated Nal'ibali (personal communication, August 2012).

Unfortunately, many children don't have storybooks or other materials in their languages, or have a difficult time connecting with trustworthy adults to share stories with. That's where Nal'ibali comes in as a helpful friend. "We offer free stories and resources adapted for real-life circumstances in various South African languages," says Etkin. "We are also affirming what people are already doing in their everyday lives or communities."

Be a Trusted Authority

The differences between being a *helpful friend* and a *trusted authority* come in both the substance and the style of your content. This approach may work better than the other approaches when you are trying to get reporters to call you for quotes or legislators to ask you to testify in hearings, for example. It can also work well when you want your staff to be invited more often to make formal presentations at conferences. With this approach, you present your organization's content in a straightforward, objective, well-documented way, likely with lots of facts and figures or best practices. You don't have to be stiff, but your style may be a bit more formal than in the helpful friend model. You also emphasize search engine optimization in your content strategy, so that people searching for the "right" answers or the "top expert" will find you.

Organizations that want to be viewed as trusted authorities often incorporate the production of new data or resources into their communications strategies.

The Black River Action Team (BRAT) in Springfield, Vermont, got started in 2000 in conjunction with an annual river cleanup event and has grown from a feel-good, let's-do-something organization into a trusted advocate for and authority on the health of the river. For example, Kelly Stettner, BRAT's director, says the organization has started collecting samples for water quality testing in the Black River. "I'm posting the results online for E. coli measurements, which indicate whether it's safe for swimming," says Stettner. "I'm also using Facebook to direct people to the water quality page on the website so they can see the information for themselves." She hopes this will help her raise committed funds for E. coli testing at local swimming holes and to promote a new Adopt-the-River campaign (personal communication, August 2012).

You can also build your own authority by aligning your communications with others who already have a solid stature within your community. That's the approach that the Gyalwa Gyatso Buddhist Center in Campbell, California, takes. "We're a spiritual organization, a Buddhist center in the Tibetan tradition. Our job is to provide our students with tools for their spiritual improvement," says Dave Jeffords, president of the board (personal communication, August 2012). "As such, we often use our recognized masters, such as the Dalai Lama, Lama Zopa Rinpoche, and recognized lay authorities in our Facebook posts."

To improve its visibility as an authority, Scholarship America began writing *The Scholarship Coach*, a blog published on the *US News & World Report* website. The blog provides scholarship application tips and resources for students. After about eight months of publishing, this nonprofit packaged the first six months of posts into an e-book and offered it via download. "After more than a year and a half, we are getting ready to publish our third compilation and are starting to see awareness of our organization growing exponentially," says Janine Fugate, vice president for marketing and communications for Scholarship America. Scholarship American also hosts an archive of the blog on its own website and has redesigned the organization's business cards to include scholarship application tips on the back, along with a QR code that links to the blog or to a scholarship application tips video. "We've seen a significant increase in our web traffic and social media followers since launching the blog," says Fugate (personal communication, August 2012).

Michael Buller, director of editorial and creative services for the Dana-Farber Cancer Institute, is using this trusted authority approach to reach out beyond the traditional Dana-Farber network of patients and families, staff, physicians, and donors. Content marketing really comes into play when trying to reach people who don't already have a relationship with Dana-Farber or who don't have cancer. "Nobody wants to come to Dana-Farber unless they have to," says Buller (McDermott, 2013; personal communication, February 2013). So the goal is to create a general awareness of Dana-Farber as the best choice if people ever do need a cancer center, and to emphasize the importance of going to a national comprehensive cancer center like Dana-Farber.

In order to build trust and recognition as an expert, Dana-Farber is creating content that resonates with people who don't have cancer. This includes content that answers such questions as, What are some tips for preventing melanoma?, or, How can I have a cancer-fighting diet? Those topics work because most people can relate to them. But creating a voice is not just about the content; style and tone are important too.

"We know it's important to take the buzzwords out of the copy, whether we're talking to the worried well or to cancer patients and families," says Buller. "We're not always successful, but when we are, it's because we avoid talking in the health care clichés of 'world-class care,' 'multidisciplinary care,' and 'patient-centered approach.'"

"We're at our most authentic—and effective—when we worry less about getting our positioning statements into our blog posts, and more about just answering our readers' questions and worries," says Buller. "When we think about our experiences as friends and family members of cancer patients, or as cancer patients ourselves; when we recall the confusion, the anxiety, the questions, then we can understand how we need to talk to that segment of our readers."

Providing good information is itself an important goal. "Even if readers never come to us; even if there's no measurable return, it's still important for us to provide this information because it's helping people. We hope it's part of the effort to prevent the cancers that can be prevented," says Buller. "And that's an important part of who we are too."

Be a Reliable Performer

While individual program participants may be attracted to nonprofits that position themselves as helpful friends, and influencers to nonprofits seen as trusted authorities, it's more likely that using your content to position your organization as either a *reliable performer* or *innovative changemaker* will work best in fundraising.

If you want to use your content to show donors that what your nonprofit does works, and it works day in and day out, you can focus on content that demonstrates that the organization is a reliable performer, a safe bet for their charitable dollars or volunteer hours. Your content could focus on storytelling that shows the impact your nonprofit has over and over in people's lives, before and after stories and images, and testimonials about its effectiveness. You should likely stay away from controversial or political topics and focus more on the bread and butter of accomplishing your mission. The content strategies of reliable performers constantly close the feedback loop with donors—"you gave, so thank you, and here's what we made happen with your support, and we'll do it again tomorrow."

Children of the Nations' vision is to "raise children who transform nations." "Success stories are the biggest part of what we do communications-wise. It is our number one goal to communicate to our partners that their partnership and their money is indeed doing what we say it is," says Pam Wright, the organization's former director of advancement (personal communication, October 2012). "We want our partners to feel like they are investing in the children. And with investments, investors expect reports on how that investment is doing." Partners respond to the stories directly. "We get pretty regular feedback that they love the stories, or are so encouraged by them, or so excited for a program or project that is moving forward," says Wright.

Be an Innovative Changemaker

If you think about those nonprofits that we might call the *rock stars*, their content strategies often position them as innovative changemakers. Like the reliable performers, innovative changemakers also focus on results, but the problems they tackle often have much more drama—or perhaps these organizations are simply better at weaving drama into their storytelling! Instead of just results per se, they talk about real, lasting change, especially when it's hard to get there. Innovative changemakers have no problem with flaunting the ways they are bucking the system or ignoring conventional wisdom.

The content strategies of innovative changemakers are sometimes personality driven, through a charismatic spokesperson or founder, for example. Scott Harrison, the founder and CEO of Charity: Water, often shares his backstory of being a New York City club promoter who turned to helping others to save his own life. "Faced with spiritual bankruptcy, I wanted desperately to revive a lost Christian faith with action and asked the question: What would the opposite of my life look like?" says Harrison on the "Scott's Story" page of the nonprofit's website as he describes what led him to found the organization (Harrison, 2006). His contagious enthusiasm and confidence that individuals can work together to bring safe, clean drinking water to everyone around the world takes center stage (along with water shooting out of wells) in many of the organization's videos.

St. Jude Children's Hospital also relies heavily on its celebrity founders, the late Danny Thomas and his daughter Marlo Thomas, and spokespersons like actresses Jennifer Aniston and Sofia Vergara and athletes Michael Strahan and Shaun White. They ask us through the annual Thanks and Giving campaign to "give thanks for the healthy kids in your life, and give to those who are not."

But you don't always need a charismatic spokesperson or leader to position yourself as an innovative changemaker. You can choose your own words and the "crowd" you hang out with to do the same thing.

In the late 1980s, DePaul Industries in Portland, Oregon, shifted from a sheltered workshop model that employed people with disabilities to an affirmative business model that provides real jobs, competitive wages, and career tracks for people with disabilities. Business growth creates the social good, not the other way around. While DePaul Industries is a nonprofit, over 97 percent of its revenue is earned from successful staffing, packaging, and security business units. The organization focuses on providing best-in-class value to its customers—its nonprofit mission is considered a hidden strength.

To cement this idea that DePaul Industries is much more than just another charity helping people with disabilities, the organization is working to present itself as an innovative changemaker. "We've done a number of posts on our blog about positioning ourselves as socially entrepreneurial," says Sarah Royal, outside marketing specialist for DePaul Industries (personal communication, August 2012). "We also are on Twitter, tweeting and sharing #socent links." The organization refers to itself as a "company" in its marketing and emphasizes the economic value of employing people with disabilities, rather than the social or charitable value.

Or Come Up with Your Own

You can customize these four starting points by replacing the adjective in front of *friend*, *authority*, *performer*, or *changemaker* with another word, such as any of these:

Ambitious	Hardworking	Punctual
Considerate	Intrepid	Responsible
Cooperative	Involved	Responsive
Determined	Loyal	Tenacious
Flexible	Meticulous	Tolerant
Focused	Neutral	Trustworthy
Frugal	Observant	Versatile

Of course, you can change those four nouns too! The goal is to decide on a clear voice that can be used to guide your content marketing decisions.

> ## Stop, Think, and Discuss
>
> Which best describes your organization's personality: helpful friend, trusted authority, reliable performer, or innovative changemaker?
>
> Is there a better combination of one adjective and one noun to describe how you would like your organization to be perceived?
>
> Do you see good ways to connect this personality to your content marketing goals and objectives?

Customizing Your Voice with Tone and Style

While you should try to maintain a consistent voice, your tone and style may change, and sometimes quite often.

Tone is the attitude or mood of your communications. As a mother, I can take a serious, perhaps even threatening, tone when talking to my kids about cleaning their rooms but a sympathetic and nurturing tone if they've had a bad day at school. Yet my voice remains that of the mother in both cases.

Your nonprofit probably has a serious but hopeful tone when it talks about the great need out there, but a more celebratory, cheerful tone when it talks about its successes.

Review the following list of words to see which ones best describe the different tones of voice that your organization may use.

Affectionate	Friendly	Respectful
Balanced	Fun	Serious
Candid	Humble	Soulful
Caring	Loving	Sympathetic
Cheerful	Opinionated	Tactful
Concerned	Optimistic	Thoughtful
Confident	Positive	Warm
Decisive	Practical	Witty
Enthusiastic	Rational	

Style is the manner in which you share your voice and tone. For example, I have a very casual style with my family, and I'd say I'm pretty casual overall professionally as well, especially compared to other consultants who take a more formal approach.

Which style is your organization most likely to use?

Authoritative	Descriptive	Journalistic
Businesslike	Detailed	Lyrical
Chatty	Eloquent	Persuasive
Concise	Emphatic	Rhythmic
Conversational	Flowery	Simplistic
Crisp	Formal	Succinct
Casual	Informal	Technical

Stop, Think, and Discuss

How can you further customize your voice or personality with different tones or styles? Where and in what ways would these tones and styles come out through your communications?

One of the biggest problems nonprofits face with making their various tones and styles appealing to their participants, supporters, and influencers is jargon. It's especially tough for organizations that deal with complicated policy or technical details. Tracy Moavero, development and communications coordinator at Policy Matters Ohio, says that's one of the most difficult challenges of working for a think tank. "I've worked in policy on the state, national, and international level, and the biggest challenge is writing for what I half-jokingly call 'normal people.' It's easy to get stuck in the jargon of your issue area, especially if you are immersed in the UN or Capitol Hill," says Moavero (personal communication, August 2012).

It's also difficult to put a human face on some issues or tell a story about them that others can relate to. "I worked on nuclear disarmament for a long time, and it's hard to write about the ongoing dangers without wearing people out. It can also be mind-numbingly technical," says Moavero. Now she works on state-level economic issues, which she says are somewhat easier but still challenging because there are no specific success stories tied to individuals. "We try to focus on values instead," says Moavero, "such as talking about funding education so every student has a fair chance to succeed, or changing our tax policies so the average worker doesn't have an unfair burden."

Finding an appealing voice, tone, and style can be difficult in situations like these, but it can be done. Take Grist, for example.

Taking on Big, Serious Issues in a Funny Voice

Grist's tagline is "a beacon in the smog." Here's what you'll find at the top of the "About" page on this nonprofit's website:

Laugh now—or the planet gets it.

You know how some people make lemonade out of lemons? At Grist, we're making lemonade out of looming climate apocalypse.

It's more fun than it sounds, trust us!

Grist has been dishing out environmental news and commentary with a wry twist since 1999—which, to be frank, was way before most people cared about such things. Now that green is in every headline and on every store shelf (bamboo hair gel, anyone?), Grist is the one site you can count on to help you make sense of it all.

John Atcheson, the chief operating officer at Grist, explains that humor was part of Grist from the very beginning. "The global climate catastrophe is not fun, but there is so much doom and gloom, and most people are not going to read it. So we really try to have fun with it, but not make fun of it," explains Atcheson (personal communication, November 2012). But trying to maintain that personality can be difficult, especially in times of rapid growth, as Grist is going through now. "We generate a lot of content. We have a core staff, but a bunch of contributing editors across the country too, and it can be hard to maintain a consistent tone and level of irreverence," says Atcheson. But it's important that Grist maintains that voice.

"Something may be important and well written, but we'd still prefer everything to have a little bit of attitude to it," says Atcheson. That humorous voice is important because it's now what regular readers expect, and they will miss that spark if it's gone. At the same time, Grist would miss an opportunity to engage new people too. "Our writers typically have deep knowledge about what they are talking about, but we want the content to be unique and memorable for people," says Atcheson, who says that maintaining humor and irreverence across the writers is a constant effort—from the screening and coaching of new writers to the ongoing review and encouragement of existing writers.

There's serious intent behind the pun headlines and goofy photos. The strategy is to attract as many new people as possible with very accessible content, deepen their understanding with explanatory journalism and news, and drive a high-level conversation with deep-dive reporting and analysis. But it's an imprecise path, says Atcheson, and Grist is constantly trying new things to see how readers will react.

"If you have base level content with a very simple basic tie into an issue like climate or food production, that helps. You can be funny and entertaining and engaging, and just touch the issue around the edges," says Atcheson. That kind of content is more likely to get attention and be more shareable. Grist focuses on generating that kind of content because it is broadly appealing and interesting, qualities that bring much more traffic to the website and social media pages. From there, Grist has a chance to bring visitors into the fold and to tie them into deeper content. "From the lighter content, you want to try to generate questions where someone is seeking an answer, and then you can inform them and get closer to the wonky stuff," says Atcheson. "But you aren't just going to make that jump. We are constantly working on how to move people along."

Bringing Out Your Personality in Social Media

Many nonprofits have found that social media is the best channel in which to experiment with and hone an organization's personality. That's been true for the

Humane Society of the United States (HSUS). Social media gave the HSUS an opportunity to humanize a brand that has been around since 1954 and is considered by many to be "old school," says Carie Lewis, deputy director, online communications (personal communication, October 2012).

"Our mission is 'celebrating animals, confronting cruelty,' and we do a lot of work on the confronting side. So we wanted to use social media to bring out that celebrating side. We've tried to create a persona of being responsive and fun, but caring about the core issues too," says Lewis. One example is putting the community manager's face on the organization's Twitter background. "You see immediately that she has a dog, and so you can relate to her as a fellow pet owner."

Responding personally to comments is extremely important to building this personality. "People will write in and tell us how much they love us and we will write back, 'We love you too!,' but you wouldn't get that kind of response from us over the phone or email," says Lewis. HSUS gets many of the same questions over and over and has a list of standard responses. For example, many people will post to the HSUS Facebook page when they have lost their dog. "We share tips on our website for what to do, but we are also very compassionate," says Lewis. "We'll say that we hope their dog comes home soon and to keep us posted. It's not just a cookie-cutter answer. We really do tailor it to the individual."

No Matter Your Personality, Add the Three G's

I first developed the three G's as a way to help nonprofits understand what they should be doing in social media. But they also work really well for an overall content marketing strategy, regardless of which communications channel you are using.

The three G's are be genuine, be generous, and be grateful.

Be Genuine

Your participants and supporters are not interested in connecting with a 501(c)(whatever). They are interested in connecting with people who share their values, people who can help them, or people who are fighting for the kind of change they too want to see in the world. It's all about being real.

You can be genuine by letting staff members' personalities shine through in the nonprofit's content, which will help your organization to build rapport with participants and supporters. Let people know how staff feel about what's happening in the world. Express some opinions, instead of just sharing facts. Take people backstage, and let them see what's really going on behind the scenes.

Be Generous

It's all about being a helpful human. Think of communicating as gift giving—are you a good gift giver who thinks about the people on the receiving end and what they want or need? Or are you a bad gift giver, thinking about your own needs and treating communications as just another chore on your to-do list? Listen carefully and constantly to your supporters, and then respond in kind. Empower them with helpful information and resources, even if those materials have been created by other, "competing" nonprofits (this type of generosity makes you look smart, confident, and in the know).

Be Grateful

Being grateful is what you do in response to generosity from others. You can say thank you directly, or you can do what I call "blowing kisses" throughout the day. Share a link to someone else, retweet a message, or otherwise pass on information from others who have been kind to you, as a way of saying thanks. Tell stories not just about your organization and its clients but about its fans and followers too. Show them how much they really mean to you.

Stop, Think, and Discuss

What could you do in your communications to demonstrate that your nonprofit is genuine, generous, and grateful?

Why It Matters: You Need Them to Recognize You

Developing the voice and the tones and styles that help you achieve your content marketing goals will take time. But it will pay off because people will come to think of you as that helpful friend or trusted expert. This is essential to standing out in the crowd of faceless 501(c) organizations. We can all describe the personalities of the favorite people in our lives. Wouldn't it be great if your supporters could describe your organization as their favorite nonprofit in the same way?

Chapter Six
Carrying the Load
How to Staff Your Content Marketing Strategy

> **This chapter is about . . .**
> - Leading your content marketing team by coaching rather than controlling
> - Creating a culture where everyone is a marketer
> - Making it easy for others to help you

When people backpack in a group, they divide up responsibilities pretty quickly, based either on taking turns or on who is best at specific tasks. It's a team effort and so is your content marketing strategy.

You really can't be the single voice for your organization, and you shouldn't want to be. You are better off helping others (whether they be staff, board members, volunteers, or social media fans) to become better messengers for your organization's cause than trying to control them or do it all yourself.

That's sometimes a challenge, depending on how others in your organization see marketing and communications. Maybe they think marketing is slick or fluff. Maybe they just don't "do" marketing. Maybe they appreciate the need for it but think it's your job, not theirs.

It's your job to help others see that everyone in the organization is in fact involved in marketing because everyone has an impact on how others perceive the organization. Their activities and behaviors affect the organization's relationships with its participants, supporters, and influencers, oftentimes more than your communications pieces do.

The Role of the Nonprofit Communications Director

The role of a communications director is extremely varied. When I've looked at the language used in job descriptions, I've found the whole gamut of assignments, from "managing the brand" to "updating the Facebook page." More often than not, I believe, the role is really best described as translator, navigator, and coach.

You Are a Translator

Nonprofit communications directors have to take what's going on in their organizations, regardless of how complicated, wonky, boring, or private it may be, and translate it into words and images that people outside the organization can relate to.

This may also mean translating any urgency or panic that staff members feel into a plan of action. Sean King, director of marketing and communications for Youth Education in the Arts, calls it "mid-level manic" when a colleague needs help right away and insists that she needs to get her latest campaign, project, or appeal on "the top of the page" or "on Facebook more" or "in an email to go out in the next hour." In this case, says King, it's your job to advocate for those who would be on the receiving end of those communications and to act as a gatekeeper while coming up with a reasonable plan. "You have the larger view of the organization's goals and universal communication plan. Be protective of the plan, but flexible enough to adapt to manage whatever arrives with a request like these, whether it is self-inflicted or a true emergency," says King (personal communication, November 2012).

It's also your job to do the reverse: to translate what's happening outside your organization and make it meaningful for the program staff. They may be hearing about buzzwords like *social media engagement* and metrics like *click-through* and *bounce* rates and not have the foggiest idea what these mean and how they are relevant to the success of the organization. Translating why engagement matters and why the organization cares about the metrics that it uses is another important part of your job.

You Are a Navigator

In today's media environment, your organization has to make choices about which communications channels it will emphasize and which ones it will leave alone (at least for now). But to make those decisions intelligently, the organization's leaders need someone to help them navigate through all those choices. That's part of your job too. If you need a visual aid when you're talking with them, just hold up one of the infographics that show all the social media channels available today, and say, "I'll navigate us through this mess."

The people you are communicating with—your participants and supporters—also need you to help them navigate your organization. Are you mapping out a path for them so they can see how to get more involved with your organization? Are you connecting the dots for them so they can see how their personal action of a $25 donation or participation in one of your events leads to much bigger collective change that makes the world a better place?

You Are a Coach

With the sheer amount of content that you need to create and the number of communications channels that you need to manage, you really can't do it alone. One approach is to serve as the gatekeeper, so that all content goes through you before it gets published or posted. If basic standards of good communications are not being met, you may need to play that role early on or at least with certain staff members. The same goes for larger organizations—because of the sheer amount of content that might be posted daily to your organization's Facebook page, for example, someone has to play the gatekeeper role.

But ultimately, you want to transition into being more of a coach. You should help program staff learn about the best ways to produce content about their programs for the best results. You should work with fundraisers to see how they can expand and repurpose their donor communications. You'll be more successful if everyone on the team is contributing, with your coaching. Even if you do remain in a gatekeeping role as well, the content that meets you at the gate will be of much higher quality.

Jereme Bivins is the digital strategy and emerging media manager for the Foundation Center, where he works with five regional offices across the United States while also maintaining the voice of the national office. Bivins updates the Foundation Center's main Twitter account and Facebook page, and staff in the regional offices handle those offices' social media accounts (personal communication, February 2013). That means you'll get a different "flavor" from each office, but one that's still consistent with the Foundation Center's overall voice, which Bivins describes as that of a "neutral expert."

He tries not to lead conversations but to have an active voice in them. He also likes to connect people who express interest in particular nonprofit or philanthropic topics with resources at the Foundation Center and at other organizations. Staff across the various offices share content over Yammer, an internal social network, and through a multimedia content calendar. They also coordinate projects over the phone as needed. Yammer is especially useful in keeping the five national offices updated while reducing the amount of time spent in meetings or over email, says Bivins.

Because each regional office has its own personality and expertise, Bivins sees his role not as dictating what should be said and when, but rather as talking about opportunities and suggesting specific tactics in an ongoing, productive conversation.

Stop, Think, and Discuss

In what ways can you lead your content marketing team as a translator, navigator, or coach?

Helping Staff Understand the Basics

Many program people honestly don't know what marketing really is or even recognize a good story when they see it. That's OK—consider it your job to help them understand the basics, which makes it easier for you to do the harder stuff. Get into the habit of training, supporting, and appreciating your program staff.

An easy way to start a group conversation about marketing is to ask the kinds of questions that your staff and board might be asked by people they meet at parties or old acquaintances they run into at the grocery store.

The goal of this exercise isn't to make sure people have the organization's talking points memorized. It's to help them talk about the organization in a way that feels very natural to them yet is consistent with how you want the organization to be portrayed.

I recommend that you have an open discussion about the following questions in sessions with staff and with board members, and then do some role playing where people practice answering them, in pairs. Change the pairs and do it again. As people listen to each other's answers, they will learn to refine their own answers. I do this exercise regularly with a board that I serve on, and it helps keep everyone current.

What do you do? Encourage people to answer this question not only with their own job description but also with some information on the nonprofit too.

What's different or special about your organization? While this question might not be asked in exactly this way, the answer you've practiced may still be a good follow-up when you are having a conversation with someone. If your nonprofit is similar to another one but with a twist, it's fine to mention that other organization that is better known.

Whom do you help? Always bring your description of your work back around to the people (or animals) involved in the cause, even when your work isn't direct service work. It's much easier for people to remember ideas when they associate them with people, rather than thinking of them in the abstract.

How do you do that? Have a quick story or anecdote (or two or three) at the ready, to illustrate how you do your work. Listen to your program staff talk to see if you can hear parts of a story arc, for example. Or watch for stories that seem to ignite a really passionate response from staff. As you identify these good marketing elements, explain to the program staff why you think they are so interesting or compelling. Interview your staff to get the details, and explain why you are asking the questions you are. As they start to see the process working, they'll begin to understand it and better understand what you need from them in order to do your job.

Creating a Culture Where Everyone Is a Marketer

Beth Ann Spiegel, fund development and communications associate of The Arc of Atlantic County, used the following four-step process to create a culture where everyone is a marketer (Spiegel, 2012). Feel free to use this example as a guide for creating a culture in your organization that respects and understands marketing as a vital way of achieving your nonprofit's mission.

Step One

Make sure your nonprofit's executive leaders value marketing and understand that every employee is a potential ambassador, or marketer, of the organization. To get buy-in from The Arc's leaders, Spiegel invited them to attend the Nonprofit Marketing Guide webinar *Helping Your Staff and Board Become Great Nonprofit Marketers*.

Step Two

Identify an opportunity to address employees in person. The organization Spiegel works for is a county social services agency with a large residential program for people with intellectual and developmental disabilities, so it has a workforce of more than 260 people. The only opportunity Spiegel had to get the attention of that many people at once was the annual staff retreat. Leadership staff invited her department to host a half-hour session on "accidental marketing" at that retreat, which was a great opportunity to gather and share valuable information. Of course, having people attend smaller staff meetings would be ideal for building more personal relationships with staff, so if you have time to do that, go for it. This would be a great chance for staff to get to know and trust you.

Step Three

Develop your agenda for the meeting. Your colleagues will have many different perspectives, depending on the program area they work in. But they all have one thing in common—they are working to promote the organization's mission. Emphasize that in the meeting. Help them see that you're not just some annoying person trying to get others to help you do your job. Stories and experiences are what compel people to support nonprofit organizations, and direct support staff are the key holders of those stories and experiences.

The following agenda is based on the one Spiegel used for her session at The Arc's staff retreat:

- **Introduce yourself and explain what you do**. Even the colleagues you see every day may not really know how much detail your job entails. Earn their respect by briefly covering your department's responsibilities, with emphasis on how your communications job benefits the nonprofit's mission.

- **Ask people what they think of when they hear the word** *marketing*. Maybe they think of the annoying people who call them at dinner time asking for money. Maybe they think it has nothing to do with their job, or that it is fluff—unnecessary and something the organization could do without. Define marketing for them, and ask them to answer this question about their own organizational role: "What value does our organization and my work in particular provide to society?" Get each person thinking about his or her impact in broader terms.

- **Explain how and why you communicate that value**. Nonprofits use storytelling and crafted messaging to communicate value in order to generate good feelings among staff about their work and to bring in volunteers, donations, new hires, new clients, and so forth. Every employee is sending a message when he is working or talking about his work that could potentially affect the nonprofit.

- **Provide time for discussion**. Now, get staff thinking about some of the messages they're sending when they're talking about their work, and what messages they get back. Spiegel's group already knew there were a lot of misconceptions about who they are, whom they serve, and what they do, so they developed their questions based on that knowledge. She gave them seven minutes to fill out their questionnaires together, and afterward she asked them to share their thoughts. They received a lot of great feedback that they can now use to craft better messaging and to develop tools that will make it easier for employees to be consistent when communicating about their work.

- **Tell your own stories**. Offer two or three short stories showing how marketing has already benefited the organization. One of Spiegel's accidental marketing stories described how The Arc's CFO knocked on the wrong door when responding to a furniture donation offer and got to talking with the residents about the agency's work. The neighbors were so impressed that shortly afterward they became volunteer partners in The Arc's Special Olympics golf program. They loved their experience and became reliable and generous donors, and later the husband even joined the board. He and his wife recently made one of the largest gifts received by the agency's ongoing capital campaign to date. All this happened because of an enthusiastic employee who knew what to say and how to say it.

- **Closing**. Ask staff to share their own stories about marketing, and how it may have helped their program. Thank them for all that they contributed, and remind them again of how you plan to use the stories and other information that they have contributed.

Step Four

Follow through! After the meeting, get to work right away on developing tools to address the challenges your colleagues face when communicating about their work. Thank them for their help in a follow-up email or memo, and send them any tools you may already have that they have not received. Spiegel identified an opportunity in new-hire orientation to distribute messaging materials so that all The Arc employees can be on the same page from day one.

If possible, you could also follow up by attending smaller staff meetings for more one-on-one story opportunities.

The bottom line is to show your colleagues that you respect their work and their busy schedules, and provide tools to make it as easy as possible for them to give you those compelling stories that ultimately will make everyone's work more successful and rewarding.

Facilitating a Board Retreat on Marketing

I was asked to facilitate a board retreat for Gaston Day School. Liz Minor, the school's director of development, gave me a lot of leeway in structuring the agenda. She told me that she had great board members who were very willing to help with marketing the school but who also felt that they didn't know how to do that exactly; they didn't know what to say or when or to whom.

Here are six principles I used in structuring the agenda for the daylong retreat (Leroux Miller, 2012), and you can use these for your board retreats on marketing too.

1. *Focus on what they already know.* People get anxious when they think you want them to memorize something, like a mission statement. Instead, focus on what they already know by heart, because it's already in their heart! At the Gaston Day School retreat, we spent most of the morning talking about two ways to think of their messages as board members. The first way was simply "sharing the love" about Gaston Day. They practiced talking to each other about "why I love Gaston Day" and then discussed, as a group, what they had said to and had heard from each other. The second way was storytelling. All the people in the room had at least one story to share about how Gaston Day had changed their own life or their child's. I asked volunteers to share stories, to increase the overall story repertoire of the board.

2. *Give what they know a little more structure.* I asked them to pair off three times and to share why they loved Gaston Day School, so that each of them explained it to three people and heard three people's explanations. (I picked up this exercise from Gail Perry.) This allowed board members not only to practice but also to refine their statements by adding points or rephrasing

their own reasons by incorporating better phrasing they might have heard from someone else.

For the storytelling exercises, I shared the three classic story plots, including the various elements within those plots. By making sure their stories have all the essential elements, they can turn an otherwise ho-hum story into one with lots of emotional staying power.

3. *Keep the concepts simple.* You aren't going to turn people into marketing experts during a one-day retreat. You have to pick and choose, and you have to simplify. I wanted the board members to get a general grasp on what I meant by marketing, but not to get overwhelmed by it. So I didn't present the ten-part marketing plan outline I sometimes use. Instead I focused on the quick and dirty version: who are you trying to reach, what do you want them to do, what's the message to get them to do it, and how do you deliver that message? I simplified it even further by saying that they, the board members, were the messengers. After a quick brainstorming session on audiences and calls to action, we were able to spend the rest of our time on the message (in this case, the personal testimonials and stories).

4. *Connect the concepts to the real world.* Board members are busy people. When you take up a good chunk of their day, you need to ensure that they see how the material you are covering is relevant to them outside the retreat. The final hour of the four-hour retreat was dedicated to this. We started with a discussion of situations where they could use the "why I love Gaston Day" message and specific stories to work Gaston Day naturally into a conversation, for example, if a friend is complaining about the state of public education or a coworker is talking about relocating her family to the area.

5. *Address their practical concerns.* I also left half an hour open on the schedule for a *sticky situations* session where, as a group, the board members were able to troubleshoot some scenarios they had faced: for example, "what do you say when someone complains about a particular thing?" This was also a great chance for board members to provide staff with some input on concerns that people had raised with them as board members.

6. *Make it highly interactive.* I saw my job as providing a framework that the board members could fill in with their own ideas and experiences. While setting up the framework did include some training that required me to speak for a few minutes at a time, most of the day was participatory and interactive. We did solo exercises, share pairs, and whole group brainstorming and discussion. Several board members thanked me specifically for making the retreat so interactive. This is so important with adult learners. If they can practice something, they are much more likely to really learn it.

Stop, Think, and Discuss

Try to identify a few times during the year when you can get your whole staff or board to focus on marketing. Can you add this activity to a staff meeting or retreat agenda?

An Easy Way Others Can Help: Storytelling Stringers

Allison Monnell was once the community relations director for Chemung ARC, an agency that supports people with developmental disabilities in the Finger Lakes region of New York. Chemung ARC's challenge was capturing good stories about the people they support and figuring out how to best share them. With more than seven hundred people supported by the agency and a staff of more than four hundred across thirty different locations, the agency had to be methodical in its approach. Because the agency distributes an internal e-newsletter to its staff each week, and because this newsletter is the primary source of news and communiqués throughout their agency, Monnell thought this the best vehicle to share their stories (personal communication, April 2013).

She set about assigning satellite reporters at each of the agency's locations whom she called *stringers* from the old newspaper term for a freelance reporter who was paid by the column inch, which was measured by string and turned into the publisher at the end of each month. She chose frontline staff who are privy to the personal triumphs of the people they support each day and set up a rotation schedule, asking each stringer to commit to a year by submitting at least two stories per year. She stressed that creative writing skills were not necessary; she just wanted the nuts and bolts: who, what, where, when, how, and why. Editing was left to Monnell, and of course, pictures were encouraged.

Kira Johnson, Monnell's successor at Chemung ARC, maintains the stringer schedule to solicit stories for the internal newsletter. Johnson also believes that building relationships with staff throughout the agency is essential to enlisting their help in promoting agency successes (personal communication, April 2013).

"I have set out to meet everyone by participating in staff meetings across the agency, dropping in on recreational events, and joining self-advocacy gatherings, for example. It is essential that our staff sees firsthand that I am involved and invested in their work. I am not somehow separate from them, sitting in a far-removed administrative office. I am part of the team."

This approach has been successful for the agency. In Johnson's first five months on the job, Chemung ARC has appeared in a dozen published articles. Many of the story ideas were submitted to Johnson by staff. "We have always circulated the news internally. But you can't be afraid to share your successes with the media. You never know what might capture their interest," Johnson said.

Stop, Think, and Discuss

Could you put a storytelling stringers program in place at your organization? How might you customize it for the way your organization works?

Supporting Your Team with a Marketing Bank

You can support your marketing team by giving them materials that make it easier for them to follow through and to complete work in ways that are more compatible with your marketing strategy.

A marketing bank is a single location where you store all the files that you need and that you are often asked to provide to others. Building a marketing bank will save you tons of time, because you'll always know where to look for that logo, program description, color palette, and so forth. And you can also send staff and volunteers right to it, so you aren't constantly forwarding files to others, saving even more time. You can store your bank on a shared drive, ideally where others can access it remotely.

Here's what belongs in your marketing bank.

Logos in Various Formats

It seems that not a day goes by where I don't see some raggedy, blurred, or skewed nonprofit logo on TV or in print that looks like it has been sent through a fax machine three times. Don't lift your logo off your website or from a word processing document and expect it to look good elsewhere. Instead, create several different files of your logo so you have the right files for the right uses. For example, you should have a color version and a black-and-white version. You should have web versions and print versions.

Find your original artwork files. They are most likely Adobe Illustrator or Photoshop files. Once you find them, label them "original" in the filename so you know not to change them. Then make copies, and start saving them in different formats and resolutions appropriate to various uses, putting "web" and "print" in the filenames to help you keep them straight.

For online use the resolution should be 72 ppi (pixels per inch). So if you want your logo to appear as 1.5 inches square on your website, the dimensions would be 108 pixels by 108 pixels (that's 72×1.5). Save web resolution files as jpgs, gifs, or pngs. Use these on websites, on blogs, and in email.

For print use, the resolution should be at least 300 ppi. So your same 1.5 square-inch logo on a piece of paper would now be 450×450 pixels (300×1.5). Save these as eps or tiff files. You can also use jpg files, but just make sure that the resolution and size are set high enough.

For TV, I recommend sending the highest-quality logo you have and letting the company you are working with adjust the size and resolution to match its needs.

If you can't find your original artwork files, get them redrawn. Either ask your graphic designer to do it or find a volunteer or college student who knows Adobe Illustrator. You'll need to know which fonts you used or be willing to have the designer take a guess. Unless your logo is extremely complicated, it will probably take a designer about an hour to redraw an old logo. The $100 to $200 you spend on this will pay for itself by making your organization look much more professional.

Photos

With every photo, include the caption, sources, photographer's name, and any restrictions.

Bios and Head Shots

Have biographies and head shots for all key staff and board members—anyone who is considered a public face of the organization.

Boilerplate Text

All those chunks of text that you use over and over should go in your files. That includes your mission and vision statements, plain-English descriptions of your programs, your history, your elevator speeches, staff bios, press release boilerplate, organizational frequently asked questions, and anything else that you find yourself frequently copying and pasting.

Calendars

Put copies of all your calendars in your marketing bank, along with links to organizational master calendars and also editorial calendars.

Editorial and Design Style Guide

Much time is wasted correcting inconsistencies in everything from your branding (including how staff use the nonprofit's logo, colors, or fonts) to preferred editorial styles—does anyone want to argue about serial commas? Spare yourself and everyone else who creates content for you the misery of these arguments by creating style sheets.

An *editorial style sheet* is a chart you fill out showing how you will use, format, and spell certain words. You can also include rules about abbreviations, capitalization, acronyms, and anything else related to how words, numbers, and punctuation appear in your publications. Include anything and everything that you end up correcting when editing someone else's work. Here are some common decisions to record on your style sheet.

- When do you spell out numbers? Under 10 or under 100?

- Do you use periods in acronyms or not, such as *USA* or *U.S.A.*?

- Do you hyphenate certain words? For example is it *e-mail* or *email*? *Decision-maker* or *decision maker*?

- How do you format phone numbers—with parentheses around the area code or not?

- How do you format email addresses—are they all lowercase or are capital letters OK?

- How do you format website addresses—with the http:// and www. or not?

- How do staff's proper names appear in print? As Robert or Bob? With a middle initial or not?

A *graphic design style guide* puts in writing all the various decisions you've made about how things should look both in print and online. While many of the same decisions will be reflected in a *cascading style sheet* (CSS), they are not the same document. A CSS is written in code for your website, producing a consistent look across your web pages; a graphic design style guide is written for humans to read, especially those who aren't familiar with code or even technical design terms!

Here are the kinds of decisions that should be on your graphic design style guide:

- What fonts will you use for headlines, subheads, body copy, and captions? What point sizes will you use, and when is it appropriate to use boldface, italics, and underlining? You may decide to use different sets of fonts, sizes, and styles online and in print, so note where staff should use which sets of guidelines. You may also choose some display fonts, to be used for big signs, graphic headers, or event invitations, for example. Include notes on the spacing, such as how big margins should be and how much space should go between the bottom of the headline and the top of the body copy.

- What's your organization's color palette? You should also select a limited number of colors (think three to six, not including black and white) for your palette. That doesn't mean you will never use any other colors, but you should start with this set and stray from it only when additional colors are clearly called for. Each color you pick will have a few different codes, or modes, depending on which process you are using.

  For online use, you'll want at least the RGB and the HEX codes for the colors. For example, the purple I use at Nonprofit Marketing Guide is 196–175–232 in RGB mode (RGB stands for Red-Green-Blue). But it's #C4AFE8 in HEX, or Hexidecimal or HTML, color codes. For print use, you'll probably want the CMYK values (for four-color process printing) and the closest Pantone color value.

- How should images such as logos and photo be used? On your design style sheet also make notes about how you want images to appear. Are they usually right or left justified? How much margin should surround a photo or graphic? Where do the caption and the credit lines appear, and how do they look? Describe how and when your nonprofit's logo and name can be used. For example, should it always appear in a certain corner of the page? What colors can it be printed in? Can it be printed in reverse (such as in white on a black background)? Can background colors show through the white space in the logo, or not? What uses are unacceptable?

- What are your standard layouts or templates? What kinds of things do staff, board members, or volunteers create on their own? If your organization has preferred layouts for items like letterheads, envelopes, business cards, basic website pages, press releases, flyers, PowerPoint presentations, and so forth, include templates with instructional notes in your design style guide.

Checklists

Short checklists are simple, easy tools to help ensure that the work of your marketing team meets your quality standards. You can create checklists for specific types of communications (for example, email newsletters) or for various processes (for example, how a program staffer can get something on the communications director's to-do list).

Publication Archive

Back issues of newsletters, flyers, annual reports, brochures, invitations, press releases, and so on should all be in your marketing bank.

Facts and Stats

Have up-to-date facts and figures about your cause and your organization ready to go; include sources where appropriate.

Links to Your Accounts and to Others

Your files should include the links to your organization's accounts on Facebook, Twitter, YouTube, and the like. They should also include other useful links, such as links to your favorite resources, ones that you want others to take advantage of too.

Models

Both examples and finished products can be very helpful to beginning marketers. Have examples of do's and don'ts available to give to people, whether they are from your organization or another nonprofit. Models can help people see what you are shooting for, as well as what to avoid. Annotate your models with the specifics of what's good and what's not.

Stop, Think, and Discuss

What's missing from your marketing bank? Create a to-do list that includes all the items needed to fill the gaps.

Creative Briefs and Job Requests

Creative briefs and job requests can also be extremely helpful in minimizing conflict when people are communicating needs and also their expectations of each other.

A *creative brief* is usually a form that team members will fill out together to ensure that everyone is in agreement about the goals for a specific communications project. Creative briefs typically ask team members to address these questions:

- What is it? What is the deliverable?
- What is the goal or purpose of the communications piece?
- What is the single most important thing it should communicate?
- Who is the communications piece for (specific participant or supporter groups, for example)?
- What is the specific call to action?
- Is there a specific voice, tone, or style for this piece that should be reflected in copy or design?
- What gap is this piece filling in our existing communications line-up?
- How will success of the piece be measured?
- Who is the primary decision maker on this piece? Who else is working on it?
- What budget and additional resources will be made available?
- What are the deadlines for the first, intermediate, and final drafts?

If other people in your organization put work on your plate (for example, if your organization serves as an internal agency for program or fundraising staff), then you might also put a *job request* procedure in place.

Diane Greenhalgh, director of web services for the Pulmonary Hypertension Association (PHA), used to compile requests that came in from staff via email, putting them into an Excel chart. But key information—particularly deadlines—was often missing, sending her department searching to fill in gaps and prioritizing by educated guesses.

Now the association has implemented an electronic case submission form that saves time and energy and prevents confusion. Each individual who needs Greenhalgh's department's help submits a request that goes directly into a password-protected database that staff can access online. This results in a list of cases and deadlines in an easy-to-use chart format that is available to everyone.

It also links to pages with more detail—all the information that was submitted with each project, fields indicating project status, who is assigned to the case, and any case notes. "We now require key information be included in project submissions. We make this easy through a simple online submission form, and we have what we need to know from the beginning," says Greenhalgh (2012).

She suggests that you standardize the requests coming from your coworkers with some key information, which will likely include the following:

- Draft due date, if applicable (provides time for editing before final deadline)

- Preferred final due date

- Must-be-final due date (to help you prioritize when you have too many projects at the same time)

- Details about the deadline, including any promises made

- Attachments with supplementary materials

- Who should be cc'ed throughout the process of filling the request (to eliminate unnecessary emails)

- Indication of urgency on projects needed in the next day or so

You can customize this list for your particular projects. For example, Greenhalgh's system is for web projects, so she asks what the page title, description, and friendly URL should be.

"In addition to organizing incoming jobs," says Greenhalgh, "communication is key to making your internal clients happy and to keeping yourself informed so you can manage your priority list." She suggests that you develop patterns for regularly checking in with staff on a broad basis, not just on a particular project. In these interactions, find out if they need help with anything, solicit feedback on your process, and ask them for updates on their projects, including materials they expect to submit soon so you can set aside time for them.

"We hold monthly meetings with each department to exchange this kind of information," says Greenhalgh. "We've formed an advisory committee to our web department, too, and this group's ideas helped us develop our case management system."

Sharing information with all key players openly also helps projects flow more smoothly. "Here in PHA's web department, we automatically send a copy of each case submission back to the person who sent the request, inform them of who is assigned to their case, and provide a login to the system online where they can see all the cases we are managing, check the status of their cases, and read case notes," says Greenhalgh.

Stop, Think, and Discuss

Could implementing a system of creative briefs or work orders help to eliminate some conflicts within your nonprofit?

Dealing with Resistance

One of the beefs that I hear from program staff is that their communications people are sooo slooow. Bring in the communications people, they say, and it takes forever to get anything done. By the time it's done, they complain, it's too late.

Of course the same is true in reverse too. Communicators who want to news-jack a story complain that it takes days on end to get a quote approved. Or that they can't get program people to give them good stories to share.

What's going on here? There are few factors at work, some within our control as communicators, and some not.

There are different sets of quality standards. It's not uncommon for program staff and communications staff to have totally different opinions about what constitutes an acceptable level of quality. Just how big a deal is a typo or bad grammar? Does it really matter that the flyer doesn't bear any resemblance to the brand guidelines or anything else that's being promoted now? Just how much detail is really needed in this piece? Try to get on the same page about goals and expectations well before the deadline.

There's no appreciation for the dirty work. So much of our daily work—both on the program side and the communications side—is dealing with technical minutiae that no one really appreciates unless he or she is responsible for it. While you and your coworkers don't need to fully cross-train each other on the hundreds of little steps that appear to outsiders as just three or four big ones, a little education about each other's actual workday wouldn't hurt.

It's harder than it looks. Writing, design, and other creative skills come easier to some than to others. Even for those with natural talent, it can take quite a bit of time to get something just right. It's hard to be brilliant on a moment's notice. Photographers take hundreds of photos to get just the right one.

There are too many layers of review. Most people think they have a keen sense of taste when they really don't. This is especially true when it comes to copywriting and design. For example, unless your executive director has been trained in direct response copywriting, he or she probably shouldn't have the final word on your direct mail appeal letter. Some people love to tinker, and they will happily wordsmith you well past your deadlines.

It happens in a black hole. Part of the reason we become so impatient with each other is that we don't see any progress. Think about ways that you can be more transparent about the steps you take and your progress on them.

Why It Matters: You Can't Do It as Well Alone

Marketing is one of the best nonprofit jobs out there, but sometimes it sure doesn't feel like it. Along with better results for your organization, you'll also improve your own job satisfaction by investing time in developing the skills and cooperation of your marketing team—which includes everyone in your organization.

As part of this effort, develop your own culture of appreciation, especially for others who don't really feel that helping you is part of their job. Make "blowing kisses" or lavishing praise on people for their specific marketing contributions and accomplishments a regular part of your routine.

In parts 1 and 2 of this book, I discussed some of the major strategic shifts you should consider making in the way your organization approaches its communications. The next three parts of this book are about implementing that shift.

In part 3, you will chart the course for your journey by preparing your content marketing plan. The plan consists of three documents:

- *The big picture communications timeline* (chapter 7), which notes the events and milestones that drive your nonprofit's communications, along with the primary calls to action you want to make and the major stories you want to tell over the course of the year.

- *A core topics list* (chapter 8), which identifies the topics or themes that you want to be known for.

- *An editorial calendar* (chapter 9), which charts the communications channels you will use and how frequently you will use them. You'll use what you learn from creating your big picture communications timeline and core topics list to fill in your editorial calendar.

I suggest you complete your editorial calendar by using a *mapping and merging* approach that applies the *rule of thirds* to your content marketing:

- One-third of what you publish can be *original content* you map out in advance, based on your timeline and core topics.
- One-third can be *repurposed content* (Chapter 10), which allows you to share your content more effectively while saving you lots of time and energy.
- One-third can be *merged content* (Chapter 11), which consists of those things you can't plan for in advance. While you can't predict the specifics, there are several major categories of last-minute content that you can be on the lookout for and ready to handle when the times comes.

Chapter Seven
Mapping It Out
Sketching Out Your Big Picture Communications Timeline

> **This chapter is about . . .**
> - Identifying major events and milestones driving your communications plan
> - Understanding how your primary calls to action affect your plan
> - Thinking about the big stories you want to tell on your journey

It's dangerous to descend into the wilderness without a plan. If you are backpacking overnight, especially for more than a few days at a time, you should always tell someone else what your plans are and generally where you will be, so he can meet up with you or find you in case something goes wrong.

The same applies to your communications plan. Everyone in your organization needs to have a general sense of what the ebb and flow of communications looks like for your nonprofit. Some people need more details than others, but everyone should understand what I call the *big picture communications timeline*. It helps you, and others, to see all the big parts, both moving and immobile, that will affect your communications.

FIGURE 7.1
Big Picture Communications Timeline

This is best done on a big whiteboard, but you can also do it with a big sheet of paper. I think sketching it out off-line works best. Once you are done editing, you can clean it up as you move it online.

Since this is a timeline, pick your starting and ending points. A year, with tick marks for each month, is a good place to start (figure 7.1), but if another time range makes more sense for your organization, use that. If you work in politics or advocacy, or in fields like disaster response where you need to react quickly, you may prefer to look at only three months at a time. Don't worry if you have more confidence in what you add during certain times of the year than others. That's not unusual, and you can always edit and add to your timeline later.

Let's start plotting it out.

Identifying Big Events and Milestones

Look at the calendar that your organization, your participants, your supporters, and the rest of the world are living with. What holidays, seasonal events, or other regular occurrences have a big effect on your communications?

For animal shelters, the start of kitten season, when stray cats start to have their litters, is mid-spring (most kittens are born between April and October). Food banks benefit from the many food drives held in November and December, but their shelves are often bare during the summer, when the people and organizations who typically organize food drives (including schools) are busy with vacation plans.

Nonprofits that offer after-school sports should chart the season openers and championship games for the various sports leagues they play in, as well as summer and holiday school breaks. For organizations that do political work, the election cycle is often important, so they will put down filing deadlines, primary and general election dates, and times when the legislature or other governing bodies are in session.

The boxes with dotted lines on the timeline show how you might add these items over which you have no control to your timeline (figure 7.2). Of course, the exact placement and size will vary from organization to organization.

Next, add the big events that are within your control (figure 7.3). Start with events that your organization hosts, including everything from annual fundraisers, workshops or conferences, member meetings, and major performances to lobby days. Then add on the similar types of events that others host but that you cosponsor or otherwise participate in in a major way. I'm not talking about events that one of your staff members might attend as professional development, but those events that your whole organization is involved with as a core part of what it does.

Stop, Think, and Discuss

What big events happen and what milestones are reached every year in your organization? What special events will happen or milestones will be achieved this coming year?

Identifying Your Primary Calls to Action

Now let's think about your most likely and most important calls to action. What is it that your nonprofit most needs other people to do during the course of the year? When will you be asking people to do things such as register, volunteer, or donate? You can't ask everyone to do everything all the time—even if that's what you really want! Try to be as specific as you can.

When I ask nonprofit staff what they want other people to do, I often hear words like these:

be more proactive	engage	promote
believe	help	share
buy in	network	support
collaborate	participate	understand
connect	partner	work with us
educate		

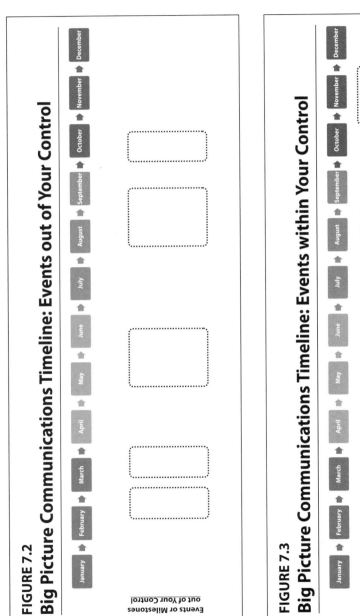

FIGURE 7.2

Big Picture Communications Timeline: Events out of Your Control

January → February → March → April → May → June → July → August → September → October → November → December

Events or Milestones
out of Your Control

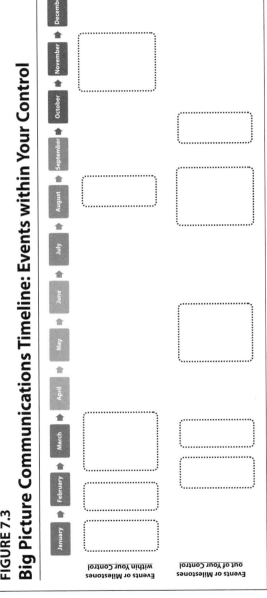

FIGURE 7.3

Big Picture Communications Timeline: Events within Your Control

January → February → March → April → May → June → July → August → September → October → November → December

Events or Milestones
within Your Control

Events or Milestones
out of Your Control

While this kind of language is acceptable in goals and benchmarks, it does not work as a call to action because it is too vague.

There might be ten different ways that someone could "partner" with you or "support" your program. What is it that you actually, physically, visibly want someone to do? If you were making a thirty-second video of someone carrying out your call to action, what would people see happening in that video? The more specific your call to action, the more likely it is that people will understand what you want and actually do it.

Another way to tackle vague calls to action is to apply David Allen's Getting Things Done or GTD approach. The GTD model was designed for personal time management, but you can also use it to make your calls to action more specific. Allen's concept of the *next action step* helps you break big jobs down into many baby steps that you then put in order. You focus on just one step at a time.

Let's say you've been disappointed by other organizations in your coalition who are not "participating," and no matter how often you ask them to "engage," they still don't. It could very well be that your definitions of what it means to "participate" and "engage" are quite different from theirs, and therefore your call to action is ineffective.

Instead you might need to ask them to perform these actions:

- Add the coalition logo to their website.

- Send senior staff to quarterly coalition meetings.

- Provide quotations for coalition press releases.

- Include an article about coalition activities in their newsletter at least twice a year.

In this case, you'd really be giving them multiple calls to action, probably in the form of a checklist to follow.

Sometimes the order of the steps matters and sometimes it doesn't. When it does matter, it's usually best to provide a step 1, step 2, step 3, and so forth format.

When you're asking people to take multiple steps, you'll need to make a strategic decision about timing: will you give them just one step at a time, or will you give them the whole list of steps at once? Depending on how complicated the process is, you might decide to limit your messaging to step 1. Then when people have completed that step, you can talk about step 2.

Take, for example, messaging by domestic violence shelters to women who are being abused. Many of us without professional experience in that field might say the call to action is, "Leave the jerk who is beating you." It's specific and filmable. But it's also too hard and unrealistic for the women who need to perform the action. A short checklist or step-by-step guide might work better, with items such as, "Write down or copy important information like Social Security numbers and bank accounts," or, "Let a trusted friend know what is happening, so she knows to check on you."

The same idea can apply to fundraising. Your first message to a potential new supporter of your organization really shouldn't be, "Give us money." Talk about earlier steps on the path to engagement, things like signing up for an email action alert or liking your Facebook page or attending an event or downloading a resource guide from your website.

You don't need to map out all your calls to action, or the full ordered list or checklist, on your big picture timeline, but to the extent that your calls to action do change over time, try to add them to your chart (figure 7.4).

Stop, Think, and Discuss

What are the main things you'll ask people to do over the course of the year? Don't use generic words like "help" or "support" us, but devise more specific calls to action, such as, "register for the training workshop," or, "donate via the Year-End Direct Mail Appeal."

Identifying Your Major Story Arcs

On top of these events and your primary calls to action, you can then layer on the major story arcs in your organization, roughly approximating when they happen. What are the major stories that play out every year as you deliver your programs and services? What's the seasonal to-do list like in your organization? These stories are often tied to events and calls to action that you already have on the calendar now, so start there.

FIGURE 7.4

Big Picture Communications Timeline: Main Calls to Action

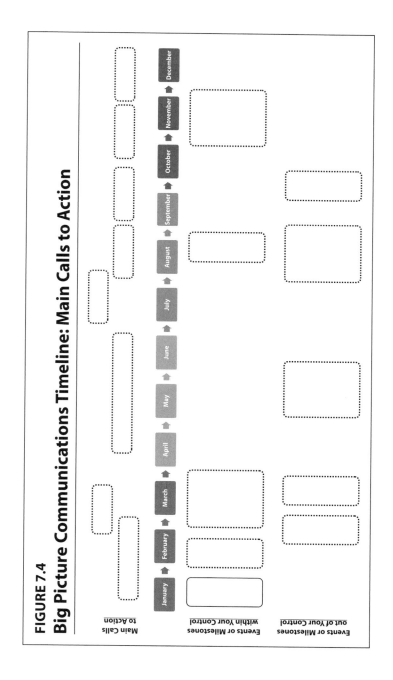

If you have a favorite weekly TV comedy or drama, you are familiar with the concept of the *story arc*: what happened last week influences what happens this week, and that influences what will happen next week. You could typically look back at the end of the season and identify several story arcs that played out over that season. Smaller, one-time events will happen in each episode but a few larger story arcs will continue from episode to episode. That's what keeps you coming back, and what makes you catch up on missed episodes through webisodes or DVR recordings. Soap operas are perhaps the ultimate users (and abusers) of the arc, but you see them in dramas and comedies too.

What if you could create a story arc over a series of weeks or months that kept your supporters hooked? What if they just *had* to open your email newsletter to see what happened next?

We often see communications arcs in advocacy and fundraising campaigns. For example, the Humane Society of United States has blogged from the ice during the Canadian seal hunt. Greenpeace chronicled the construction of its new *Rainbow Warrior*, the ship it uses to monitor the high seas for activity like illegal whaling or dumping.

Even if your work is less dramatic, you can surely envision a beginning, middle, and end to some of your campaigns, programs, or stories. When you share that beginning, middle, and end, you've created a story arc. If you tell a good story, usually by taking people behind the scenes, they will want to see how it turns out, and will want a stake in creating a happy ending with you.

What are your big stories that unfold over weeks or months? Might you

- Follow one school or one teacher throughout the school year, showing how your work is helping that school or teacher?

- Share in a counselor's journey through a summer camp?

- Follow a set of foster parents as they begin fostering a new child for you?

- Watch the renovation of a community center, or chronicle how a green building is designed and constructed?

- Watch a legislative battle unfold?

- Chronicle the life of a new client or volunteer as she works through your programs?

During a workshop for the Land Trust Alliance, I asked participants to identify a big story for the summer by completing this title: "The Story of_____." People worked together in small groups to brainstorm this list:

- The story of creating a public park
- The story of protecting a special piece of land
- The story of farmland preservation
- The story of receiving the BP settlement funding and restoration of the Gulf
- The story of our fundraising event
- The story of our upcoming public forum
- The story of our strategic planning process

Stop, Think, and Discuss
What big stories can you tell over the course of several months or even a whole year?

Breaking a Story into Its Beginning, Middle, and End

Once you have a story concept in mind, you can start breaking the story down into its beginning, middle, and end, so that you can take your participants or supporters along with you as the story unfolds. Sometimes thinking in terms of the beginning, middle, and end is enough, but at other times it helps to add even more structure.

For example, let's say a Friends of the Library group holds an annual used-book sale every May. The group has already marked the sale weekend on its big picture communications timeline and started its calls to action to get people to donate books and then to buy other books. Now it's time to build out the story around the book sale. If the group treats the book sale as the end of the story, asking the community for donations of used books in February and March could be the beginning of the story, and sorting and organizing the books in April could be the middle.

Or the group could treat the book sale (or any other spring fundraiser) as the beginning of a story about fundraising for upcoming programming. In that case, the end of story might be a new Story Hour series in the fall. The middle of the story, in the summer, could be the selection of books, authors, and activities for the series.

Going back to the Land Trust Alliance workshop, the farmland preservation story was broken down into planting, growing, and harvesting as the beginning, middle, and end, an approach that wraps the literal story in metaphor and so is especially nice for telling that particular story. The group that worked on the BP settlement and Gulf Coast restoration story defined the beginning, middle, and end as getting the money and planning how to spend it, purchasing land and habitat for wildlife, and demonstrating how we can make protecting birds and fish a way of life.

You can give your stories even more structure by relying on fiction techniques. For example, maybe your story arc can follow the classic three-act structure:

Act I. We meet the main character and learn his situation and aspirations. Characters are most often the people who are helped in some way by your nonprofit. In Act I there is usually some sort of incident or disturbance that changes the character's goal and sets him on a difficult path, with no easy way back.

Act II. The character's situation changes further, often because he hits small and large obstacles. He will eventually hit rock bottom or a breaking point, but there will be a small glimmer of hope.

Act III. The character will face the final obstacle and (usually) overcome, but often not before one final battle. At the climax, he succeeds.

Act II or Act III is where your nonprofit typically comes in as the supporting cast, helping the character overcome some of the obstacles. But remember, the story is the character's from start to finish, so don't make it all about your nonprofit once you've introduced the organization into the story. Remain in the supporting role, and wrap up the story with the character's triumph.

You can expand on the three-act structure with this six-step story summary, from the book *Plotting Simplified: Story Structure Tips for the Break-Out Novelist*, by Eddie Jones (2011).

1. Portrait: Show your lead character's normal life.

2. Crisis: Show the great disturbance that disrupts his life.

3. Struggle: Your lead character tries to restore order to his life.

4. Discover: Your lead character reaches a moment of realization.

5. Change: Your lead character's life is transformed. Hint at the lessons he's learned.

6. Portrait: Show your lead character's new life.

Jones points out that the characters usually want to get something or get away from something, and this conflict is essential to creating a powerful story. He defines conflict as tension: "Your lead must be opposed by something: person, natural force, inner demons. Your story's main problem is the primary source of dramatic conflict. No hurdles, no conflict—no story. Conflict moves the story forward and shapes your character. Opposition from characters and outside forces brings your story to life. Through your lead's struggles, he will grow or shrink but never remain the same."

Even if you don't know exactly how each of your stories will unfold, take a guess at it. Draw those story arcs across your timeline (figure 7.5). This will allow you later to structure your communications over several weeks or months, hooking your supporters and keeping them invested in how the story ends.

Stop, Think, and Discuss

Where is the conflict or tension in your stories? What are the characters in these stories trying to get or to get away from?

Breaking Story Arcs into Individual Stories

Story arcs that span several weeks or months can also be morphed into content that you can use for your newsletter or website. Let's take a look at one process you might use to break down these larger stories into smaller, individual stories that can be placed on to your editorial calendar (I'll get into editorial calendars in chapter 9).

FIGURE 7.5
Big Picture Communications Timeline: Story Arcs

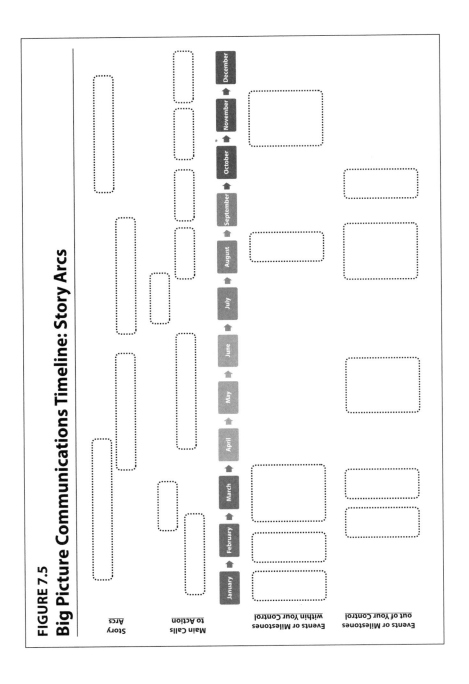

Let's say you have a story arc that covers the experiences of ten new volunteers with your nonprofit. Start by thinking about some of the touch points or milestones they are likely to reach during this journey. For example, the volunteers connect with the nonprofit in several different ways. They attend an orientation together. They do their first assignments. Some have life-changing experiences. You start to see some of the results of their work. Some volunteers move on; others renew their commitment. There's a beginning, middle, and end to the arc, with plenty of opportunities for conflict or tension. Remember, conflict can take the form of inner struggles or battles against institutions or stigmas, as well as interpersonal tension.

Now think about the different ways to tell smaller stories along that arc, hitting on the major touch points. Keep in mind that many of the real details will probably change as events actually occur. That's OK. Sketch out the arc and the stories on it the best you can for now. For example, maybe you will choose to follow three of the ten new volunteers more closely to get their backstories and to interview them more intensely than the others during their time with you.

Next you schedule when you can tell these stories via your various communications channels on your editorial calendar. Think about the best ways to share these stories over the weeks or months in your e-newsletter, on your blog or website, and on Facebook, for example. Do you put one volunteer in each channel or mix up their experiences? Think about how you will maintain the arc, and give readers enough information to get them hooked and waiting for the next update from you.

Finally, as the deadlines for your newsletter and other communications channels come near, you will adjust your plans as needed and share the real stories. Link back to previous episodes of the bigger story, so those who join in midstream can easily catch up if they like.

Stop, Think, and Discuss

What are some beginnings, middles, and ends—or touch points—in your major story arcs? Can you think of a few specific articles that you could write for each of those touch points?

The Big Picture Communications Timeline for Lillian's List

This section presents the process that, as a board member, I helped the staff at Lillian's List walk through. Lillian's List is a political action committee that recruits, trains, and helps elect progressive Democratic women in North Carolina to the North Carolina General Assembly and Council of State.

Before our conversation, Lillian's List staff had made up the communications plan as they went along, typically not looking more than a couple of weeks out at a time. While they certainly had ideas about what they would likely talk about at different times of the year, it had never been written down so they could see the flow or how the different components fit together. The concept of a story arc that tied all their communications together was also new.

Our meeting took place in November 2011, and our goal was to map out the organization's big picture communications timeline from that time through the November 2012 election. Figure 7.6 displays the actual big picture communications timeline that we created, first on a big whiteboard in a conference room and later in a Google Doc. What looks neat and organized now took more than two hours of conversation with lots of messy writing and erasing and rewriting on the whiteboard.

After talking a little bit about the organization's goals—to get more women elected and to rally the sisterhood of progressive women across the state to financially support those political campaigns—we drew a calendar from November to November. We then listed the events and milestones out of our control: the period when candidates could file for running for office, the primary and general election dates, and the 2012 Democratic National Convention, which would be held in our state. Next we added the events we could control, including some key board meetings, fundraising events, and candidate trainings. We wrote down what we knew at the time and made adjustments later as we got more information.

Next, we talked about the story arcs (labeled "Messaging" in the timeline) and calls to action (labeled "Fundraising"), almost at the same time. It's not unusual for the elements that will end up on your timeline to be discussed out of order. It's natural that as you are discussing events, for example, you'll have some clear calls to action in mind. It's OK to bounce around, but be sure to come back more

FIGURE 7.6
Lillian's List Timeline

Take Back the General Assembly by Electing TEAM LILLIAN!

Unofficial Goal: Put the Sisterhood to work to create a statewide and sustained embrace of "Team Lillian" with a dramatic increase in bunding, including smaller online donations.

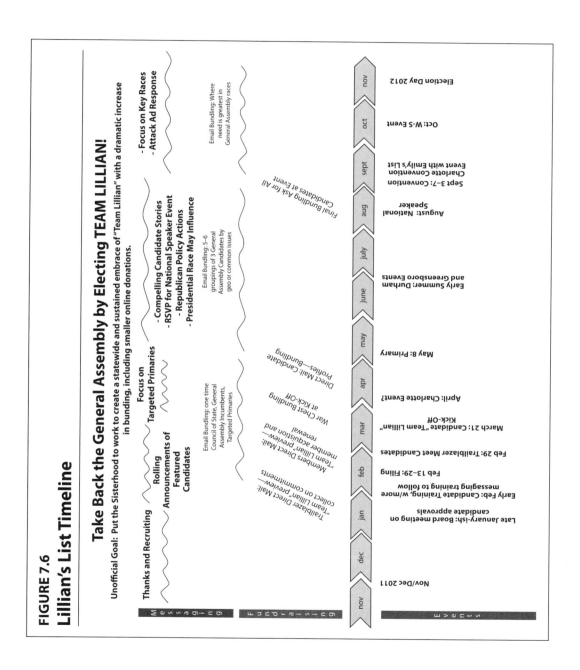

Messaging

Thanks and Recruiting

Rolling Announcements of Featured Candidates

Focus on Targeted Primaries

- Compelling Candidate Stories
- RSVP for National Speaker Event
- Republican Policy Actions
- Presidential Race May Influence

- Focus on Key Races
- Attack Ad Response

Fundraising

Trailblazer Direct Mail: "Team Lillian" preview—collect on commitments

Members Direct Mail: "Team Lillian" preview—member acquisition and renewal

War Chest Bundling at Kick-Off

Direct Mail: Candidate Profiles—Bundling

Email Bundling: one time Council of State, General Assembly Incumbents, Targeted Primaries

Email Bundling: 5–6 groupings of 3 General Assembly Candidates by geo or common issues

Final Bundling Ask for All Candidates at Event

Email Bundling: Where need is greatest in General Assembly races

Events

Nov/Dec 2011

Late January-ish: Board meeting on candidate approvals

Early Feb: Candidate Training, w/more messaging training to follow

Feb 13–29: Filing

Feb 29: Trailblazer Meet Candidates

March 21: Candidate "Team Lillian" Kick-Off

April: Charlotte Event?

May 8: Primary

Early Summer: Durham and Greensboro Events

August: National Speaker

Sept 3–7: Convention Charlotte Convention Event with Emily's List

Oct: W-S Event

Election Day 2012

nov | dec | jan | feb | mar | apr | may | june | july | aug | sept | oct | nov methodically to each of the major categories (events, calls to action, and story arcs) one by one to make sure you haven't missed anything and to ensure that all the elements line up in a way that makes sense.

For Lillian's List, we decided to tell one story over the course of the full year: how we worked to get more women elected. The beginning of the story was about recruiting women to run, leading up to the filing deadline. At the same time, we were also thanking supporters for what they did in 2011, so the first part of the story was labeled "Thanks and Recruiting." That was followed by announcing which candidates Lillian's List was choosing to feature, which is Lillian's List terminology for endorsing a candidate and supporting her with a campaign contribution. After that, we knew some of our featured candidates would have tough primary races, while others would not. So instead of talking about all our featured candidates in the spring months, we decided to focus on a handful of women in tough primaries.

Next in our conversation, we decided to place the end of the story on the timeline. The end was obviously Election Day and celebrating any wins in the immediate aftermath.

That left the middle of the story, which covered about six months of content. What would we talk to our supporters about after the primary but before people really focused on the general election in November? In many communications plans, this is the *muddled middle*, where the story loses focus. To build out this part of the timeline, we thought about past election cycles and what we thought would likely happen in this one. We also looked back at the events we had noted.

We saw four major touch points:

- Introducing the featured candidates in more depth to our supporters

- Encouraging registrations for a major event

- Getting our supporters fired up in response to policy actions taken by the General Assembly and congressional Republicans (we didn't know what those might be exactly, but we were confident that these groups would propose things our supporters would strongly oppose—and they did)

- Keeping supporters informed about the influence of the presidential race (because North Carolina was a swing state and was hosting the Democratic National Convention).

We also knew from history that it was highly likely that big money from both inside and outside North Carolina would be injected into several of these races in the form of negative attack ads against the featured candidates.

Finally, we went back to our calls to action section and listed three direct mail campaigns and two major statewide events where we would fundraise. Then we layered on how we would use email to encourage supporters to make online contributions to the featured candidates (known as *bundling* in political fundraising).

"Going through the exercise of mapping out our year-long communications plan with a story arc really helped us see our efforts in a totally different light," says Carol Teal, executive director of Lillian's List (personal communication, February 2013). "We are now making decisions that build on our mission and tell our story in an engaging way, instead of just reacting to the topic of the day."

Why It Matters: You Have to Get Your Story Straight

If you want people to grow to love you, you need to provide communications that give them something to grab onto and to follow. Sketching out your big picture communications timeline gets everyone in your organization on the same page, so that the story people outside the organization hear and see is consistent and makes sense over time.

Chapter Eight
What You'll Talk About
Deciding on the Core Topics You Want to Be Known For

> **This chapter is about . . .**
> - Identifying and creating content on the topics you want to be known for
> - Categorizing those topics into evergreens, perennials, and annual color
> - Combining what you want to talk about with what your participants, supporters, and participants want

Back in chapter 5, I talked about your trail name, or the personality you would become known for along the trail. The topics that you talk most about go hand in hand with that personality.

For some nonprofits, mapping out the big picture communications timeline is enough. But if you are going to take full advantage of all that content marketing has to offer to you, then you need to create a list of core topics too. This list will guide many of the specific decisions you will make about what goes on your editorial calendar.

Developing Your List of Core Topics or Themes

Your list of core topics or themes will drive your content strategy in many ways, by determining

- How you optimize your organization's website for search engines
- How you fill in gaps on your big picture communications timeline
- Whether reporters think to call you for quotes when they are working on various stories
- Whether you come to mind when a friend asks another friend if she "knows anyone who. . ."
- How board members and other supporters describe the organization's work to their own networks

    Several considerations go into creating this list.

    1. What are the most obvious topics, given the work your nonprofit does?

    2. What are some related topics, especially those likely to be top-of-mind issues with supporters and participants, even if they aren't especially important to your organization?

    3. What's the competition for "owning" the primary terms that name or describe these topics? Who comes up first on the search engine results for these terms?

    4. Do you have the capacity to produce content on these topics?

I recommend that you brainstorm with your staff to create your initial list of topics, and then go through the process of narrowing it down to your top ten topics (not necessarily in order of importance).

If ten topics seem too few, you can create a second-tier list as well. If ten topics seem too many, I encourage you to go back and learn more about what your participants, supporters, and influencers care about and value. I believe every nonprofit should be able to come up with a list of ten topics or themes it wants to be known for, at least in some way.

Let's say your organization is called Tabby Cat Rescuers. You all love tabbies so much that you and your staff came up with more than thirty topics, but you have combined them and prioritized them into this list of core topics:

- Where to adopt a tabby
- What tabbies are available for adoption right now
- What to do if you find a lost tabby
- How to help tabbies
- How to care for your own tabby
- Why tabbies are special
- How to help tabbies get along with other pets
- How to care for wild or feral tabbies
- Whom to call if you have to give up your tabby
- The history of tabbies

Stop, Think, and Discuss

What topics do you want to be known for? What kind of competition exists on those topics? Can you narrow those topics down to a top ten topics list?

Three Kinds of Content: Evergreens, Perennials, and Annual Color

Even though your organization wants to be known for all the things on its core topics list, it doesn't make sense to treat these topics equally in your content marketing strategy. For example, some of the Tabby Cat Rescuers topics, like adopting and volunteering, involve direct calls to action, while others, like the history and why tabbies are special, are more informational.

To better understand later what needs to go into your editorial calendar and how, I recommend that you break your list of topics down into three kinds of content, using gardening metaphors: evergreens, perennials, and annual color.

Evergreens stay fresh from season to season. Much of your basic website content will be evergreen content.

Perennials come back year after year but do require regular maintenance, especially when they are growing and in bloom. Many of the topics informing your newsletter and blog content will be perennials.

Annual color is short lived but full of that extra oomph! Much of what you do in social media will be annual color.

There will be some overlap when a topic has both evergreen and perennial content, so don't worry about drawing the lines too clearly.

You can maintain your core topics in a separate list or chart, or you can add them to your big picture communications timeline (figure 8.1). Table 8.1 shows how Tabby Cat Rescuers might break down and categorize a few of its core topics. Let's take a closer look at each content category and the ways in which Tabby Cat Rescuers could divide up its list to make it more manageable.

Reliable Evergreens: Content with Staying Power

Evergreen content is information that stays fresh from season to season, much like an evergreen tree. You may not need to change it at all, or you may make just minor tweaks from time to time.

Evergreen content on your specific topics will often take these forms:

- How-to articles or tutorials
- Top ten or "best of" lists
- Core principals, ideas, or values
- Best practices
- Frequently asked questions (FAQs), with your best answers
- Trends, timelines, or historical accounts

Producing evergreen content is essential for a variety of reasons, not least of which is that it makes your job easier! As a nonprofit communicator, you can use

FIGURE 8.1

Big Picture Communications Timeline: Core Topics by Content Category

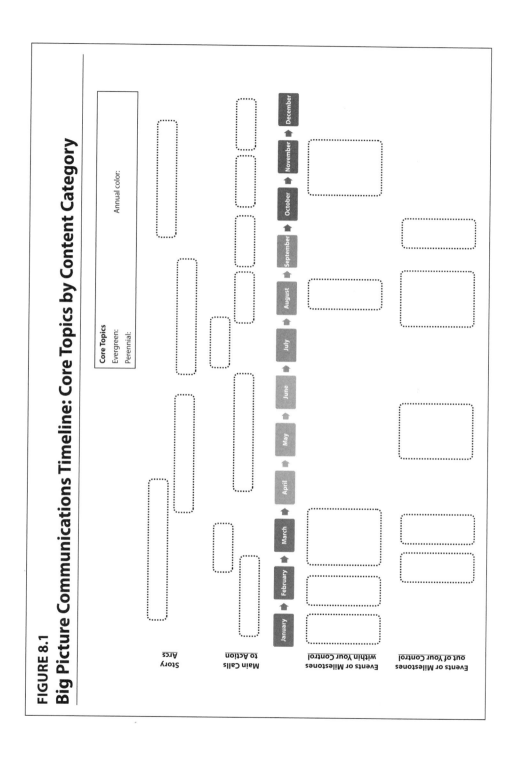

TABLE 8.1 Tabby Cat Rescuers Core Topics by Content Category			
Core topic	**Evergreen**	**Perennial**	**Annual color**
Where to adopt a tabby	Directory—update only as needed.		Share Facebook updates from our key adoption partners.
How to help tabbies	Top ten ways to help.	Regular features in newsletter and blog.	Include stories about star volunteers, and the like.
What tabbies are available for adoption right now		Weekly newsletter feature.	Feature individual tabbies on Facebook and Twitter.
The history of tabbies	Single web page—update only as new research becomes available.		Include trivia questions on tabby history.

evergreen content in many different ways to carry out your content strategy, but it's most likely to be present on your website.

Evergreen Content on Your Website

In many cases evergreen material will be the heart of your website. Think about why visitors come to your organization's site. You might ask yourself, what questions do people have that we have great answers for?

Your answers will lead naturally into creating content for search engines too, because many Internet searches are made by people looking for answers. Even though Google is paying more notice to fresher content than it used to, you still want to develop a set of core pages on your site about the primary topics your nonprofit wants to be known for.

Evergreen content is great for improving your search engine optimization, because—if that content is genuinely good—others will link to it over the course of many months and even years, creating more authority for these pages, which is a factor in how highly your content ranks in search engines. In other words, evergreen content is great link bait. People love to link to and share how-to articles, lists, and the like. That's why it's better to create a core set of pages on your site with evergreen content, and to make only minor modifications to those pages over time, without changing the URL, than to create a brand-new page every time you need to make an update.

That doesn't mean you can't blog about changes—that's a great strategy too, because you get the benefits of being timely. But that timely blog post should then link back to the core evergreen content on your website.

You might also think about organizing your evergreen content by placing it around the primary landing pages (the pages people most often link to from emails or social media) on your site. For example, if you have a clear-cut list of calls to action that you use over and over, you can create landing pages that are mostly evergreen, with a little space at the top to edit with some timely content.

Let's say you need volunteers year-round. You could create a landing page where 80 percent of the content addresses, for example, how to apply, basic tasks that volunteers do, and FAQs, and it never needs to change much. But the top 20 percent of the page you might change on a seasonal basis so that it feels fresh. You can also change the photography you use on pages to show the changing seasons, which makes the content feel timely, even if you don't change many of the words.

This doesn't preclude you from developing short-term, campaign-specific landing pages too, especially for online fundraising campaigns, for example.

Evergreen content doesn't change very often, but that doesn't mean you should just set it and forget it. You can get a lot of mileage out of your evergreen content if you approach it correctly.

Let's take a look again at the Tabby Cat Rescuers core topics list. What topics are likely to stay the same year to year with just minimal maintenance? I'd say "why tabbies are special" and "the history of tabbies" are definitely evergreen content. Some of the other topics will likely have at least some evergreen content on the website too. For example, the organization might maintain directory pages with lists of "where to adopt a tabby" and "who to call if you have to give up your tabby" that are updated only as needed.

Furthermore, there are likely to be some basic how-tos or tips that don't really change much in such other topics as "what to do if you find a lost tabby," "how to help tabbies," "how to care for your own tabby," and "how to help tabbies get along with other pets."

Tips for Getting the Most from Your Evergreen Content

Invest Time Up Front to Save Lots of Time Later

Because your evergreen content is going to last a long time and you'll want to link to it and repurpose it, invest some time and energy into creating your evergreen pieces. You want them to be really good. Do your research, edit your drafts well, and write strong *microcontent* (headlines, bolded and linked text, and so forth).

Think about repurposing as you write. Evergreen content is perfect for repurposing and reposting. Evergreen pieces tend to be longer than other content, so as you write, imagine ways that you might easily break this content into smaller chunks. This may affect the way you structure the longer piece. Because it's timeless, you can always repost a link on Facebook or Twitter to some of your evergreen content on slow news days or when you are too busy to come up with something new. Another technique that works well is to put a quick, fresh anecdote at the top of a newsletter article or blog post and then fill in with or link back to the relevant evergreen content.

Match Evergreen Content with Calls to Action

Your evergreen content will likely bring more traffic to your site than other content does because you'll be repurposing it and linking back to it, not to mention the search engine traffic. That's why it's important to include a next step on those evergreen content pages, whether it's signing up for a newsletter or contacting the organization's staff. Think about using a call to action that itself is somewhat evergreen.

In addition to posting the evergreen content on your website, you can add a timely sentence or two to the top and distribute it via email or your blog. For example, a Tabby Cat Rescuers newsletter article might say something like this: "Last week, a volunteer mentioned she was having trouble with her tabby hissing at her dog. Here are our top ten tips on how to help tabbies get along with other pets." The content on the website wouldn't include that first sentence but would start with the second one. That way, even though the main content is evergreen it feels timely in the newsletter because the first sentence refers to last week.

Link to Related Evergreen Topics on Your Website

As you build out your evergreen content, you'll see how the various pieces of it are related. Go back and do some internal linking of these pieces on your website. For example, in addition to the list on helping tabbies get along with other pets, the Tabby Cat Rescuers might write another list on helping tabbies adapt to a new baby or overnight visitors and then it would add links from one piece to the other, typically at the bottom of the article under a heading such as "Related Topics." As you build out your site, your evergreen content will serve as the anchor content for other, more timely pieces.

Set Reminders to Update Statistics or Other Data Likely to Change

It's best not to use stats or other data that can change often in your evergreen content. You want these pieces to hold true for a good stretch of time. But if you do create content with data—from an annual survey, for example—simply set a reminder in your calendar to update that content next year when fresher data are likely to be available.

Build Evergreen Maintenance into Your Workflow

Build time into your schedule to review your evergreen content, especially the material that gets good traffic, two or three times a year. That way, as necessary, you can tweak the language, make any corrections, add newer examples, and update the call to action.

Stop, Think, and Discuss

Which of your core topics are mostly evergreen? Which topics are likely to have at least some evergreen content? List several evergreen article ideas for each core topic.

Perennial Favorites: Long-Term Content You Actively Tend

With your evergreen content in place, now think about the topics that people always want to talk about or that you want to maintain as top-of-mind topics. Unlike evergreen content, perennial content will require you to spend a fair amount of time each year creating new material. You may go a little deeper into a topic, share new examples, or focus on new developments and trends in the field. Once you have your basic website built out with evergreen content, perennial content will likely take up most of the space dedicated to original content on your editorial calendar.

If you are regularly listening to your community, whether via surveys, polls, focus groups, or website analytics, you can use the feedback to develop your perennial content. For example, you can create multiple-part blogs or email newsletter series that function like story arcs.

Let's say you begin to see a pattern in when your organization's program participants start to think about a certain topic. You could create a series of blog posts or newsletter articles and start publishing the series a few weeks before the time participants' interest usually starts to kick in. The participants will be pleased with how well the organization knows them and how helpful and insightful it is!

For example, Tabby Cat Rescuers could create a blog series in the spring on caring for newborn tabby kittens. In the fall and winter, it could develop a series of tips on helping your tabby to safely enjoy Halloween, Thanksgiving, Christmas, and other year-end holidays. If you don't have the expertise to create certain specialized content, this is a great opportunity to tap into your larger network by curating content produced by others, asking guest bloggers to provide content for you, or creating an interview series with experts.

Regular features, sometimes called *standing heads*, are another great approach for delivering the new or latest updates on perennial favorites. Think of standing heads as a category of content, often in a particular communications channel, that you can include in your editorial calendar. They can grow into beloved traditions in your publishing schedule. Standing heads provide numerous advantages:

- Hand-wringing and office debates about content will be minimized.

- You will know what kinds of content you need to produce, so you can watch for ideas that fit those molds.

- As you write more and more of a particular category of article, you'll get better at it and will produce better articles, faster.

- Most important, your readers will start to look forward to your content because they will know what to expect.

Tabby Cat Rescuers, for example, might decide to create the standing head "Tabbies Ready for Adoption" for their weekly newsletter. This article would always appear in the newsletter in the same spot each week.

Wordless Wednesday is a popular meme that many nonprofits use as a standing head in their blogs or Facebook editorial calendars. To participate, you simply post a picture or two without much, if any, explanation on your blog or Facebook page. Kathryn Doyle, communications director at the California Genealogical Society, often uses Wordless Wednesday blog posts to highlight the work of volunteers. Others use them as caption contests or quizzes, encouraging readers to add the words themselves in the comments. ASPCApro.org will often post pictures of curious items found in animal shelters, asking readers, "What is this?," or, "What's going on here?" Days later it will update the post with the correct answer, often including additional educational links.

Another way to connect your core topics list to your big picture milestones is to map out when you will focus on specific topics—likely your perennial top-ics—throughout the year (figure 8.2). If you see yourself focusing on kitten care in the spring, for example, you could add that to the timeline.

Stop, Think, and Discuss

Which of your topics are perennials? How can you tackle those topics with a series of articles? Can some of the topics be used to inspire regular standing heads in your newsletter?

FIGURE 8.2
Big Picture Communications Timeline: Core Topics by Content Category and Time of Year

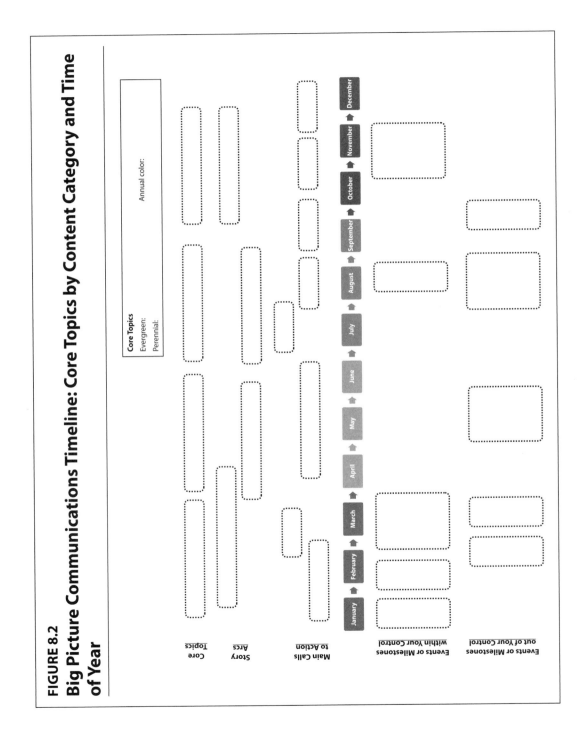

Annual Color: Short-Term, Splashy Content

The third content category for your core topics list encompasses your shorter-term priorities as well as lighter content that's meant to engage your audience in something fun. You can use annual color content to start conversations in social media, and if they take off, you can turn them into longer pieces, for your newsletter, for example. While you will likely create some original content in this category, most of it should be less labor intensive, so think about ways that you can use curated or repurposed content to fill in your annual color (I'll talk about both curating and repurposing later in the book).

Let's suppose that Tabby Cat Rescuers has received a grant to do some additional work around helping wild, or feral, tabbies. While the organization doesn't see this as a big part of its mission, it does want to conduct a two-month campaign on the issue and, afterward, turn any content created for that campaign into evergreen advice on its website. It might also produce lots of short, timely social media updates on specific cats that have been found or that are ready for adoption.

Stop, Think, and Discuss

Which of your topics are likely best treated as annual color, meaning that you will talk about them in little timely or splashy chunks, often primarily in social media?

Combining Your Priorities with Their Interests

You know that you are supposed to listen to your participants and supporters and give them what they want to hear from you. But you also have your own agenda full of information you want them to have. How do you bring the two together?

This is a challenge for many nonprofits, especially those that serve a professional community. "We try to offer a mix of things we know are popular, like social media, data visualization, data in general, and the cloud in particular. That gets people in," says Brett Meyer of his experience at the Nonprofit Technology Network (personal communication, February 2013). It's not unusual to have 500 to 1,000 people taking a free webinar on those topics. "But we really want them to be more interested in topics like mobile, IT governance, and privacy issues. These are so important, but people don't want to spend time on them."

This reminds me of an email conversation I had with my daughter's guitar teacher. My child was not thrilled with the process of learning guitar by picking one string at a time, and she wanted to quit the lessons. What she really wanted to do was strum along to a bunch of pop songs. But, of course, she didn't have the skills to play any song at all. So I discussed this with her teacher, and he said he would try to combine more "instant gratification with responsible pedagogy." In other words, he would give her some of what she wanted, so she would stay engaged in learning, while also continuing to teach her the fundamentals that she needed to learn so she could meet her own goals of playing her favorite songs.

Let's say you work for a national nonprofit that provides education and training to local nonprofits in its field; perhaps they are chapters or affiliates of the national organization. On the one hand you want to be responsive to what the local groups say they need because they are the boots on the ground. On the other hand you are the national expert, and you want the local organizations to focus on topics that you deem important—and in fact, many of the locals do look to you to help them figure out what they should be learning.

I worked with one national alliance whose members are community based and regional nonprofits. The national alliance wanted to start a newsletter for board members of all these local groups. They wanted to talk about lots of responsible pedagogy topics like board governance and financial accountability. I strongly encouraged them to include healthy amounts of instant gratification topics to address the concerns that are front and center with board members. Those might include such questions as, how do I ask other people, including my friends, for money?, and, how do I tell our executive director that he's not doing a very good job in certain areas? By soothing the pain points, the national group will build trust and open the door to equally important but less exciting conversations about bylaws and bookkeeping.

I'm working with another national organization in a similar situation, but it is focusing on the content strategy for its blog and e-newsletter, which will be based on content on its website and in its webinar series. The problem is that there are literally hundreds of relevant topics to cover. So which ones should this nonprofit focus on? The ones the locals ask about most, which tend to be the more basic or mundane issues, or the ones the national organization believes the locals need to know about to be more effective long term? Which should drive the content strategy?

The realistic answer is a combination of both. Your nonprofit can meet people's needs for basic information or for tips on the hotter topics du jour while also sharing the content that it feels is essential or "stretching" for participants and supporters.

Putting Some Cheese Sauce on That Broccoli

Here's another way to think about it: you can put some cheese sauce on that broccoli. The broccoli is what you want to talk about, because you know it would be good for your participants, supporters, and influencers (PSIs). But they may not feel the same way. What they want is some delicious cheese. So your content strategy can combine the two by putting some cheese sauce on the broccoli.

Here's one approach I suggested to a client that might work for you as well.

On a quarterly basis, in conjunction with your program staff, come up with a list of topics that your organization wants to cover in its educational programming or communications, whether those communications take the form of new blog posts, website downloads, webinars, or training videos. You then pick the top five specific topics from your list. These will most likely be subsets of the larger topics on your core topics list. This is the broccoli.

Next, you'd look at sources that give you clues about what your PSIs are interested in right now. You could look at recent keyword searches that brought traffic to your site, as well as searches within your site. You could also look at comments on your blog and your Facebook page. My client regularly presents webinars, so I suggested that the client's staff look at webinar chat or evaluation surveys for hints too. You then compile this information into a separate top five list. Remember, this list is based solely on popularity with your PSIs, not on what you want them to know. This is the cheese sauce.

Now you have two lists of five topics each. Combine them into one list, eliminating the overlap. Let's say that leaves you with eight different topics.

To develop your content strategy for the coming quarter, ask these questions for each topic:

- *Can we—and do we want to—provide a significant amount of new information on this topic in the coming quarter?* If your answer is yes, sketch out what the editorial calendar might look like. Topics that were on both lists are prime candidates for this kind of attention.

- *If we don't want to provide new content, can we review and update our basic evergreen or older or outdated content on this topic?* If your answer is yes, identify which existing content can be updated or repurposed.

- *If we don't want to work on this topic at all, can we at least create a landing page for that traffic with referrals to other organizations?* If your answer is yes, spend an hour on it, and be done with it.

You will then repeat this process quarterly. Over time, you will build up a library of evergreen content and resource pages that meet the needs your participants and supporters identify for you (because, as Marshall Field said, "the customer is always right"). At the same time, you will also create new content on the topics you think are most important (because, as Steve Jobs said, "people don't know what they want until you show it to them").

Stop, Think, and Discuss

Which of the topics you want to write and talk about are the broccoli? Which topics are the cheese? Can you combine these lists?

Why It Matters: Good Conversation Requires Substance

To get the most lasting value out of a content marketing strategy, you want to simultaneously build up your long-term evergreen content, build your ongoing communications around your perennial content, and add some pizzazz with your annual color content. This gives you much more substance to talk about with your participants, supporters, and influencers, going well beyond your events, milestones, calls to action, and story arcs. It's this combination of the work of your nonprofit as it is laid out on your big picture communications timeline and the specific core topics that your organization wants to be known for that serves as the foundation for your content strategy.

Chapter Nine
Building Your Itinerary
Designing Your Editorial Calendar and Adding Your Original Content to It

> **This chapter is about . . .**
> - Understanding that you are a publisher and a broadcaster
> - Learning how to use editorial calendars and meetings to plan and make decisions
> - Deciding which communications channels to include on your editorial calendar
> - Deciding how often to communicate

Many years ago I hiked the Milford Track in New Zealand. It's a spectacular trip into a sensitive natural environment, so only forty people a day are allowed to start the hike on the trail, or the "tramp on the track," as they say in New Zealand. You have to walk about six hours a day each of the four days it takes to complete the hike, so that you can sleep at a designated hut each night. On the last day you not only have to reach your destination but you must reach it by a certain time, because it's the boat dock with your ride back to civilization!

Though you are walking in what feels like wilderness, you have a very specific itinerary to follow in order to meet your goal of finishing. Similarly, your editorial calendar is your itinerary for your content marketing journey.

You, the Media Mogul

Nonprofits are now expected to share all kinds of content (stories, how-tos, calls to action, videos, and so forth) through multiple communications channels (online, in print, and in person). But it's not just about the content—you are expected to participate in conversations with your community too. The mainstream media are now just another communications channel. You don't have to rely on newspaper or magazine publishers exclusively anymore because you can publish your own website and blog. You don't have to rely on radio and television broadcasters anymore because you can post videos to YouTube and produce podcasts and live Internet radio shows.

You are the publisher. You are the broadcaster. You are a media mogul— we all are!

That's how Sean King, director of marketing and communications for Youth Education in the Arts (YEA!), views his job. "Our strategy is part advertising agency, part youth service agency," says King (personal communication, November 2012). For the past two years, YEA! has connected with both millennial program participants who play in marching bands and their parents. "Our approach to content is similar to that of any web-based multimedia publisher," says King. "We create a mix of messages and delivery channels for every part of our community. Providing content in written, video, and photo form is time consuming, but it is important to capitalize on the strength of each of the different mediums."

King juggles curation of what he calls a never-ending overabundance of content generated at rehearsals and performances, with careful tracking of what's attracting the most viewers and the resulting activity. "YEA! constantly monitors which messages and approaches work, always experimenting with content ranging from serious to silly to get the right balance of positive buzz that helps us disseminate the important message of the day and build our brand," says King.

Even in this fast-moving environment, King regularly makes time to "plan the work, then work the plan." "Any nonprofit plan or timeline has to be a live, interactive document that tells the story of what's planned, but also what was actually executed," says King.

An editorial calendar will help you move from plan to execution.

Why You Need an Editorial Calendar

What content goes out via email, and how is that email repurposed to Facebook? What channels are you going to use online to promote your nonprofit's in-person event? How are you encouraging your supporters to discuss the content you produce, and how are you taking what you learn in that conversation and using it to create new content? When is this all happening, and who will make sure it does?

Don't leave this all to chance or make it up willy-nilly. The thinking you've put into your big picture communications timeline and core topics list won't come to fruition on its own. While your process should be flexible to allow for lots of last-minute changes that you will have to merge in, you do need a process. An editorial calendar, coupled with regular editorial meetings, is that process.

Editorial calendars help you in seven important ways.

Editorial calendars help you stay focused on your goals. It's easy during strategic planning time for everyone to sit around and agree that the organization should be doing more work on, let's say, reaching out to families with young children. But if everyone on staff is used to working only with individual adults, it's easy in the pressure-packed days of the real world to slip back into old patterns and to write articles relevant mostly to those adults. If families with young children are important, put them on the editorial calendar so the expectations are there for all to see.

Editorial calendars help you turn ideas into action. Behavioral scientists tell us that when we put something in writing and we say exactly what we're going to do, when we're going to do it, and where we're going to do it, we're more likely to actually do it. So even if you use your editorial calendar more as a planning tool than as day-to-day guidance for your to-do list, completing it is still a valuable exercise because it helps you move from the idea stage to the implementation stage. Similarly, if you find yourself coming up with lots of good ideas for content but not following through on them, create a placeholder on your editorial calendar sometime in the future where you can put the idea. That way you won't lose it, and when the future time approaches, you can decide whether it is really worth pursuing or not.

Editorial calendars help you prioritize. You probably can't do everything that's being asked of you. You can't even do everything that you want to do. By mapping your opportunities to communicate in a grid or on a calendar, you start to see the real limitations that surround you. When new assignments come up, it's then possible to say, "OK, I can do that, but show me what on this editorial calendar we are going to delete or move to make room for this new assignment."

Editorial calendars can help you enforce deadlines. If you feel that you are constantly waiting on other people, a shared editorial calendar that is regularly reviewed in an editorial or staff meeting can remind people that their assigned piece fits into a larger picture and that they have a responsibility to the organization as a whole. A calendar will make it easier to point out the implications of missed deadlines.

Editorial calendars help you draw some boundaries. Planning with an editorial calendar will also help you rein in staff who are communicating too often. No, you can't email everybody every day! And you can't email supporters fifteen things in one email, as much as you may want to. An editorial calendar will help you and the rest of your staff see what's realistic, what's possible, and what's respectful of the organization's community. You'll see how many slots you have to fill.

Editorial calendars can help you break down silos. If your marketing and communications office is separate from programs or fundraising, an editorial calendar can act as the umbrella that forces you and your colleagues in other areas to huddle together. Sharing an editorial calendar will help to ensure that all the messaging going out from the organization, regardless of who is sending it, is consistent. Otherwise, messages from different parts of the organization are likely to create confusion among participants and supporters.

Editorial calendars help you create consistent communications. When you use an editorial calendar, it's much easier to see where you are communicating too little or too much, and where you are covering too many topics or overdoing it on one topic. It helps you smooth out the flow of communications so it feels more comfortable and consistent to both the staff producing it and the participants and supporters receiving it.

You may have noticed that I said an editorial calendar can "help" with all of these things. It is, however, more like a lasso than a magic wand.

Finding the Right Tracking Process

Editorial calendars can be extremely simple or highly complex. That simple word processing table or spreadsheet you've been using forever might still work. I used something like the calendar in table 9.1 with a client for many years. In this example, the standing heads, or article categories, go down the side, and the months go across the top. You then fill in the specific topics in the boxes. You can also add who is responsible for the article and the deadline for the drafts.

But to properly manage the overall communications flow produced by multiple staff members and being delivered to supporters through multiple channels, you need something more robust.

Strongly consider a web-based solution that allows out-of-office (and ideally mobile) access to the calendar files. That way everyone you give access to can

TABLE 9.1
Sample Editorial Calendar for a Monthly Email Newsletter

	January	February	March	April
Breaking news				
Member profile				
Tip of the month				

log in no matter where they are. This approach is also much more collaborative, because the documents aren't stuck on one person's desk or computer.

The next decision is really one of personal preference: do you prefer to see topics, assignments, channels, and dates at a glance in a spreadsheet layout, or do you prefer to organize this same information on a calendar? Both can work equally well, but your viewing preference will help you decide which tool to use.

If you prefer spreadsheets, the simple solution is a shared Google Docs spreadsheet. Use a new tab for each month or quarter. If you prefer a calendar view, set up several Google calendars in one account (one calendar for each communications channel). This allows you to layer the calendars on top of each other so you can see everything at once, while using the distinct color of each calendar to identify the channel.

Whether you prefer the calendar or the spreadsheet, you can also upgrade to many of the various online project management tools. Some of these tools lean more toward the spreadsheet model, while others are more calendar based, so choose one that is functional for the way you think.

Formats for Nonprofit Editorial Calendars

During a series of webinars in late 2012 and early 2013 on communications trends, I asked 1,163 nonprofit representatives what their editorial calendars looked like, and found no clear preference for format. Here are the results.

What Does Your Editorial Calendar Look Like Now?

Have a shared spreadsheet that others can view or edit	18%
Have a shared calendar that others can view or edit	19%
Have a handwritten, paper, or online version for myself only	25%
Have a plan, but it's all in my head	18%
Don't plan content or use an editorial calendar	20%

Organizing Your Editorial Calendar

Once you've made the spreadsheet or calendar format decision, you need to think about the internal structure of your editorial calendar. Most nonprofits build out their calendars to emphasize at least one of these aspects.

The communications channel (*where*). Create a separate editorial calendar for each major communications channel that requires a significant amount of content, such as your newsletter or blog. You can also create an editorial calendar to note when you'll post new content to Facebook or Twitter.

The participants, supporters, and influencers (*who*). You can also organize editorial calendars by audience. If you have multiple, distinct audiences (such as teachers, parents, and students) and you want to ensure that you communicate with each of them regularly, you might create a calendar for each audience, with your channels down the side and your time frames across the top. If you have several groups of people whom you're trying to reach out to and you're concerned that you may unconsciously favor one group over another in your communications, this method will help you find the right balance.

The program or topic (*what*). You can also organize editorial calendars by program when you have several different programs and you want to make sure you are spending an appropriate amount of time communicating about each one. Just as with the audience-oriented calendar, you can list your programs down the side and dates across the top, and fill in the boxes with channels and specifics about the content you'll deliver there.

You can add more detail to either spreadsheets or calendars, based on what you feel is most important to track.

For example, in a calendar format, you might use abbreviations or codes that are easy to scan at a glance. If you have layered calendars and each calendar is a different communications channel, you could use something like "P: Workshop Preview" to indicate that an article about a workshop is to be written for parents; whereas "T: Workshop Preview" would indicate that the workshop article is to be written from the teachers' perspective. Or you might draft a headline for each piece instead of simply listing the topic.

You might also wish to indicate a level of priority. While you may plan out what you think is a reasonable calendar of blog posts for the coming month, reality always has a way of mucking up your plans. If you highlight the boxes on the grid or the calendar that are *must-do's*, in contrast to *would like to do's*, you will more easily see ways to adjust the schedule when time or space gets tight.

Some people also like to include on the editorial calendar the subtasks that are required (researching, interviewing, drafting, reviewing, designing, publishing), who is responsible for each step, and due dates. Or you might like to see which pieces are in which stage (planning, in progress, waiting for approval, ready to go) at any given moment.

However, that level of detail can quickly fill your calendar with extraneous information, and it may make seeing the essential information about participants and supporters, message, and channel much more difficult. If that happens, you may decide to put certain details in another document or in fields that are available only when a calendar item is fully opened.

Using Spreadsheets and Calendars Together

At Nonprofit Marketing Guide, we use both a spreadsheet and layered Google calendars. The spreadsheet is like a big picture timeline, organized week by week, with the major categories of work across the top (figure 9.1). Specific dates and assignments are noted in the grid. We also use some color coding.

For the day-to-day tracking of what goes into our weekly newsletter, daily blog, and daily social media updates, we use Google Calendars (figure 9.2). In addition to listing the topic, we put initials in front of the topic to indicate who is responsible for drafting the content. When the item is ready for review, the initials are replaced by a slash mark (/). When the item is published or sent, we change the single slash to two slashes (//). This coding allows us to quickly see the status of all the items on the calendar. In truth, we use this system mostly for our blog and e-newsletter, while doing the majority of our social media updates on the fly. When we want to be sure to remember to put a particular post on Facebook or Twitter in the future, we will usually schedule it with a tool like HootSuite, but we also occasionally include it on the calendar.

FIGURE 9.1
Content Plan Spreadsheet Page for Nonprofit Marketing Guide

Blue=Live Green=Kris to do Orange=Kivi to do	Mentoring Topics	CharityHowTo Webinars	Our Pass Only	New Content	Freebies/Free Webinar	Pass Marketing	E-Clinic	Public Speaking Topics
JANUARY	Audience				2013 Trends Report—Main Report			
Dec 31–Jan 4			Changes to Make in 2013 (1/3)					
Jan 7–11		Thank Yous (1/8)	Thank You Letter Makeovers (1/10) They can attend webinar at CHT on 1/8, ask them to submit examples by end of day 1/8.					
Jan 14–28		Annual Reports (1/15)						
Jan 21–25		DIY Audit (1/23)						
Jan 28–Feb 1		NEW DECK Writing Short (1/29) – update existing	Advanced FB (KK, 1/31)	?s and examples: audit and interviews				

(Continued)

FIGURE 9.1 (Continued)

Blue=Live Green=Kris to do Orange=Kivi to do	Mentoring Topics	CharityHowTo Webinars	Our Pass Only	New Content	Freebies/Free Webinar	Pass Marketing	E-Clinic	Public Speaking Topics
FEBRUARY	Messaging				2013 Trends Report—Additional Reports		Direct Mail	
Feb 4–8		Thank Yous (2/5)	Feedback and Fine Tuning Topic E-Newsletters (2/7)			Audits		(2/6) Webinar for MT Assoc of Nps on Audits
Feb 11–15		Annual Reports (2/12)	Writing with Emotions (KZ, 2/13)				Ahern Direct Mail Training	
Feb 18–22		DIY Audit (2/19)	Release Audit E-book for sale	Measuring Networked Nonprofit (Beth Kanter, 2/20)			Ahern Direct Mail Coaching	
Feb 25–Mar 1	FINAL BOOK DRAFT DUE FEBRUARY 28							(2/27) NC Grant-makers on getting board to talk about right things to right people

FIGURE 9.2
Editorial Calendar for Nonprofit Marketing Guide

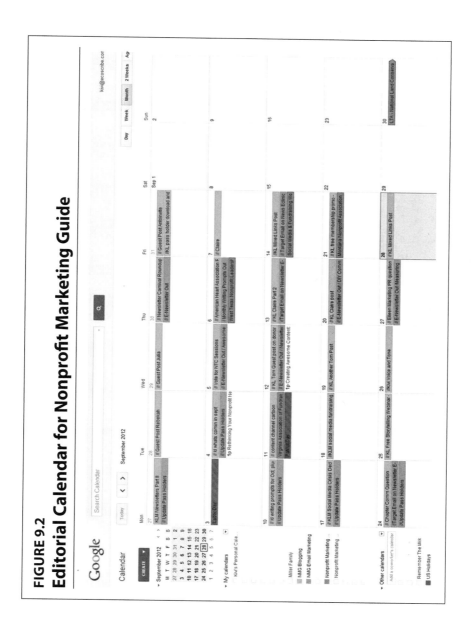

Stop, Think, and Discuss

Do you and others in your organization have spreadsheet brains or calendar brains, or both? Who needs to see what level of detail?

Planning Ahead: How Far Out Should You Look?

Regardless of how you structure your calendar, pick a realistic time frame. What is realistic will vary from organization to organization. The length of your manageable time frame will depend on such things as how quickly things change in your organization and whether you typically know what will be happening six months from now or not.

Your nonprofit may have reliable programming that doesn't change a lot from year to year. In that case, you'll be able to look further out than the staff will at nonprofits that are, for example, active in legislative advocacy and must deal with situations changing hour by hour in the state legislature or in Congress. Organizations that must respond in real time to breaking news or disasters will also tend to plan for the short term.

How Far Out Do You Plan?

During a series of webinars in late 2012 and early 2013 on communications trends, I asked 1,163 nonprofit representatives how far in advance their detailed communications calendars went. A little over 30 percent said one to two months, and 28 percent said more than two months at a time.

One to two weeks	10%
One month	19%
Two months	12%
More than two months	28%
Don't plan detail in an editorial calendar	31%

While everyone's process is a little different, many nonprofit communications directors find it most useful to think about their bigger communications goals month-to-month (and up to three months at a time, including roughing out an editorial calendar), but they make the decisions about what actually goes out or online and when on a weekly basis (such as during a weekly editorial or staff meeting). In organizations that are driven by real-time events, week-to-week decision making can often turn into day-to-day decision making.

As a default, start with a quarterly calendar. Try to predict what your major messages and calls to action will be over the next three months. Adjust as you go, adding a month or two at a time to the discussion. Remember, you will first map out your major content from your big picture communications timeline (chapter 7) and core topics list (chapter 8). You'll leave space for repurposing your original content (chapter 10) and some space for wildcards, content you'll end up merging in later (chapter 11).

Letting Your Editorial Calendar Evolve

Your editorial calendar process will evolve over time. Cristina Chan, the grants and communications director at CompassPoint Nonprofit Services, has seen her group's editorial calendar evolve from a spreadsheet to project management software to a calendar format (personal communication, December 2012).

"We tried out the spreadsheet-based editorial calendar and it didn't quite work for us in the end. We loved how comprehensive it was—breaking communications into projects and channels and keeping track of evergreen topics and project arcs, etc. But because it was so in-depth and because we have so many projects and channels, it quickly became unwieldy for us to manage simply," explains Chan. Schedules for the various CompassPoint projects change frequently. "We would plan out communications activities for a given project like a research study or a program launch," says Chan, "and inevitably the timeline would shift or another item would take precedence." That meant a lot of cutting and pasting and revising in Excel, which became too time consuming and difficult to keep up to date. CompassPoint then tried a popular online project management tool but, after a month, staff knew that wasn't going to work well either.

"We decided to go back to the tracking process we initially started with—an Outlook calendar—while we shopped around for another solution," says Chan. "But that first solution, with a few tweaks, turned out to be the best one for us."

CompassPoint now has a communications calendar in Outlook that the entire communications team can access and that everyone on staff can view. But in reality, says Chan, only she and the communications assistant use it regularly. "We thought it would become this much-used tool across the staff so that they could track what they each needed to prepare for communications, but in the end people prefer to have the communications staff tell them when they need to get us something or vice versa," says Chan. "With their busy schedules, it means one less thing they have to pay attention to."

"We have color-coded our channels (including newsletter, blog, e-catalog, e-blast) and have them calendared according to the regular timeline that they drop each week or month," says Chan, with e-blasts being an exception in that they are merged in as needed for press releases or special program announcements for certain groups. While the calendar has a color code for social media, staff typically don't calendar those items. "Social media has become a standard 'muscle' of our communications team so we automatically move certain things onto social media, and onto our homepage, after they appear in our e-newsletter," says Chan.

At the outset of every program, program staff draw up a timeline of activities with related communications activities, and Chan slots them into the appropriate communications channels and times on the calendar. If there are changes, she can easily cut and paste content into different channels or just drag the item to another day on the calendar. "This system also allows us a lot of flexibility to drop in spur of the moment content item requests from partners and funders," says Chan.

Planning a Reasonable Amount of Content

Just how many communications channels should you include in your editorial calendar, and how often should you update them? The number of channels you choose multiplied by the frequency with which you use them to send content and update them gives you the total number of slots that need to be filled with content.

For example, let's say you do a twice-a-month email newsletter with three articles in each edition. Two newsletters × three articles per newsletter = six content slots. Perhaps you also send a single-topic email twice a month in between your newsletters. You are now up to eight slots for content. Maybe you also blog three times a week, which means you would average twelve blog posts per month. Add your newsletters, emails, and blog posts together, and you have twenty content slots to fill.

According to the *2013 Nonprofit Communications Trends Report*, "lack of time to produce quality content" is the biggest challenge nonprofit communicators are facing (Leroux Miller, 2013). This begs the question, what is a reasonable amount of quality content to expect from a nonprofit communicator?

What's reasonable for your nonprofit will be way too much for some nonprofits and way too little for others. What's reasonable for each organization depends on several factors:

How ambitious your goals are. How many different kinds of participants and supporters are you trying to reach? And with how many different messages and calls to action? How quickly and to what extent are you trying to increase turnout or raise money? Limiting the kinds of participants and supporters and the number of things you want them to do (your calls to action) is the first thing I recommend to overworked communications staff because these two factors have such a huge ripple effect on everything else.

The role of content marketing in achieving those goals. Just how important is the content you produce to achieving those goals? For example, if your organization is trying to establish itself as an expert on a topic, be seen as the go-to source of news in its field, or build a grassroots network of citizen advocates, then you are going to need to create a lot more content than the staff will at a nonprofit that provides direct social services to clients who show up at the door primarily via a strong referral network and word of mouth.

The level of resources available to implement the plan. If your nonprofit doesn't have the staff capacity, including time and talent, along with adequate financial resources to get the work done, then its goals are unreasonable. Plain and simple. Too many nonprofits create pie-in-the-sky plans that they don't back up with resources. That often creates negative situations where (1) everyone knows the plan is a farce, and so there is little accountability for anything, or (2) people get branded as failures even when they've done their very best work. It's certainly fine for a plan to have stretch goals, but only if everyone understands the difference between stretching and breaking.

The difficulty of the topic and the storytelling. Some nonprofits do really complicated, technical work that takes some time to understand and translate into plain English. Others do highly personal work that requires a very careful, deliberate touch. In certain fields and in certain situations, it simply takes longer to tell the story. This is especially true when communications staff are not particularly fluent in the organization's particular programs and services.

The frequency preferred by your community. If you pay attention to both what supporters and participants say about your content when asked and what they actually do with that content, you'll also get some good feedback on how much and how often you should be communicating. It's wise to track both what supporters and participants say and what they do. Donors often complain about getting many requests for money from nonprofits. But closer examination of that concern, according to Cygnus Applied Research (Burk, 2012), reveals that donors do not define oversolicitation as a certain number of asks per year but rather as being asked to give again before learning what happened with the previous donation. If donors receive information about results created by their last gift before being asked again, a higher quantity of asks doesn't feel unreasonable.

Stop, Think, and Discuss

How much new, original content do you think it is reasonable for your nonprofit to produce in a week or a month?

Selecting Communications Channels: The Big Six

Now that you have a sense for how much content you can likely produce overall, you need to decide which channels, and how many, you will use to distribute that content.

At Nonprofit Marketing Guide, we conduct an annual survey asking nonprofit communicators to predict what they will do in the coming year (Leroux Miller, 2013). For three years now, 2011, 2012, and 2013, the surveyed nonprofits have identified the same six communications channels as "very important" (figure 9.3). Websites, social media other than blogging, and email marketing are the most important channels, followed by in-person events, media relations/PR, and print marketing. Podcasting, mobile apps or texting, phone calls/phone banks, paid advertising, and photo sharing were selected as the least important communications tools for nonprofits in 2013.

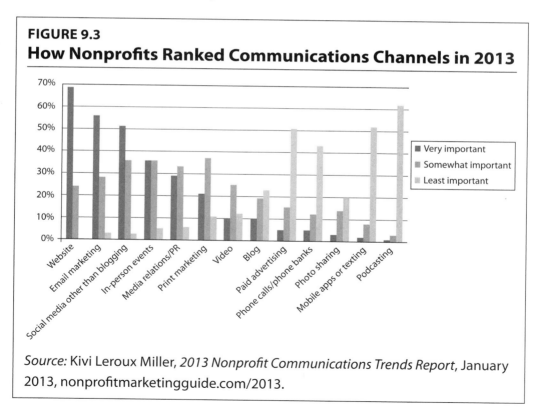

FIGURE 9.3
How Nonprofits Ranked Communications Channels in 2013

Source: Kivi Leroux Miller, *2013 Nonprofit Communications Trends Report*, January 2013, nonprofitmarketingguide.com/2013.

While the Big Six remain the most important tools as a group, we did see some shifts within the rankings of importance in 2013.

- In 2013, when we combined the "very important" and "somewhat important" rankings, social media other than blogging edged out email marketing for second place after websites (table 9.2).

- In 2012, in-person events were ranked as very or somewhat important by 66 percent of participants. In 2013, that grew to 74 percent.

TABLE 9.2
Relative Importance of Communications Channels to Nonprofits

	Very important + somewhat important	Very important	Somewhat important	Least important
Website	93%	69%	24%	0%
Social media other than blogging	87%	51%	36%	3%
Email marketing	84%	56%	28%	3%
In-person events	72%	36%	36%	5%
Media relations/PR	62%	29%	33%	6%
Print marketing	58%	21%	37%	11%
Video	34%	9%	25%	13%
Blog	29%	10%	19%	23%
Paid advertising	19%	4%	15%	51%
Phone calls and phone banks	17%	5%	12%	43%
Photo sharing	17%	3%	14%	20%
Mobile apps or texting	10%	2%	8%	52%
Podcasting	3%	0%	3%	62%

Source: Kivi Leroux Miller, *2013 Nonprofit Communications Trends Report*, January 2013, nonprofitmarketingguide.com/2013.

- In 2012, media relations/PR was ranked as very or somewhat important by 57 percent of participants. In 2013, that grew to 62 percent.

- In 2012, print marketing was ranked as very or somewhat important by 67 percent of participants. In 2013, that fell to 58 percent.

- We also saw big jumps over 2012 in rankings for video and photo sharing.

When we factor in budget size, the order of importance of the most popular communications tools doesn't vary significantly, with a few minor exceptions. When looking at the very important rankings by nonprofits with budgets over $1 million (figure 9.4), you'll see that the mobile apps or texting channel ranks higher than paid advertising, phone calls and phone banks, and photo sharing.

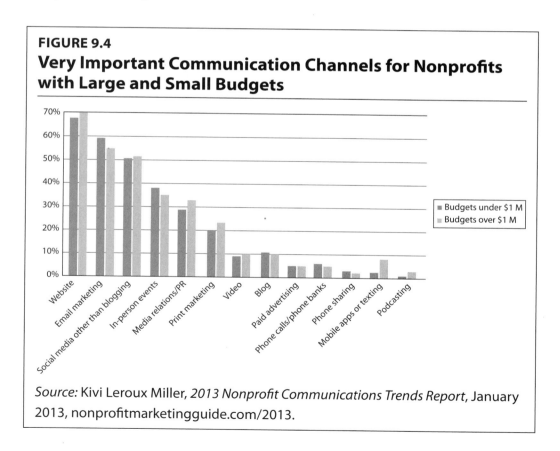

FIGURE 9.4
Very Important Communication Channels for Nonprofits with Large and Small Budgets

Source: Kivi Leroux Miller, *2013 Nonprofit Communications Trends Report*, January 2013, nonprofitmarketingguide.com/2013.

The biggest differences come in just how important smaller versus larger organizations say the tools are. For example, nonprofits with budgets under $1 million were more likely than larger organizations to rank email marketing and in-person events as very important. Nonprofits with budgets over $1 million were more likely than smaller organizations to rank websites, media relations/PR, and print marketing as very important.

Facebook remains king of nonprofit social media, with 94 percent identifying it as a top social media site. Twitter was selected as a most important social media site by 62 percent of nonprofits, followed by YouTube at 42 percent, and LinkedIn at 24 percent.

Nonprofits said they were most likely to add or experiment with Pinterest, followed by a three-way tie for second place among Google+, LinkedIn, and YouTube.

Finding the Right Frequency of Communications

Once you pick your communications channels, you need to think about how often you will update them. Let's look at what's typical for email and direct mail communications.

According to the *2013 Nonprofit Communications Trends Report* (Leroux Miller, 2013), monthly emailing to a typical person on an email list is the most popular frequency expected by nonprofits in 2013 at 42 percent, followed by every other week at 17 percent, quarterly at 15 percent, and weekly at 14 percent. This changed only slightly from 2011 and 2012. More than three-quarters of nonprofits (76 percent) plan to email their typical supporters at least monthly, which is down slightly from 78 percent in 2012 and up from 75 percent in 2011.

Not surprisingly, the more important a nonprofit believes email to be as a communications tool, the more frequently it will email. Those nonprofits planning to spend most of their communications time on email fundraising or advocacy appeals or email newsletters also expect to email supporters more frequently than other nonprofits do.

Of the nonprofits that ranked email as a very important tool for 2013, 84 percent will email at least monthly, with 39 percent emailing every other week or more often. Conversely, among those ranking email as only somewhat important, 70 percent will email at least monthly (up from 66 percent in 2012), and 29 percent will email every other week or more often (up from 22 percent in 2012).

Of the nonprofits that said they would spend most of their time on email newsletters, 83 percent said they would email supporters at least monthly. Of the nonprofits that said they would spend most of their time on email fundraising or advocacy appeals, 77 percent will email supporters at least monthly.

Quarterly direct mail to the typical person on the mailing list is the most popular direct mail frequency for nonprofits, at 39 percent (the same percentage as in 2012), followed by twice a year at 22 percent (down from 31 percent in 2012). Only 11 percent expect to send direct mail to their typical supporters at least monthly (down from 12 percent in 2012), which means that a total of 50 percent will send direct mail at least quarterly.

Of the nonprofits that ranked print marketing as a very important tool for 2013, 14 percent will send it at least monthly, and 66 percent will send direct mail at least quarterly.

Of the nonprofits that said they would spend most of their time on print newsletters, 15 percent said they will send direct mail at least monthly, and 75 percent will send direct mail at least quarterly. Of the nonprofits that said they would spend most of their time on print fundraising appeals, 11 percent will send direct mail at least monthly, and 68 percent will send direct mail at least quarterly.

Producing Good Content Takes Time, So Choose Wisely

Using a list of twenty choices (not including "other"), I asked nonprofits to choose which types of content they expected to spend most of their time producing in 2013, limiting their answers to five choices (figure 9.5).

Email newsletter articles, Facebook updates, event marketing, and website articles top the list. Nonprofits with budgets over $1 million were more likely than nonprofits with smaller budgets to say they would spend time on print fundraising appeals, print newsletters, annual reports, and press releases. Nonprofits with budgets under $1 million were more likely than nonprofits with larger budgets to say they would spend time on event marketing and presentations delivered in person.

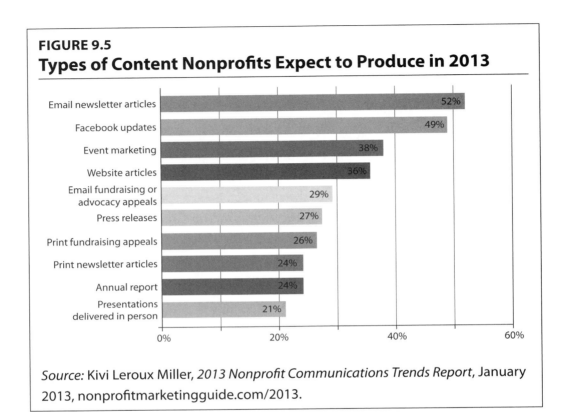

FIGURE 9.5
Types of Content Nonprofits Expect to Produce in 2013

Source: Kivi Leroux Miller, *2013 Nonprofit Communications Trends Report*, January 2013, nonprofitmarketingguide.com/2013.

Using a list of thirteen choices (not including "other"), I asked nonprofit communicators to identify their biggest challenges, limiting their answers to three choices.

Lack of time to produce quality content and lack of budget for direct expenses topped the challenges list, followed by inability to measure effectiveness, lack of clear strategy, and producing engaging content.

Not surprisingly, nonprofits with budgets under $1 million were much more likely to identify lack of budget for direct expenses as a big challenge. The smallest nonprofits (those with budgets under $250,000) cited lack of budget for direct expenses 51 percent of the time, while only 33 percent of nonprofits with budgets over $10 million did so.

Nonprofits with budgets over $1 million were more likely than nonprofits with smaller budgets to identify difficulty integrating communications channels, producing enough content, and lack of buy-in or support from managers as big challenges.

Still Not Sure? Start Here

Here's one example of what feels like a reasonable list of work for one generic communications person, not including everything else that comes along with a full-time job, such as attending meetings or conference calls that are only tangentially related to your work, all the various reporting you have to do, dealing with incoming calls and email, office drama, fire drills (real and imagined), and your turn to clean the break room refrigerator.

This list also assumes a good deal of repurposing of content between channels, which I'll cover in the next chapter.

- A monthly e-newsletter
- Print communications, four to six times a year (maybe a short newsletter, an event marketing device, or an appeal letter)
- A blog or website update, at least twice weekly
- Social media updates, at least once a day
- An annual report
- A few special projects over the course of the year (such as producing a special report or guidebook)

Stop, Think, and Discuss

When you combine your number of channels and the frequency with which you update them, how does the result look to you?

Does it feel like a reasonable amount of work?

How Much to Map, How Much to Merge

Trying to fill all of the slots in your editorial calendar with new, original content is a bad idea. Not only will you burn yourself out, but you'll also find that it's hard to get your message through because you are talking about too many different things.

You'll need to adjust this to your organization, but a reasonable goal is to map out two-thirds of your communications, leaving one-third of the spots on your editorial calendar open for what you'll need to merge in as required. The mapped content will be a mix of original content and repurposed content, leaving you with an overall content plan that might look something like this:

One-third is mapped, original, or curated content.

One-third is mapped, repurposed content.

One-third is merged content to be identified later

Tracy Moavero, development and communications coordinator at Policy Matters Ohio, knows that her communications calendar will revolve around certain annual events. Since she works at a think tank, government budget deadlines are big days. "February 1 is the big day when the White House makes its annual budget request to Congress, also referred to as Rollout Day," says Moavero. "Then everyone spends that week reading the parts of the budget that apply to them and either making press statements about what's good or bad or making plans to lobby key members of Congress. Those of us who work on budget and revenue use Tax Day as a communications hook too." Moavero knows this will happen every year so she can plan around it (personal communication, October 2012).

But not everything is predictable, so Moavero knows she'll likely have to merge various topics into her communications schedule, even if she has no idea what those topics and their channels might be. For example, she couldn't have predicted that there would be a major turnaround when the Ohio state legislature passed an antiunion law. "Providing research and data on public sector jobs and unions became a top priority since we needed to counter misinformation about what those workers earn and other related matters," says Moavero.

Using Editorial Meetings for Final Calendar Decisions

Planning is great, but at some point, someone has to make a go or no-go decision. Maybe that's you, and you alone. But the odds are that other people on your nonprofit's staff want a say too. That's where editorial meetings come in. This is where you confirm whether what you mapped on your editorial calendar is still right, and how to merge in anything new.

How often you meet with staff depends on how fast moving your working environment is. Some organizations meet every other week, some weekly, and some daily. Some have special meetings for just this purpose, and others include fifteen minutes on the agenda to talk about content at each staff meeting.

The online communications department at the Humane Society of United States (HSUS) has grown from a staff of eight in 2006 to thirty-five today. As Carie Lewis, deputy director of online communications, puts it, "We can't just shout over the cubicle wall anymore." HSUS's online communications team uses two different procedures to manage its editorial schedule (personal communication, October 2012).

The first is an editorial calendar in Outlook, which Lewis says works well because HSUS is an email-heavy organization, so staff are using Outlook all day long anyway. The calendar is color coded by channel so that everyone can see what will be put out on each channel each day. "It's great to plan, but the plan never, ever stays the same," says Lewis, "so we are constantly changing and shifting the calendar around. Still, it's good to have the plan because that way when there is breaking news, we can get that taken care of, but still remember that we had other things to get out and that we need to reschedule those." She says the calendar is also very helpful for the occasional slow days, so they aren't caught without anything to talk about.

The second procedure is the daily noon meeting. Every day at noon, all the HSUS communications heads, along with anyone else who wants to know what's going on, gather in a small conference room for a nine-minute meeting. Though it sometimes goes longer, it's important to say that it will last only nine minutes, says Lewis, so it's clear that everyone is expected to get through his or her items quickly. After all, no one wants to be in a long meeting around lunch time.

"We go around the table, and we talk about what is going out via PR, email, the website, social media, the blogs, and video that day, followed by anything else that is happening around the organization that day," says Lewis. Communications staff who are embedded in HSUS program departments, like the companion animal department and farm animal protection department, also attend and will bring any important program news. "We will often see that we are putting out really different stuff, and that we need to change that, so we will adjust what's going out when," says Lewis.

For example, email is HSUS's top driver for advocacy action and fundraising, so if she sees that something is going out on email earlier than she expected, she will adjust what she puts on Facebook that day to match it. "We know that a lot of people on our email list are also connected to us on Facebook, so giving them that consistency means they can get the email and then talk about it on Facebook. But if there is no post about it on Facebook, they may go somewhere else." Because the meeting happens every day at noon, she and her colleagues typically wait to publish content to their channels until the afternoon.

"It really helps to break down silos, where everyone is doing their own thing," says Lewis, "and to integrate and sync our communications." While only six or seven people report every day, it's not unusual to have thirty people standing around in the room and spilling out into the hallway. "It's become the meeting that you go to if you want to know what's going on," says Lewis.

Why It Matters: You Need a Dynamic Plan

An editorial calendar helps you keep your communications goals in perspective and vanquishes writer's block. It's what connects your big picture communications timeline and core topics list to your day-to-day work. But always consider it a working draft, frequently subject to change. It's nearly always better to respond to what your supporters are talking about, or some other timely news, than to stick with a story idea you put on the calendar a month ago, just because it's there.

At the same time, don't let the day-to-day work distract you too far from meeting your strategic communications goals. Some of the real power in an editorial calendar comes from seeing how you can get all of your communications channels working together and find the best ways to repurpose your content over time so that your organization's voice is clear and consistent.

Chapter Ten
Conserving Energy on the Trail
Repurposing Your Original Content

> **This chapter is about . . .**
> - Understanding how essential content repurposing is to your work
> - Identifying content ripe for repurposing
> - Learning many easy ways to repurpose the content you create

When you are stuffing a backpack full of gear, knowing that you'll feel every ounce of it on your back for days, you make sure that as many of the items as possible can do more than one or two things. Your spare clothes become your pillow. Your soup pot doubles as a kitchen sink.

The same goes for the original content you create: make it do at least double or triple duty, if not more.

Karen Cutliff, the marketing coordinator for Legal Aid of Western Missouri, became a staunch advocate of repurposing content a few years ago, at a cocktail party (personal communication, July 2012). "We host a yearly donor thank-you cocktail party, and as part of the short program, we choose a few attorneys and paralegals to share a client story with the guests," says Karen. "One attorney told an especially poignant story and many people (including our executive director) told me that I should feature it in the next newsletter or annual report."

The only problem? Karen had already shared that same story on the front page of the organization's latest newsletter! That night convinced her that not everyone was reading everything, and therefore repurposing content makes perfect sense. Don't wait for an experience like that to make a believer out of you.

Making One-Third of Your Content Repurposed

I don't believe nonprofits are repurposing nearly enough. You want to repeat your main messages several times, across multiple channels. It's that simple. That's the only way those messages have a chance of actually getting through.

You'll need to work out the right proportions for your organization, given the number of topics you like to cover and how many people are contributing, but I recommend that one-third of your content should be original, one-third repurposed, and one-third merged in later. If you take away what you'll have to merge in later and focus on the content you are mapping out in advance, that means it's about fifty-fifty: half of what you map will be original and half of what you map will be repurposed. In my informal polls, however, I see nonprofits leaning too heavily toward original content.

I often say that if you aren't bored with a message *as a communications pro*, you haven't said it enough times. You need to repeat your messages many times before people will hear them, regardless of how monotonous that may feel to you. Granted, this isn't necessarily the easiest rule to live by. It can make parts of your job boring or annoying. But you have to resist the temptation to make it all about you and how much fun you are having.

It's Not Cheating; It's Media Mogul Genius

To some of you, repurposing might feel like "cheating" in some way. But, trust me, this is how creative professionals work, whether they are painters, musicians, or writers. They are always building off or riffing off of something they did previously—or something someone else did. And as a nonprofit marketer, you are a creative professional!

No media mogul worth her salary creates original content all the time. Instead, moguls use reruns, syndication, b-roll, and other techniques to reuse and repurpose content they've created. It not only makes their work life easier but it's smart from a marketing perspective too.

The reality is that you need to repeat your main messages several times, across multiple channels. That's the only way those messages have a chance of actually getting through. Despite your best intentions, and theirs, your supporters don't read everything you put out in its entirety the first time they see it and commit it to memory right then. They likely just give it a glance or skim it, which means you need to give them several opportunities to let that message sink in.

Repurposing, or remixing, doesn't mean you simply copy and paste everywhere, all the time. Your fundamental message stays the same. Your fundamental calls to action are the same. But you're just slightly remixing the ways that you're framing some things and the ways you're presenting some stories. This approach allows your thinking on various topics to grow, and you can incorporate those new perspectives as you repurpose old content. Repurposing allows you to incorporate feedback on earlier versions.

Quentin Smith, design/marketing specialist at Extreme Response International, is a big believer in repurposing. He estimates that only about 30 percent of the content he produces is original, with 70 percent being repurposed (personal communication, July 2012). "With limited resources, we are a strong believer in repurposing what we can in different ways to make it look new," says Smith. "Why reinvent the wheel when you don't have to?"

Extreme Response is a humanitarian aid organization changing the lives of those living in extreme situations, with a focus on orphans, refugees, dump dwellers, and people in extreme poverty. Its biggest event of the year is the Christmas Celebration; more than 11,000 people participate in communities in Ecuador, South Africa, India, Philippines, and Nepal, and volunteers travel from the United States to help. Staff members in each of the countries submit reports with all the ins and outs of the community events to Smith, who is based in Georgia.

He repurposes them into numerous Facebook posts throughout the year, especially as the nonprofit begins to promote the coming year's event. For example, a November Facebook post promoting the upcoming parties reads, "Nothing says party like getting your face painted. Guests at each of the parties will have the opportunity to have their face painted," and it includes a photo of face painting at the previous year's event. Another post reads, "Lives are changing! One of the Kids Club members at the Quito Dump has been attending since 2004 and her life has been changed," and includes a collage of photos of the child over the years.

The content repurposing continues as the community events take place over ten to fourteen days in late November and early December, depending on the location. During these celebrations staff members keep track of the number of volunteers and guests, as well as other statistics and memorable stories. The reports are reviewed by organization leaders and then passed on to Smith. He repurposes that material into a variety of different forms, including publications for the media and for supporters such as brochures, the annual report, volunteer guidebooks, and Facebook updates. "We know many of our supporters receive multiple forms of communications from us, therefore the majority of my time goes towards tweaking the content so it does not appear to be a direct pickup from the other materials," says Smith.

He advises nonprofit communicators to use their time wisely and not make more work for themselves. "Repurposing content, as well as designs, not only saves you time and stress, it also helps strengthen your organization's brand," says Smith. "Consistency is important in order to build, and maintain, trust with supporters."

Determining What's Ripe for Repurposing

According to our research at Nonprofit Marketing Guide, nonprofits are most likely to repurpose content in these three ways:

- Using newsletter content or blog posts as Facebook updates
- Turning blog posts into email newsletter articles (or vice versa)
- Turning website articles or blog posts into print newsletter articles (or vice versa)

What's the perfect repurposing trifecta?

1. One channel is clearly missing a particular type of content.

2. You know that some part of your supporters are clamoring for it.

3. You've done a lot of the work already in another channel.

Let's say the staff who contribute to your blog get really excited about a certain topic and talk about it a lot over several months. You originally thought of the topic as annual color content and didn't think much more about it until you realized that your participants were searching for information on that topic on your website. This is a perfect opportunity to take that content that was created in an organic, largely unfocused way, and to rewrite it into some solid evergreen content for your website.

Be careful, however, about repurposing from grant applications and reports to funders and your organization's board. Oftentimes that material has too much of an insider feel and may not work well on public communications channels. While such repurposing can certainly be done, know that it will take more rewriting time than repurposing a blog post into a newsletter article, for example.

Stop, Think, and Discuss
What content are you already producing that is ripe for repurposing?

Five Favorite Ways to Repurpose Content

Clever nonprofit marketers repurpose content all the time. Here are five great examples.

Use a Different Channel

If you've written a blog post, is there something you can do with that material elsewhere? Three short blog posts can be combined into one longer newsletter article. You can use a top ten list you published in your email newsletter as a starting point for a video script. Start with live audio, and record it as a podcast, video, or webinar archive. Have the recorded audio transcribed. Pull text from that. If you've written a how-to article, turn it into a top ten list. If you've written a top ten list about how to do something, rewrite it as an opinion piece or as a review.

Jennifer Charney, communications manager at Save the Redwoods League, repurposes her donor profiles. First, she'll write a story for her organization's twice yearly print newsletter, *Create Your Legacy*. That print newsletter will be posted as a pdf on the legacy giving page of the league's website, creating additional content there. Next, she'll share a link to the newsletter pdfs on Facebook. Finally, she posts stories from the newsletter directly onto the website. She does that same thing with stories from publications like the league's annual reports. "Posting links on Facebook about our print publications garners among the most 'likes' of any of our Facebook updates," says Charney (personal communication, July 2012).

Edit for a Different Audience

Also think about your different audiences and how you can put a slightly different spin on existing content for one audience to make it more relevant to another audience.

Rachel Hicks, director of programs and communications at the Archie Bray Foundation for the Ceramic Arts, began building out that nonprofit's online communications and fundraising just a few years ago (personal communication, January 2013). At the end of 2011, the Archie Bray Foundation sent one fundraising email to its full email list, without segmenting it into different groups. That email produced eleven online donations totaling $3,325 (table 10.1).

In 2012, Hicks and her coworkers on the development team thought that just by tweaking the message a bit and repurposing that single email, they

TABLE 10.1 **The Archie Bray Foundation's Email Open and Click Rate, December 27, 2011**			
Group	**Emails sent**	**Opens**	**Clicks on link**
General	2,692	606 (22.51%)	31 (1.15%)

could do better. So they decided to start segmenting the email list, hoping to improve on open rates, click-through rates, and donations. They started by pulling out the audience segments that were easiest to track in the Archie Bray Foundation's database: class or workshop participants, collectors, and past resident artists. Though those segments represented only about 20 percent of the total email list, the results were impressive. By tailoring the subject line and lead paragraph in each segment's message before getting to the annual campaign ask, which was repurposed between the different versions, Hicks and the development staff were able to push up both the open rates and the click-through rates significantly.

After that effort, Hicks sent out three rounds of email for the year-end campaign. The first two emails, on November 8 and December 12–13, went to four audience segments:

- Class or workshop participants
- Collectors
- Past resident artists
- General (everyone who wasn't in one of the three previous categories)

Each group received a different email targeting members' personal interests directly. For example, the subject line for the email to collectors was "Nurture Ceramic Artists—Support the Bray Today," and the email began like this:

> If you are like most ceramics collectors you remember fondly the
> beginning of your collection—the object that ignited your curiosity
> and began your life in ceramic art. You also relish meeting artists and
> learning about each individual's artistic path. And you have found
> that very often the Archie Bray Foundation is an important stop along
> that path, having played a pivotal role in nurturing an artist's creative
> voice.

Contrast that with the email for past residents, with the subject line "Support Ceramic Artists—Give to the Bray Today," and the following opening:

> What is your most vivid memory of your time as a resident at the
> Bray—working late in the studio; gathering for a potluck; savoring the

late summer sun on Mt. Helena? Chances are that whatever memory stands out for you, something about being at the Bray changed your life. That's the thing about it—the Bray was an experience like no other that helped us define our careers.

For the last message on December 31, everyone on the list received the same email without customization.

Through this campaign, the Bray brought in fifty-one online donations totaling $12,265, nearly four times as much as in 2011, when it sent just one email on December 27 that produced eleven online donation totaling $3,325.

"At least one person donated twice in response to these emails, first with a $20 gift and then with a second for $50," says Hicks. "We did receive one email response that said they thought that three emails were too much. Other than that, it seemed to be a great success."

Tables 10.2 through 10.4 display the 2012 year-end email fundraising by the Archie Bray Foundation for the Ceramic Arts.

TABLE 10.2
The Archie Bray Foundation's Email Open and Click Rate, November 8, 2012

Segmented emails sent November 8, 2012

Group	Emails sent	Opens	Clicks on links
Class or workshop participants	277	77 (27.80%)	5 (1.81%)
Collectors	97	36 (37.11%)	11 (11.34%)
Past resident artists	248	81 (32.60%)	12 (4.84%)
General	2,301	683 (29.68%)	51 (2.22%)
Total	**2,923**	**877 (30.00%)**	**79 (2.70%)**

TABLE 10.3

The Archie Bray Foundation's Email Open and Click Rate, December 12–13, 2012

Segmented emails sent December 12–13, 2012

Group	Emails sent	Opens	Clicks on links
Class or workshop participants	270	63 (23.33%)	3 (1.11%)
Collectors	97	30 (30.93%)	0 (0.0%)
Past resident artists	245	82 (33.47%)	7 (2.86%)
General	2,250	564 (25.07%)	27 (1.20%)
Total	**2,862**	**739 (25.82%)**	**37 (1.29%)**

TABLE 10.4

The Archie Bray Foundation's Email Open and Click Rate, December 31, 2012

One email sent December 31, 2012

Group	Emails sent	Opens	Clicks on links
General	2,868	669 (23.33%)	26 (0.91%)

Change the Perspective

You can also change the perspective, so you are telling the same story but from a slightly different point of view. Maybe initially you talked about three people whom your organization has worked with and emphasized one of them. Now you can tell the same basic story but emphasize another person in the story this time. Or if the story covers several aspects of the work the organization does, highlight one aspect while deemphasizing the others, then switch the aspect that is highlighted when you repurpose the story.

That's what Children of the Nations does. Its staff frequently write stories about the specific children the organization serves, and they repurpose those stories based on which programs they are talking about. "Because we provide well-rounded care for children, by focusing on one aspect of care (for example, feeding, medical, education, etc.) it's really easy to create completely different articles on different topics using the same child's story," says Pam Wright, former director of advancement. "Another easy way to repurpose content is to pull quotes from one story and insert them into another, instead of always trying to obtain original quotes for each article," says Wright (personal communication, July 2012).

Remake It as a Sidebar

It you are afraid that people will be annoyed with repetitive content, you can always downplay what you are repurposing by making it subordinate to other content. That's the approach that Ashlie Hutcherson, associate development director with Almost Home in St. Louis does (personal communication, July 2012). She will start with a blog post, then use a shorter version of it as an e-newsletter sidebar article, while also placing a link to the full article on the Facebook Page. "I always add something new when I repurpose my work," says Hutcherson. "Or I sum it up and make it shorter, add a picture, or make it a side story rather than a feature."

Update It from Last Year

Lots of nonprofits publish information that stays basically the same from month to month, or even year to year, except for the statistics. Grab the old article and just update the stats and republish it!

Annual events or "awareness" months are also a good time to just update older content. January is National Mentoring Month so it's an important month for the Mentoring Partnership of Southwestern Pennsylvania. For the past three years, this nonprofit has partnered with the Pittsburgh Steelers to create videos of the players talking about what their mentors have meant to them. While staff need to film new videos every year, they don't have to think of a new approach. "This idea or premise remains the same year after year, but we're always able to generate new excitement and exposure with it," says Kristan Allen, the organization's director of marketing and communications (personal communications, February 2013).

Allen says the video series grows more popular and generates more exposure for the organization every year. For example, traffic to its YouTube channel, where the videos are posted, has increased exponentially each year. "The first year we did this, our highest-viewed video was watched 440 times. Fast-forward to this year and you'll see that our highest-viewed video has been watched nearly 1,500 times and counting!" says Allen.

News affiliates have picked up the story, and she also says that "the Pittsburgh Steelers joined in on the fun by writing a story for each individual mentoring clip. These stories were posted to the Steelers.com home page and official Facebook Page (with 4.8 million likes!) each week in January and resulted in thousands of 'likes' and 'shares' for our content."

Seventeen More Ways to Repurpose Your Content

Make short stuff longer. If you started with a 200-word blog post or even a quick tweet or Facebook update, flesh that out into a newsletter article by adding some examples. Add descriptive details, get quotes from people, or share opposing points of view.

Make long stuff shorter. Pull the headline and use it as a status update. Reduce paragraphs to bullet points. Publish a teaser, and link back to the longer piece.

Change the lead. Simply start the article in a whole new way. Move something that was lower down in the article to the top. If you didn't use a quote in the first paragraph before, use one now. Open with a trend or other big picture explanation.

Round it up. Group several like items together into a new piece with a theme that you can use in a new headline and lead paragraph.

Integrate the comments. This works great with content such as a blog post or Facebook update that was originally posted where people could add comments. As you repurpose the article, fully integrate some of what you saw in the comments into the newer version.

Add your opinion. Much of what you publish is likely "just the facts, ma'am." Repurpose a newsy article by adding your commentary to it.

Recast it. Take something completely unrelated and tie it into your content. Tabloid magazines are great inspiration for this—can you tie the latest hot superstar, scandal, or headline to your content in some unexpected way?

Turn it into a drip email series or autoresponder series. Create a series of evergreen emails and turn that series into a five-day email course: for example, someone who signs up on Monday would get the first email right away, followed by the second email on Tuesday, and so forth. This is great for list building too!

Turn it into an evergreen FAQ or resource page. By stripping out time-sensitive references, you can often make content evergreen.

Make evergreen content timely. Reverse that process; add a timely update or reference to make your evergreen content seem fresher.

Create a slideshow. If you have a list of items or several bullet points in an article, turn these items and points into slides and share the resulting slideshow on SlideShare. You can also turn slideshows into videos and share them on YouTube.

Add to your standard presentations. Create slides from examples or great statistics in a content piece, and use them in presentations that your staff or board members give.

Reformat into collateral or handouts. If you mail information packets or do outreach tabling, turn some existing content into giveaways that you can share with people.

Create a quiz. Reformat information into a series of questions and answers for an online quiz.

Create a worksheet. Help readers put information from an article to use by creating an accompanying worksheet that guides them through the process of applying the information to their situations.

Offer it as a guest article or blog post. Let others use your content as is or with some minor edits.

Transform it into a back-and-forth interview. Let's say you've written an article with three points about why cats are better than dogs. Ask someone who prefers dogs to reply to your points and publish the new content as a point-counterpoint that reads like a transcript of an actual conversation. You make a point, then she rebuts or concurs, and so forth. Of course, you can also produce these back-and-forth conversations on less-contentious issues as well!

Stop, Think, and Discuss

Can you pick three to five repurposing techniques that will work easily for your organization? Can you add them to your editorial calendar now?

Repurposing Challenge: Getting More Mileage from an Awards Program

Let's say you work for a nonprofit that trains and finds jobs for developmentally disabled adults by partnering with employers large and small in your community. To help sustain those business relationships, it presents annual awards to companies that have successfully created working environments that integrate people with and without disabilities. It presents these awards during October, which is National Disability Employment Awareness Month. As the awards are presented, you talk about them in your October publications and get some press coverage. But is that it?

The awards program is a lot of work for your nonprofit, and you'd love to find a way to get more marketing mileage out of the program. Let's say you are working on a December or January edition of your print newsletter. By then, the fact that your nonprofit gave out awards in October is old news, so you would need to do what's called *advancing the story*. What's the next chapter in this story about giving out awards?

This is when it's time for some creative brainstorming. Start by looking at what you already have in front of you. Let's say your organization gave out fifteen awards. That means you have fifteen businesses and at least fifteen of your nonprofit's clients as potential next chapters.

I'd start by looking for subcategories within the whole. If you were asked to group the fifteen businesses into three or four smaller groups, how could you do that? Are a handful of them in the same industry (for example, are they restaurants or corporate headquarters)? Are some of them geographically clustered? Do some of the managers your nonprofit works with have anything in common, such as where they went to college or whether they themselves have disabled family members? Do the same thing with your nonprofit's clients, the employees with disabilities. Are they doing similar kinds of jobs? Is there a common experience or current living situation? You may need to do a little interviewing to gather additional details to help you see the best groupings.

Once you have several good subcategories, you can use them as story hooks and combine them with some of the most common article formats, like how-to articles, lists, and advice columns. Do a few interviews with the people in your subcategories, creating content that is current and forward looking while also giving additional acknowledgment to your award winners. For example, you might write an article for your e-newsletter about what five restaurant managers have learned about working with employees with Down syndrome. You could expand that article into a longer piece for your print newsletter by adding commentary from the employees themselves—either what they have learned about working in the restaurant industry or their reactions to what their employers said.

Somewhere in the story, almost as an aside, you would mention that each of the companies received an award back in October. Or you could list your organization's award criteria in a sidebar for those companies who aspire to be award winners in the future.

By writing a story in this way, you are providing useful, interesting information to your readers now, giving more exposure to your nonprofit's partners and clients, and saving lots of your time and energy by not starting from scratch.

Stop, Think, and Discuss

Look at your major programs. Is there one you don't feel you are getting enough mileage out of? How could you restructure some of the content you create for that program so you would have more opportunities to repurpose that content?

Using Technology to Reheat and Remix

Even great chefs use microwaves. You can use the tools of technology and other services to help you reheat and remix too.

Transcription services are a wonderful service for content creators. Say you produce webinars or podcasts or other forms of audio recordings. Get those recordings transcribed, so you have text to work with. Sometimes you can post the text as is and at other times you will need to clean it up a bit.

You also can use tools that let you simultaneously post content in lots of different places, such as HootSuite.com. These same tools will often let you schedule updates over time, dripping the content out on a schedule you define. That allows you to do all the work ahead of time but to share the results of that work over several hours, days, or weeks.

For example, if I want to promote a webinar, I'll often write the tweets and the Facebook updates for that webinar all in one sitting. That ensures that my message is consistent but also that I can mix up the words I use and the things I emphasize as benefits, and so forth. Then I schedule those updates in one sitting too, but they will post live to Twitter and Facebook over several days. By doing the work all at once, and using technology to distribute it, I can mix it up, and it still feels fresh to my participants.

Why It Matters: Repurposing Saves Lots of Time

You don't have a spare minute to waste, and neither do the people reading your content. That's why repurposing makes perfect sense. Take it from Wynn Hausser, director of communication for Public Advocate Inc. He says it was initially hard to get into the habit of repurposing, but now that he and his staff have created a basic process, it's much easier (personal communication, July 2012). Hausser says he first writes a blog post showcasing news articles, papers, presentations, and the like. Then he creates Facebook and Twitter posts linking back to the blog. Next he creates a short e-news item that also links back to the blog. Sometimes the process begins with a press release, which is the basis for the blog post. "Once you start doing this you will wonder why you haven't been doing it forever!" says Hausser. "It sounds like it takes a lot of time. But you do 80 percent of the work up front for the first piece so it makes for a good return on investment."

Chapter Eleven
Handling Surprises along the Way
How to Merge in What You Can't Plan

> **This chapter is about . . .**
> - Leaving room in your editorial calendar for what you can't predict
> - Building in space for experimenting
> - Preparing to take advantage of breaking news and to respond to crises

You can't plan out everything. You never know when you will climb over a rock to find a rattlesnake sunning on top of it. Or when you'll finally emerge from a thick, dark forest into a blooming field of wildflowers.

As a communications director, don't fear surprises. You'll be jumpy and nervous all the time if you do. Big picture communications timelines, core topic lists, and editorial calendars are helpful in many ways, but you can't pack them full and then expect all of that material and scheduling to play out exactly as you planned.

Instead, plan loosely, leaving plenty of play in the schedule so you have room for the inevitable changes, the unexpected, and the unpredictable—of both the positive and negative varieties. For a starting point, remember the rule of thirds, and leave about a third of your editorial calendar open to merged content.

In this chapter, I'll look at several types of content you'll often want (or need) to incorporate with only minimal planning or notice.

Preparing for Serendipity and Surprises

Leave enough room in your editorial calendar so you can take advantage of serendipity, as well as cope with those surprises that get dropped in your lap.

Unexpected events can be good or bad, and while the good ones are more fun to write about, the bad ones have to be addressed too. I have heard from non-profits who have had to scramble to write about everything from an unexpected donation and program changes to decreased funding because of the economy and damage done to an office due to a plumbing issue!

Sean King, director of marketing and communications for Youth Education in the Arts, refers to work that gets dropped into his lap unexpectedly as "hair on fire" moments, which usually originate in management meetings or board meetings. "Sometimes they are driven by competitive challenges in the market or by either real or imagined threats to funding or support, or they may spring up because the rumor mill becomes overheated," says King. Either way, he advises that you make the best of it (personal communication, November 2012).

"The reality is that nonprofit marketers must be on their toes to shelve current projects for a day or a week in order to address the needs of senior management," says King. "Embrace these opportunities as ways to flex your creativity and develop skill sets that would not otherwise be tested. Having the ability to roll with the punches and to engage with something new can be great professional opportunities."

"Keep cool. Stay calm. Move forward," says King.

Little Bets: Getting Creative and Other Experiments

Little bets are low-risk actions taken to discover, develop, and test an idea, as described in a book I highly recommend called *Little Bets: How Breakthrough Ideas Emerge from Small Discoveries*, by Peter Sims (2011). Where traditional planning emphasizes avoiding problems and mistakes from the outset, the little bets approach emphasizes finding problems and solving them as you go. It turns out that this approach is behind many of the creative innovations in our world today, from minds as diverse as comedian Chris Rock, architect Frank Gehry, and the moviemakers at Pixar. It's also how Twitter was born.

How does this play out? I think this passage from the book sums it up best:

> Practicing little bets frees us from the expectation that we should know everything we need to know before we begin. Redefining problems and failures as opportunities focuses our attention on insights to be gained rather than worrying about false starts or the risks we're taking. By focusing on doing, rather than planning, learning about the risks and pitfalls of ideas rather than trying to predict them with precision up-front, an experimental approach develops growth mind-set muscles [Sims, 2011].

Make sure you have space in your communications calendar to play around. Rather than being annoyed by people who have "brilliant" ideas, make room in your schedule for some play. Also make room for topics that might strike you! The easiest posts to write are the ones that you are emotional about in some way, whether that means you're excited, impressed, or annoyed. When the mood strikes, scrap what's scheduled and write!

I asked several nonprofiteers—staff and consultants—to share some of their favorite little bets with me in a Facebook group I participate in. Here are some great examples:

> The most expensive guided missile cannot do a thing until it's launched! I almost didn't start InvisiblePeople.tv because I only had $45 and I couldn't edit the videos. Having a background in marketing and knowing the importance of design I really thought that the quality of what I was able to make happen would not get positive attention. I was wrong. Do the best you can with what you have but launch—then repair and adjust. Today, it's best to get your campaign, product or service out than to wait until it's perfect.
>
> **—Mark Horvath, founder, InvisiblePeople.tv**

When I worked with Hebrew University, we decided to create the Facebook event, "Happy Birthday Albert Einstein," and created a video inviting anyone to send in a question to Albert Einstein—any type of question—and the Albert Einstein scholar at the university would reply to questions in an answer video. The event received over 300 comments from many countries around the world, and created huge awareness of the university online. Hebrew U. owns the rights to "Albert Einstein" the brand, and has many of its papers. So we took an asset and created an event from it.

—**Debra Askanase, digital engagement strategist,**
Community Organizer 2.0

Back when I did communications for a small, nonprofit, experimental art gallery, we had a juried show around a pretty opaque—yet fascinating—topic: syzygy. Because we were already having a bear of a time making the marketing hook, I threw it out to Twitter and Facebook (I don't think I'd even heard the term "crowdsource" yet) and asked folks to text in a definition of syzygy, with the idea that the best definition would win a membership. I wound up getting around 100 texts, and I thought it helped me in a few ways. Our social media presence was only a few months old at the time so first it helped me see if anyone was really even listening/willing to engage. Second, it helped me find some good bits for the marketing copy. But most important, it gave the audience a chance to think about the show and get their wheels turning about what "syzygy" means before they even came to see the show. Talking to people at the opening, I discovered more than a few who were excited to come to see if the jurors' take on it aligned at all with their own concept or what they'd found when they looked it up online for the contest. This was one of the first acts I did as a social media manager (who also did PR, web design, and a little bit of everything else communications related), and after that I was hooked.

—**Michael DeLong, online community**
manager, TechSoup

In order to increase awareness of UNFPA's (the United Nations Population Fund) work in crisis settings, to involve field staff in social media and grow their supporter community, we designed a way for midwives to report and share safe deliveries from refugee camps—presenting babies basically; it has really worked, you can see the increase in response levels and shares on their Facebook page at facebook.com/UNFPA. They started with 5,080 fans on Facebook and less than five months later, they had 18,333. Some of the campaign images were shared more than 4,000 times (at the time more than half of all supporters shared it). The quadruplets born in Dadaab camp are quite amazing!

—**Mari Tikkanen, managing director, M4ID**

We've seen great results at the Case Foundation on asking our community to chime in with their favorite for new cover photos, our Be Fearless imagery, etc. We've also gotten high response with little stuff like fill in the blank updates on both Facebook and Twitter, and asking folks which nonprofits we should be following or liking. Our 2012 Facebook-based promotion around Back to School was a great success: the theme of fearless books resonated, the ask to vote on a favorite was easy, the app we built was clean and user-friendly, and the associated partners (recipients of grants and promotional partners) tied all of the campaign elements together.

—**Jenna Sauber, digital marketing and communications manager, The Case Foundation**

Stop, Think, and Discuss

Which of these stories inspires something in you? What little bet can you work into some free space on your editorial calendar?

Letting a Little Bet Grow into a Way of Life

Sometimes little experiments work, and they grow into a way of life. That's what Kerry Barnes, director of development and community relations at Longview, discovered. Longview is a senior living community in the Finger Lakes region of New York. One of Barnes's biggest tasks is increasing awareness of the beautiful Longview community and all it offers. Barnes decided to set up a Facebook Page a few years ago, more or less as a lark. "I was pretty familiar with using social media for my own personal purposes, but I wasn't quite sure what role it could play in marketing a senior community," says Barnes (2011).

Her organization is fortunate in that it has an extensive daily list of events and programs for its seniors; the day's agenda makes for an easy status update. Before long, Barnes added photos of special events and happenings, making sure to post pictures within hours of an event.

Longview's Facebook Page started getting comments such as, "Wow, this reminds me of the daily schedule on the cruise I recently took!," and, "Hey—look at Dad! Glad to see you're getting out and taking part of things!" Longview had stumbled upon a great way to keep family members informed of what their loved ones were doing, without being invasive or overbearing.

Recently Barnes realized that more residents were using computers, especially to use social media. She is currently gathering data to back up her claims that the vast majority of Longview residents are regular and savvy computer users, contrary to the popular image of seniors being befuddled by technology. Particularly for seniors, computer use is vital for staying in touch with family that may be far-flung geographically. "Being able to watch real-time video from a grandchild's birthday party happening across the country or getting photos of a new baby straight from the delivery room are all appealing actions that are just not possible without the use of a computer and Internet," says Barnes. "Residents at our community who are blatantly anti-computer have no compunction about asking for help downloading photos family members have posted online."

Newsjacking: Taking Advantage of the Headlines

Sometimes the work your organization does is newsworthy on its own, and it's worth taking the time to pitch that story to reporters. But there's also another way to get your nonprofit's name in the news: *newsjacking*. David Meerman Scott (2011) has published a fast read all about the process: *Newsjacking: How to Inject Your Ideas into a Breaking News Story and Generate Tons of Media Coverage.*

It's all about what Scott calls owning the second paragraph. It works like this: a news story breaks. Journalists are under pressure to update that story for the next edition or broadcast. So while the core of the story (the first paragraph) doesn't change all that much, the second paragraph does, with additional details or insights or related quotes. That's your chance to swoop in with something a reporter can use that's related—but not necessarily essential—to the main story to freshen it up. Then your part of the story gets repeated as other media outlets pick up the story.

In the book, Scott shares an example of newsjacking by the London Fire Brigade (LFB) that's a perfect illustration for nonprofits. Remember when Richard Branson's private Necker Island retreat went up in flames, and actress Kate Winslet rescued Branson's ninety-year-old mother from the fire?

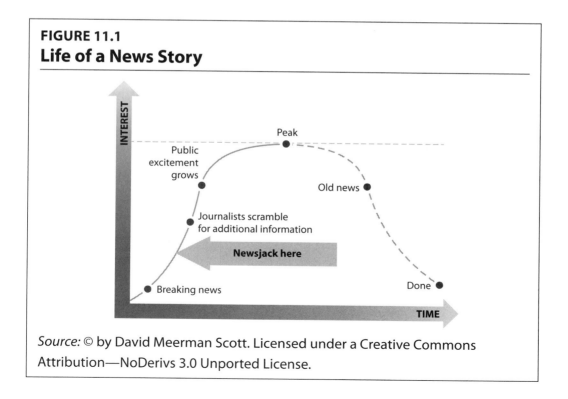

FIGURE 11.1
Life of a News Story

Source: © by David Meerman Scott. Licensed under a Creative Commons Attribution—NoDerivs 3.0 Unported License.

Here's how Scott describes the subsequent newsjacking:

Within hours of the initial reports on the fire and Winslet's role in the rescue, the London Fire Brigade offered Winslet the chance to train with firefighters at its training center. The offer was made in a story written by the LFB and posted on its website:

"The Brigade, which has over 300 women firefighters, is inviting Kate to learn how crews deal with fires and also how people can prevent fires from happening in the first place. On the proposed visit, Kate would visit the Brigade's training centre, meet trainees and experience the role of a modern day firefighter. This would include operational duties such as trying out firefighter breathing apparatus and climbing a ladder pitched against a tower block. She will also be made aware of the community safety activities that firefighting staff regularly carry out."

The London Fire Brigade newsjacked an incendiary event fueled by A-list celebrity heroism [Scott, 2011].

Your nonprofit can do the same thing! Think about it. . . . celebrities do both amazing and ridiculous things all the time. We also know that at some point in the coming months, there will be a natural disaster of some sort and a national political figure will say something really stupid. It's also likely that a business or another nonprofit (for example, a sister organization, someone you consider competition, or a national counterpart to your local group) will go through some sort of crisis or other kind of news-making change. These occasions happen over and over; we just don't know precisely when.

But when something like that does happen, could you follow the London Fire Brigade's example and offer a training or a tour, volunteer hours, or an honorary seat on your board of directors in response? Could that newsworthy event have been prevented if the person or organization involved had downloaded your handbook, taken your course, heeded the advice you offer, or lived their lives as your clients do? Remember, these offers don't necessarily have to be sincere; in many cases, humorous or satirical responses can work well too.

To make this work for you, you have to be fast. To practice being nimble, I suggest you make *newsjacking practice* a regular part of your staff meetings. Look at the recent headlines, and brainstorm how you could have newsjacked. Then when you get good at that, go for it for real! Figure 11.2 displays the process as outlined by Scott.

FIGURE 11.2
How to Newsjack

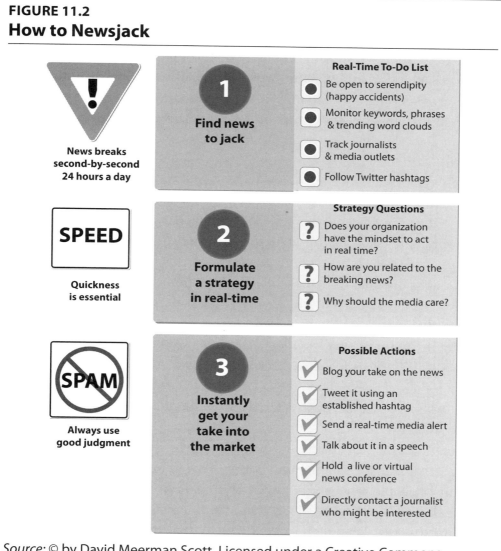

News breaks
second-by-second
24 hours a day

SPEED

Quickness
is essential

SPAM

Always use
good judgment

1
Find news
to jack

Real-Time To-Do List
- Be open to serendipity (happy accidents)
- Monitor keywords, phrases & trending word clouds
- Track journalists & media outlets
- Follow Twitter hashtags

2
Formulate
a strategy
in real-time

Strategy Questions
- Does your organization have the mindset to act in real time?
- How are you related to the breaking news?
- Why should the media care?

3
Instantly
get your
take into
the market

Possible Actions
- Blog your take on the news
- Tweet it using an established hashtag
- Send a real-time media alert
- Talk about it in a speech
- Hold a live or virtual news conference
- Directly contact a journalist who might be interested

Source: © by David Meerman Scott. Licensed under a Creative Commons Attribution—NoDerivs 3.0 Unported License.

How the Firelight Foundation Newsjacked the Facebook IPO

Remember when Facebook announced that it would go public? A few months before the initial public offering (IPO) was to take place, the board of directors of the Firelight Foundation, where Robin Dixon works as the communications director, identified a unique press opportunity (Dixon, 2012). Firelight Foundation was born from a successful IPO, and the upcoming Facebook IPO provided a highly visible way to talk about tech IPOs and the future of philanthropy, something of special interest to the Firelight Foundation. It was a great idea, but how to make it happen was the million-dollar question. Firelight decided to take three approaches to the story, creating a trail that journalists, donors, and anyone could follow up on.

First, it established the facts with a background story about how the foundation was started from a successful tech IPO. Firelight did this through a blog its director writes with *Alliance* magazine, an international magazine on philanthropy. Second, Firelight asked its founders to write an op-ed about their experience with a successful IPO that spoke to Facebook employees and encouraged their smart, thoughtful philanthropy. Finally, Firelight published a more personal side of the story from one of its founders on its blog. The response was overwhelmingly positive.

Firelight Foundation had an ideal placement for the op-ed on the day before the Facebook IPO. Since they had received only twelve hours' notice, staff immediately shifted into calling Firelight's network to let everyone know how to help. They called board members and offered cover letters, subject lines, and ideas on where to share the op-ed.

A Google alert let Dixon know when the op-ed was posted, six hours earlier than expected, and she sent the link out right away. She lost no time at all, and a handful of people started talking about it late that night on Facebook. "The response of the board was invaluable and the founders were happy to have the leadership support. They then reached out to donors, friends, and colleagues through personal emails and their mailing list. That exposure brought an entirely new round of attention," says Dixon.

In the end, the op-ed was tweeted, shared, and posted on sites that reached millions. It trended on LinkedIn, and one San Francisco Bay area TV station interviewed Firelight's founders for the five o'clock news. At least 550 people took an additional step and pushed it out further by sharing, tweeting, or emailing it. These were just the engagement numbers that Dixon could track. The next day, she posted the founder's more personal story on Firelight's blog and again asked its network to share the story and keep the conversation going. Its blog traffic tripled and its website traffic doubled.

Stop, Think, and Discuss

Take a look at the headlines from the last week or so. Could you have newsjacked any of those stories?

Brainstorm a list of news stories that are just bound to happen in the next year, where you could be ready for a newsjacking attempt.

Crisis Communications: Responding to Bad News

While you can do a fair amount of planning around hypothetical crises, until you know what you are really dealing with, you can't know exactly what to say, and you certainly won't know exactly when you need to say it until the crisis hits.

Every nonprofit should have a crisis communications plan—whether it be for a potential crisis of your nonprofit's own making or for something out of its control. It doesn't matter, because you can't ignore it either way.

Susan G. Komen for the Cure couldn't ignore that it made a program decision that enraged many of its supporters. The Second Mile couldn't ignore that its founder is now a convicted pedophile. Hospitals, schools, and other nonprofits in the Midwest and South can't ignore it when their facilities are destroyed—with people inside—during a tornado.

Whether a nonprofit can predict it or not, whether a nonprofit thinks it is controversial or not, whether a nonprofit is careful and prepared or not, every nonprofit is vulnerable to some sort of crisis. In some ways, the actual substance of the crisis is less important than whether you are ready to respond quickly and competently to it.

Your Crisis Communications Goal: Shorten the News Cycle

Let's focus on the kind of crisis that has the ability to cause long-term damage to your organization. When that kind of crisis strikes, your goal is to shorten the news cycle about it.

Nature and the news media abhor a vacuum—the story will be told, with or without you. Ignoring a crisis is one of the best ways to ensure that it will drag out even longer. Take, for example, the decision by Susan G. Komen for the Cure to suspend funding to Planned Parenthood for breast cancer screening. The first news cycle was about the backlash against the decision to stop funding Planned Parenthood. But it didn't end there. The second news cycle was about how Komen failed to respond to the first cycle. Even after the apology and reversal, the story continued on into a third cycle of "lessons learned from the Komen debacle." Now we can simply refer to the "Komen story," and most people know what we are talking about.

Don't do anything to drag out the news cycle, starting with ignoring the crisis. Also be very cautious about trying to rationalize what happened. That too can drag out a crisis much longer than need be. So what should you do instead?

Prepare for the Whens

Start with your known vulnerabilities, or what I call the *whens*—as in "when this gets out."

In your personal life, you may have skeletons in the closet or less-than-ideal members of your inner circle of friends or family. There may be embarrassing photographs or politically incorrect behavior or even illegal activity in your past. The same is true for your nonprofit organization.

Those who are in the know about these things are obligated to plan for when they become public, even if they never actually do. I recommend that you draft a brief response (think three to five sentences) for each potential situation, long before your head is spinning and your heart is racing from the adrenalin of breaking news.

Also think about any other shoes that could drop. Could one crisis lead quickly into another? Would it make sense to drop that other shoe yourself, rather than waiting for someone else to do it?

Another kind of when to prepare for is an attack on your organization for what it stands for. It hasn't done anything wrong in this situation, but it is under fire nevertheless. Social media has made it incredibly easy for anyone to express opinions about anything, which means that it should be fairly easy for you to identify some common arguments on the other side of your nonprofit's issues. When those voices decide to get aggressive and come after your organization directly, you should be ready with your response.

Prepare for the What-Ifs

When you are done with the whens (and hopefully they make a fairly short list!), it's time to plan for some *what-ifs*. Start with the crises of your own making. These can arise from mistakes, flubs, gaffes, inappropriate behavior, and so on. What if an intern were to accuse a senior staff member of sexual harassment? What if safety systems failed and a program participant was injured or killed? What if a board member were to post a racist comment on his Facebook profile? What if your nonprofit were to lose accreditation or were found to be cheating in some way?

When you are done with identifying potential crises at home, go through the same exercise for crises in the neighborhood. What if scandal were to rock another nonprofit in your building or the national organization your organization is affiliated with? What if one of your corporate supporters gets caught up in something that you need to dissociate yourself from?

For all of these situations, discuss what your nonprofit's public reaction would be. Would you take responsibility and apologize directly, or would you express regret and sadness but stop short of apologizing? Or would you stand firm, restate your position, and prepare to weather what comes next?

Stop, Think, and Discuss

What are your whens? What are your what-ifs? What do you need to do to prepare to manage those crises should they break?

How to Get It Over With

Maybe you'll do all this crisis planning and never have to use it. That's great! Consider it an insurance policy. But what do you do when crisis does strike? Here is a quick guide to getting through it and to keeping that news cycle short.

- Stay calm.
- Take an hour to sketch out a crisis communications plan. You won't regret it.
- Be honest. Getting caught in a lie creates a second crisis even worse than the first.
- Respond publicly, quickly, and from as high up the organizational ladder as possible.
- Be concise. Do not ramble your way through. Be natural but prepared.
- Be clear. Leave nothing up to interpretation.
- Get your own words online fast. This is where a blog on your main website comes in very handy. Do not rely on the media to get your message out correctly.
- Prepare for seventy-two hours of hell. Even if you are successful in containing the crisis, you won't get much else done.
- Keep any promises you make in your statements.
- Learn from what happened. Make notes on what you did right, and what you did wrong.

Why It Matters: You Really Can Predict the Unpredictable

You may feel that you can't predict the kinds of things I've covered in this chapter, but that's not true. You know something from this list you've compiled is likely to happen sometime, so budget the time in your calendar to merge in what pops up. If nothing does, then you can fall back on some of your evergreen content to fill any gaps.

You have your content strategy goals, and you know the voice and style you want to be known for. You've mapped out your big picture communications timeline, your core topics list, and your editorial calendar. You know how you'll map and repurpose your original content and merge in the unexpected.

Now it's time to do the work—to put your hands on the keyboard and create that content. This section shows you how by sharing

- Ways to create relevant content that works for here and now (chapter 12)

- Content formats and types of articles that always work for nonprofits (chapter 13)

- Ways to curate and add value to content created by others (chapter 14)

- Ways to use metaphors and humor to get your point across more effectively (chapter 15)

- Ways to use technology as you implement your content marketing strategy (chapter 16)

If you have ever had writer's block, this is the section that will cure it.

Part Four | Set Out on Your Trek:
Implementing Your Content Marketing Strategy

Chapter Twelve
Living in the Moment
Create Relevant Content for Here and Now

> **This chapter is about . . .**
> - Understanding what it means to produce relevant content
> - Recognizing how other nonprofits have made their communications more relevant
> - Looking at ways you can incorporate the six R's of relevance into your communications

Living on the trail in the wilderness forces you to live in the moment. You have no choice but to constantly respond to the environment around you. Friends who have never backpacked have asked if I get bored. I tell them that if you keep your eyes and ears open, there's no time to be bored, because you are constantly responding to the world around you.

Content marketing is like that too. You are constantly listening and watching for ways to connect and engage. Ultimately, content marketing is all about being relevant, right here and now.

Producing relevant and valuable content for your participants, supporters, and influencers sounds good. But relevancy can be hard to pinpoint because it varies so much from person to person and circumstance to circumstance. Information you may think is irrelevant right now may suddenly become relevant later tonight. You can improve your odds, however.

To make it a little easier, I've developed what I call the *six R's of message relevance*.

The Six R's: How to Be Relevant

I believe there are six primary elements of message or communications relevancy that are especially important in nonprofit marketing. Any message you are trying to get across, or any particular piece of communications, is much more likely to be relevant when

It's rewarding

It's realistic

It's real time

It's responsive

It's revealing

It's refreshing.

It's tough to be all of these at once, but if you can be at least two of the six, your odds of feeling relevant are significantly improved. Let's look at each R in more detail, with examples of how nonprofits are putting them to work in their communications.

Be Rewarding

Are the benefits or rewards for reading your content, following through on your calls to action, or otherwise engaging with your content generally clear? With nonprofit communications oftentimes, these benefits or rewards are emotional in nature. Will they make participants or supporters feel happy or proud or connected or included?

Elexa Liu, communications director at HOPE *worldwide* in Hong Kong, used to fill her newsletters with statistics that she thought summarized all the work her organization was doing. After participating in many Nonprofit Marketing Guide trainings, she decided to focus on telling a good story instead, reporting back to supporters on how the organization was using donations, sharing the vision for the future, and always thanking, thanking, thanking. The approach paid off in the form of increased unsolicited donations from supporters.

Liu tells this story: "A private individual recently asked us to submit a proposal to apply for a donation of approximately HK $400,000 (about US $51,600). She came to our centre for a visit and told us that our newsletter was what caught her attention as she researched different NGOs to support. She said most of what she read were boring facts and program details. Instead, we had a story that touched her heart, but we also laid out the vision of what we do to help the kids" (Leroux Miller, 2012c).

The vision and story were rewarding to that donor, not a bunch of statistics about the problem and HOPE *worldwide*'s workload. Remember, reward the heart first, and then let the head justify the heart's decision later with your facts and figures.

Rachel Hicks, director of programs and communications at the Archie Bray Foundation for the Ceramic Arts, experimented with her organization's Facebook Page for a couple of years before she discovered what the page's followers found most rewarding. The Archie Bray Foundation is a small but highly distinguished nonprofit in Helena, Montana, dedicated to creativity and innovation in the ceramic arts, with a highly competitive artist in residence program.

At first Hicks and others who helped manage the page would post about whatever they were working on, which included lots of exhibits and images of completed artwork. Over time, she started to have more fun with the page by posting more pictures of people, both artists at the Archie Bray Foundation and the organization's staff, sometimes wearing costumes or doing other silly things. She also started posting more pictures of works in progress that show the behind-the-scenes creative process (personal communication, January 2013). Hicks also decided to use her personal profile in a professional context and began friending artists and others in the ceramics community. This allowed her to tag individuals in photos and posts, something that she couldn't do as the organization's page administrator. She also asked staff to like and share things on the pages as individuals themselves, and she began to share more information from other ceramics organizations. "The ceramics world is a very small community," says Hicks, "so people will recognize each other's names or the names of artists they may be following over their own careers." By using both the nonprofit's official page and her personal profile, she gets the best of both worlds.

All the while, Hicks kept watching to see what people were responding to, and she concluded that it came down to two things: people responded to the artwork, especially in progress, and to other people. A review of her Facebook Insights confirmed what she was seeing.

Today Hicks says that Facebook is one of the Archie Bray Foundation's most important communications channels, especially for reaching the artist community. "While Facebook hasn't produced money from donors, it has created a lot of good community buzz. In the arts, we have many different kinds of people involved, from art collectors and major donors to hobby workshop participants and professional artists," says Hicks. "Our biggest group on Facebook is the artist community and they tend to respond to the art-in-process posts. When we post pictures, people will respond saying they know the artist, or will ask technical questions about the pieces."

That's the reward for people who follow the Archie Bray Foundation on Facebook: they get to feel personally connected, not just to the organization or the place itself but, more important, to the artists themselves and to others who love ceramics. They are rewarded for engaging with the organization's Facebook Page by feeling that they are part of this tight community of people who deeply appreciate ceramic arts.

Because of the work Hicks has put into making the organization's presence on Facebook much more personal, the Archie Bray Foundation has built a real community there, with tangible organizational benefits. For example, says Hicks, "Facebook is now the biggest tool we have for promoting applications for our fellowships and residency programs."

Helping people express themselves is also a type of reward, and creating content that makes it easy for people to share what they believe in—thereby revealing a bit more of who they are to their own family and friends—can also work for you. "We do a lot of what we call 'share graphics,' so we make these graphics with the intent to ask people to share them," says Carie Lewis, deputy director of online communications for the Humane Society of the United States (HSUS). "People want to show that they stand for something, and they want to tell that to the people that matter the most to them—their friends and family. Facebook works very well for that" (personal communications, October 2012).

Stop, Think, and Discuss
What rewards do your communications deliver to the recipients?

Be Realistic

Does what you are talking about feel possible or appropriate within the given context? Are your communications realistic in addressing any barriers to following through on the organization's calls to action? For example, do you give easy-to-follow instructions or address common fears head on?

Let's look at how you might market a monthly giving program in a way that's more realistic, by directly addressing some of the barriers to participating in those types of giving programs.

The *Cygnus Donor Survey 2012* (Burk, 2012) found that 69 percent of donors in the survey said they used an automatic deduction for some kind of bill payment, such as insurance, utilities, or loans. People who are already comfortable with this kind of transaction are more likely to be comfortable with automated, monthly charitable donations. The survey found that 45 percent of those donors who paid a bill in that way were also current or former monthly donors, while only 21 percent of the donors who did not use automatic deductions for bill payments had any experience with monthly giving.

Furthermore, the survey found that people who did not want to participate in monthly giving felt that way because they preferred not to be committed to a fixed amount over an extended period, were afraid it would be difficult to cancel or get out of if they changed their minds, and were concerned about the security of their personal information.

Based on this information, if you were marketing a monthly giving program, it would make sense to be realistic about these barriers. First, if possible, you might want to try to segment your list to focus on those people who are comfortable with automated payments or who at least have given to your nonprofit online before, which could signal their trust in secure online banking technology. Next, you might want to focus on the positives. Providing stable income for the nonprofits they supported, convenience, and reduced cost of fundraising were the top three reasons why people chose to give that way.

But if you suspect you are marketing to people without automatic bill paying experience, it may be more important to confront their fears head on. You may want to structure both the program itself and communications about it to address common concerns. For example, your messaging could include instructions that demonstrate how easy it is to change the donation amount or stop giving entirely should the donor's circumstances or wishes change.

Another good area in which to be realistic is what actually excites people and what doesn't. Helping program staff be more realistic about the ways their community will likely react to certain kinds of news is another important part of Carie Lewis's job at the Humane Society of the United States. Because she manages the editorial calendar for Facebook, program staff will ask her if she can push out an announcement of some kind about their work.

"Every single time, I ask, how does this benefit the community? What is the value for them? Or what can they do to change this?" says Lewis. For example, if the business development department creates a partnership with a hotel, department staff might ask Lewis to show the hotel some love on Facebook. But expecting the community to get excited about the announcement of some corporate partnership isn't realistic.

"It doesn't line up with our mentality," says Lewis, who will then quiz the staff about whether the hotel is pet friendly and could offer a coupon to entice people to stay there with their pets, or whether HSUS could ask its Facebook fans to tell their own pet-friendly hotel stories. "We have to think about how we can get people involved in that content or give them some kind of benefit, rather than just throwing it out there," says Lewis.

Because she asks the same questions all the time, the pitches coming from program staff are getting much better. But sometimes the right answers aren't there, and Lewis has to be realistic, and say no to the request.

Be Real Time

Do your nonprofit's communications feel current and real time, and do they generally make sense given what else is happening around the recipients?

Tying your communications to what's already in the news can be extremely effective, because it feels so relevant to your audience. One study found that open rates for advocacy emails containing an "issue du jour" are more than double the rates for those that do not pertain to a currently relevant issue (Daigneault, Davis, and Sybrant, 2011). The response rate for emails containing an issue du jour is better too, increasing from 10 percent to 25 percent. (Review the section on newsjacking in chapter 11 for more tips.)

Rachel Hicks at the Archie Bray Foundation is a strong believer in the power of real-time communications. "With my iPhone, it's so easy to take pictures and post them right away. I can take a picture and post it as I walk out the door," says Hicks. Sometimes though, she has to contain her excitement, because what's real time for her may be downtime for her Facebook community, for example. "If I post something early in my work day, like 9:00 AM, no one sees it," says Hicks. So she'll hold the post until the afternoon or evening, which produces better results.

Because she has built her organization's page into a genuine resource for the ceramics community, Hicks also says she considers it a personal challenge to be the first organization in that community to share breaking or hot news from other organizations. "I want to reshare the good stuff I hear before a lot of other organizations do and it feels like old news," says Hicks, so she has Facebook open all the time.

Julie Seewald Bornhoeft, director of development and community relations for WEAVE, which assists victims of domestic violence and sexual assault in Sacramento, California, found a good way to connect with WEAVE's supporters in the midst of a public uproar about some candidates' comments about rape during the period before the 2012 General Election. "We created talking points around 'rape knows no political affiliation' to try to reframe the conversation outside of the politics," says Bornhoeft. "What we found was that supporters of all political persuasions respected and appreciated us trying to put the topic on neutral grounds. We had bipartisan support, but were still able to call out really ridiculous and inappropriate statements made about sexual assault. Because these were hot-button issues, they generated a lot of response, but in a manner that allowed us to be an expert without becoming overtly political" (personal communication, December 2012).

Stop, Think, and Discuss

How can you connect more directly and more quickly to what's happening in the news? How can you make your communications feel more timely?

Be Responsive

Do your communications appear to be responsive to your participants and supporters? In other words, can they tell by the content that your nonprofit has been listening and taking what it's heard into account?

Being responsive—and in real time—is a hallmark of the social media strategy used by the Humane Society of the United States. "We read every single comment and every single Facebook wall post that people put on our page," says Carie Lewis. "If people just wanted to read your content, they would go to your website. On social media, it's really important [for you] to pay attention to them."

HSUS staff have an ambitious goal for reacting to posts that they believe do require a response: under two hours on Facebook and under thirty minutes on Twitter, during normal business hours. If the issue is important, it doesn't matter what time it happens. "If you find the right person to do this work for you, they will take such ownership of it, and they will deal with anything that comes up, even outside of the normal day. We'll text each other if something is going on," says Lewis. "Facebook and Twitter never sleep, so the HSUS social media team is cross-trained to handle a crisis or urgent situation, which happens a couple of times per month," says Lewis, even when the situation occurs in the absence of the community manager or Lewis herself.

Demonstrating that you are responsive also plays out over relationships that you build over weeks, months, and years too. Since Beth Ann Spiegel began working as the fund development and communications associate for The Arc of Atlantic County, she has been trying to improve participation in the annual Step Up For The Arc Walk (Spiegel, 2011). It's your typical peer-to-peer fundraising event, but no matter what she tried, she couldn't get past the 200 participants and $20,000 raised threshold in any significant way. She tried new incentives, contests, attractions, and pretty brochures to encourage participation, but none of these tactics seemed to work.

It finally dawned on Spiegel in 2011, thanks to the active engagement of two families in particular, that one big reason The Arc was failing to attract families of people it served was that it hadn't built the type of relationships that would inspire these families to get involved.

It wasn't that the families of the 700 people The Arc served didn't care about The Arc and what was done for them and their loved one. It all boiled down to The Arc's lack of attention to getting to know the families it was trying to attract, how those families perceived The Arc, and what might motivate them to participate. Spiegel shares the stories of two families as examples.

Dina, who had passed away early in 2011, had been one of The Arc's most beloved and engaged clients. Dina's mom, Mary Ann, had a strong desire to give back to The Arc, so she called Spiegel to do some brainstorming. After they tossed around a few ideas, Mary Ann agreed that forming a walk-a-thon team in memory of Dina would be the best way to remember her. The loss of her daughter also provided Mary Ann with a great sense of urgency to make a difference for the organization that had helped her child. Spiegel remained in contact with Mary Ann regularly in the months leading up to the event, making sure she was there to answer all of Mary Ann's questions.

By the day of the walk, Dina's team had grown to nearly sixty people—all wearing handmade shirts with a photo of themselves with Dina on the front—and had raised nearly $6,000. This was by far the biggest team The Arc had ever had at its annual walk and the most touching example of support for someone it had served. The Arc staff immediately started getting amped up for the 2012 walk and plotting a strategy for raising a lot more money.

The second example involves Lisa, the mother of a teenage girl who had been receiving a few hours of help from The Arc each month in the form of in-home respite care since she was little. Lisa also happened to be a server at the local deli where The Arc's CEO ate lunch regularly, so they had a chance to get to know one another.

One day the CEO asked Lisa why she didn't enroll her daughter in more of The Arc's programs, especially the five-hour Saturday program designed to give parents a break and kids a fun, nurturing environment in which to socialize and learn. Lisa didn't think her daughter's behavior would make her a good fit for that program, an opinion the CEO wanted to hear nothing of—"at least give it a shot," she said. So Lisa did, and it was the perfect match. Lisa's daughter now not only attends the weekly kids program, she also attends a bi-weekly program for teens and has made many friends. This has helped the daughter and her family tremendously, and Lisa is not shy about expressing that.

When it came time to develop a new agency video, The Arc asked Lisa if she'd give a testimonial in the video. She agreed and spoke very sincerely about how she wished more families could benefit from The Arc's services. The Arc's relationship with Lisa evolved even further when it came time for her daughter to attend Step Up For The Arc, as the Saturday program children and their staff always do. While most of the parents who send their children to the walk make a modest contribution, Lisa didn't hesitate to set up an online fundraising page and set her goals high.

She and her daughter beat their goal and came into the next year's event even more energized. She offered to provide her signature on a cover letter that accompanied The Arc's event mailer inviting people to participate. She also set her goal even higher than the year before and beat that too. Lisa became The Arc's top individual fundraiser, bringing in more than $2,500 from more than sixty people.

Stop, Think, and Discuss

How can your participants, supporters, and influencers tell from the communications you send that you've been listening to them? Should you establish some response times? How can you listen more carefully?

Be Revealing

Do your communications reveal new or interesting or surprising insights or take people behind the scenes? Do they help people see or understand or participate in something they would enjoy that they wouldn't otherwise know about?

"I think the appeal of the 'new' is human nature," says Julie Seewald Bornhoeft of WEAVE. "Our supporters, especially on Facebook, are very loyal and have a solid understanding of what we do. If we are just sharing information, we get moderate response. If we frame anything as new or needing their input, the engagement increases."

For example, she once highlighted some toiletries and clothing that had been donated to WEAVE's safe house. "We shared pictures of what was donated and then asked our supporters what they would like us to include in a welcome basket for families. We receive these types of donations several times a month and have been providing the basics to families at the safe house for years. But when we framed it around a new idea—the welcome basket—and asked for input, we saw the feedback spike immediately," says Bornhoeft. "People love to share information they believe will help you. For me, it's a matter of looking past what I think I know and allowing others to engage."

Infographics are becoming a popular way to provide insight into an organization as well. Data that would normally be relegated to boring pie charts or lengthy reports is now easily understood and shared.

Julia Reich of Stone Soup Creative created infographics for her client Legal Information for Families Today (LIFT) to draw attention to the problems existing in the New York State Family Court system (personal communication, February 2013). As Reich says, "We knew recipients were familiar with the organization, but probably did not know the extent of the problem existing in Family Court and the specifics of the work LIFT does." Using the infographics LIFT staff were able to tell a story about LIFT and the people it helps in a way supporters had never seen before. "We began with an outline of the problems in Family Court and then came up with a lot of facts and numbers that helped make our case, like the number of filings per year compared to the number of Family Court judges," says Reich. "But we came up with too many facts and too much text, so we had to cut back to focus on the bare bones text and imagery that would make the most impact, touch just the right nerve, and encourage people to donate."

Stop, Think, and Discuss

How can you reveal more of what your participants, supporters, and influencers find interesting? Can you make a story or other information you think is old feel new again?

Be Refreshing

Are your communications refreshing to hear or see? Do you share your messages in a style or tone that is both authentic and perhaps pleasantly surprising?

It's been well documented through a variety of experiments, including several of my own at Nonprofit Marketing Guide, that nonprofits as a whole do a terrible job of thanking donors. In my experiments, I received follow-up communications beyond the automated email receipt from only about a third of the organizations I gave to.

Because it happens so rarely, when donors are properly and effusively thanked, they notice, and they find it refreshing.

Theresa Swartwood, director of public relations and marketing at Cross-Lines Community Outreach, Inc., is investing time in changing the way her organization approaches thank-you letters. Swartwood has started sending thank-you letters once a month with a personal note, and she considers the response nothing short of amazing. Several donors have called and said they look forward to her little personal notes of appreciation, which she writes by hand in the white space to the right of her signature (Leroux Miller, 2012a).

Swartwood also personally calls any individual or business that makes a donation over $200. "I did this with a new donor and it blew her away," says Swartwood. "She supports ten other charitable organizations, but we were the first one that called within three days of her donation. She was so impressed with our prompt and personal call that she says we are now in her top five organizations." Their executive director, Roberta Lindbeck, also sends within three business days a personal letter to any donor who contributes $500 or more.

While the ideal might be to get thank-you notes out within seventy-two hours, if you can't make that happen, what can you make happen this year? Every little bit of progress in this department will make a big difference, as you can see from Theresa Swartwood's story.

Kathleen Kennedy, program and development coordinator at the Coalition for Sonoran Desert Protection, shared a similar story. While the coalition has always sent out a hard-copy thank-you letter the same week a gift is received, it recently began following the letter with a personal phone call. Kennedy says the phone calls have been very well received and have even resulted in some productive dialogue about the organization's work and offers to volunteer (personal communication, December 2012).

The coalition is also experimenting with sending donors high-quality photos of some of the wildlife species it works to protect, as an extra thank you. The photos are taken locally by remote, motion-activated cameras that the coalition's volunteers maintain. "At first, we sent the photos only to our higher-dollar donors, but once we realized the low expense of the photos, we expanded the strategy to all our donors," says Kennedy. The coalition has also sent photos with fundraising letters and with thank-you letters, adding its logo, website, and an inspirational slogan to the photo as well. "Our supporters have even requested more copies to give out to their friends," says Kennedy.

Mark Horvath, founder of InvisiblePeople.tv, shared with me (on Facebook in October 2012) his experience with being emotionally honest on Twitter and how refreshing people found it.

> Early on I built the @hardlynormal brand by being emotionally honest at all times. I remember when I first started I would be candid about not only an issue, but my own personal life. A few people would respond "you can't say that," yet a significant amount of other people would tweet back "that's exactly how I feel but I was too scared to share, thank you!" Of course, at the time my house was being foreclosed on and I was eating $1 pizzas to survive. It was the start of the economic crisis and I had a lot of content to share that people could relate to. I really do believe being vulnerable had a huge impact on my original growth on social media channels.

My point is this: I really believe we are all screaming to connect to others. Nonprofits and brands that give a little personality to their social media find more engagement. I think being vulnerable can be an important content tool when used right, especially if you make a mistake, which we all will! As organizations grow the levels of risk they can take online also changes. But I do urge everyone to continue to take the risk of being vulnerable at some level. It's how we connect as humans.

You can also pleasantly surprise your supporters in refreshing ways by using humor (see chapter 15 for more examples). Jennifer Stevenson is the marketing, public relations, and development director for the Bergstrom-Mahler Museum in Neenah, Wisconsin. This glass museum is located on a large lake. "In May, we have a hatching of lake flies. They are disgusting tiny creatures that live for only a few days, but in that time cover nearly every inch of horizontal and vertical space within a half mile of the lake shore. It is a local phenomenon," says Stevenson. "So I do an installment of the e-newsletter *Overheard: Conversations with Lake Flies*, where I Photoshop images of lake flies talking about museum events. It gets laughs and I get to be weird," says Stevenson (personal communication, October 2012).

Stop, Think, and Discuss

What could your nonprofit do to add a more refreshing voice or personality to its communications?

Bringing the Six R's Together

I received many emails from nonprofits after Hurricane Sandy hit the East Coast, with content all over the map, from direct pleas for assistance for those affected to educational and advocacy emails tying severe weather to climate change. In looking through them all, one stood out: an email I received from the Washington Humane Society (WHS) the day after the storm passed through Washington, DC (figure 12.1).

FIGURE 12.1
Washington Humane Society's Hurricane Sandy Email

Dear Kivi,

After a night of howling wind, pouring rain and more than a few lights flickering, we are relieved to report that in spite of Hurricane Sandy, all of our animals remain safe and sound.

Because of you, we are able to serve the animals of our region 24 hours a day, seven days a week - even during natural disasters like hurricanes.

Our shelter staff remained with the animals at our adoption centers all night, as they do every night. Our team, along with our dedicated volunteers have been busy ensuring that every animal in our care is safe and warm, and receiving all the comfort they need. Additionally, our Humane Law Enforcement Officers and Animal Care & Control Officers have been criss-crossing our streets day and night - even in the worst hours of the storm - in search of, and assisting, animals in need.

All is peaceful in Kitty City. Despite the raging winds and rain three cats were adopted yesterday.

We may be the hands and feet, but *you* are the heart and soul of the Washington Humane Society. You are the reason we are able to make a difference in the lives of so many. We depend on you and so do the animals of our region.

Thank you for your compassion and support for the animals in our care.

Wishing you warmth and security during these recovery days of the storm.

Most sincerely,

Lisa LaFontaine
President and CEO

This gloomy, rainy day hasn't dampened volunteer Delores Hamilton's and Ellia's spirits! A huge thank you to our volunteers who braved the storm for DC animals!

It's rewarding. It credits the donors. "We may be the hands and feet, but you are the heart and soul. . . . We depend on you and so do the animals of our region."

It's realistic. It doesn't ask for money, which would have been in bad taste given how little damage there was at this facility compared to the devastation in New Jersey and New York.

It's real time. It came out the day after the storm.

It's responsive. It reports back to supporters on how the animals fared, which the WHS knows from experience is of great concern to their donors.

It's revealing. It includes visual proof and takes us behind the scenes. It doesn't just tell the story—it shows it, complete with photos of a kitty sleeping with rain hitting the window behind and a volunteer in rain gear taking a dog for a walk. It reinforces how trustworthy the WHS is. Staff get the job done no matter the circumstances. The email talks about volunteers walking dogs and kitties getting adopted in spite of the bad weather.

It's refreshing. After this disaster, area donors expected (and likely received from other organizations) desperate pleas for help. Because this was good news, and a positive message about how preparation pays off, it was refreshingly different from other messaging at the time.

I was curious as to how the email came about. Since the storm was on everyone's radar for a few days, I wondered if the WHS had planned to do some kind of update like this in advance. So I talked to Darcy Levit, director of major gifts (Leroux Miller, 2012b).

Levit told me that the email wasn't planned. The morning after the storm, she was struck by the fact that so many staff had spent the night at the shelter—many more than the usual overnight crew. "There were sleeping bags everywhere," she said, all to make sure that the animals were cared for no matter what happened. While there was some flooding, there was no major damage.

She thought it would be a good message to share with supporters, so she and other staff brainstormed some ideas for what to include in the email that morning, and then set about making it happen the same day. She checked the master calendar and with the events team to make sure there weren't any conflicts with sending an email that day.

She then emailed shelter staff asking for pictures taken around the time of the storm. Levit says staff routinely take lots of photos and know they will often be used by the communications and fundraising staff, so she quickly had the examples she needed.

"The intent was to communicate [to donors] that their dollars are hard at work, at all times, without asking for more in the email," says Levit. You'll notice that the email does include one very soft ask (the linked word "support"), and WHS did receive some gifts.

But better yet were the email replies to the message. Levit says she received many messages in reply to the storm email, from donors grateful to get an update on the animals, and she shared those with the frontline staff. She considers herself the facilitator or the conduit between the donors and the staff who are making the good work happen. The staff share stories with her to share with donors, and when donors send encouraging words back, she forwards them on to staff.

Stop, Think, and Discuss

Take a look at the last email you sent to your list. How many of the six R's of message relevance did you include? How could you have added more relevance to that email?

Why It Matters: We Pay Attention Only to What's Relevant

The conventional wisdom is that we each see about three thousand media messages a day. We pay attention to about fifty-two of them. We positively remember only four. You can keep throwing your messages out there, but until you figure out how to get people to not only pay attention but also to positively remember them, you won't make a difference. Creating content that's relevant is how you connect and engage.

Chapter Thirteen
Your Swiss Army Knife
Reliable Nonprofit Content That Always Works

> **This chapter is about . . .**
> - Using tried-and-true article formats for nonprofit content
> - Sharing results and successes without bragging
> - Telling better stories
> - Using fill-in-the-blank headlines (when you are really stuck)

It's always good to have an all-purpose tool like a Swiss Army Knife at the ready on a long hike. You never know exactly what you will need it for, but having it with you gives you the confidence that you'll be able to fix just about anything.

That's how I feel about the types of content I'll review in this chapter. These formats and these approaches to your content are like that Swiss Army Knife: pull them out when you are in a bind and odds are you'll figure something out!

Eleven Favorite Types of Articles

Here are what I consider the tried-and-true, best article formats for nonprofits.

How-to articles. "Tricks of the Trade." "Step by Step." "Your Road Map." In an easy-to-follow format, provide your readers with clear directions on how to do something related to the issues your organization works on. Is there something your readers could do on their own to advance your mission? Do people call your nonprofit asking how to do certain tasks?

Advice columns. "The Answer Man." "Dear_____." "Ask_____." "The Experts Speak." It's a basic advice column, but with your own twist. If people call your nonprofit for advice, use some of those questions in your content. Encourage readers to send in their own questions. You might try rotating the job of answering the letters among experts in your organization or field. You can also write humorous, fictional questions with subtle true-life lessons in the answers.

Frequently asked questions. "Now You Know." "FAQs." "Afraid to Ask?" Pick a topic and write down five to seven of the most common questions you hear about it. Then provide your answers. This is a great way to share information about your organization's programs and to answer common questions about your organization as a whole.

First-person accounts. "What I've Learned." "In My Own Words." "In My Experience." Hearing about an experience directly from the person who lived it is usually more interesting and believable than hearing someone else talking about it. Ask someone with a good story to share to write an article or essay in the first person (that is, using the words *I*, *me*, and *my*). Or you can write the article in the third person (that is, using *he*, *she*, *him*, and *her*), being sure to use lots of direct quotes from the subject of the article.

Lists. "Our Top Ten." "The Countdown." People love lists. They can be made up of just about anything and can be used to provide advice, offer checklists, or simply entertain David Letterman–style. Depending on the focus of your organization, you might issue releases on the top ten "ways to improve_____," "ways to avoid_____," "most common_____," or "easiest_____." Fill in the blanks with whatever is appropriate to your group and mission. List your top ten in read-at-a-glance bullet points.

Take a position—and get out there with it. If you can write something that people can't say for themselves for whatever reason—because the thoughts just haven't coalesced in their own heads yet, or because it would be politically unpopular in the office—they will love you for it. Strong opinions are also naturally interesting and engaging, even if you don't personally agree with them (if you have any doubt about this, you obviously don't watch cable news, which is based entirely on this reality). Position articles can also take the form of reviews or recommendations, with titles like "Picks and Pans" or "We Checked It Out." Share your thoughts, both positive and negative, on the books, websites, news reports, places, and events your readers are likely to be interested in.

Respond to someone else. Look at what else is going on in the world around you, from media headlines to your trade press and favorite bloggers to what your friends are talking about on Facebook and Twitter. Look at what's coming up on your schedule. What can you write in response to what you see? Sometimes it can literally be a response ("Jack said this on his blog, but here's what we think . . ."). At other times, your response may be inspired by something a colleague has written, even if what you write doesn't end up addressing that person's article directly.

Do a roundup. Another quick way to create content is to round up a bunch of (often unrelated) ideas. You can do these in traditional roundup posts, where you present several news blurbs, anecdotes, or links you recommend. I think roundups work best when you can add a little perspective or value, such as indicating how the individual items are related or why you are sharing them.

Debunk myths or conventional wisdom. The media love a contrarian point of view. If you see an issue in a way that differs from the conventional wisdom, share your thoughts and point out the flaws in those widely held views. You can call articles like this "Fact Versus Fiction" or "Their Myths, Our Reality." What are the common misperceptions in your field? Are there any tales you wish would die forever? Lay out the fictions and the facts for your readers.

Add some clarity. People are so overwhelmed with information and details and all the ifs, ands, and buts that they are often paralyzed by it all. If you can add some clarity, so people know where to start and where to focus, they will love you. Help your readers keep up with the latest lingo in your field. You'll be surprised how many people have questions about special terminology but are afraid to ask. Put events, statistics, and other information in context for your readers by reporting on trends in a specific segment of your field. What patterns do you see developing? What issues are people talking about now more than before? Do the research for your supporters on the best places to find the things or people they might be looking for. If you've recently conducted a search for something, odds are your readers may need to do the same search themselves.

Offer a local angle on national news. In the wake of a national election, natural disaster, or groundbreaking scientific discovery or achievement, explain how the national news will play out locally in your organization and community. Offer your executive director or a board member as a source for local angle comments.

Stop, Think, and Discuss

Looking at this list of article formats, which two or three could you add to your repertoire?

Monthly Writing Prompts to Get You Started

To help you overcome nonprofit writer's block, we at NonprofitMarketingGuide.com have created a free newsletter called *Monthly Nonprofit Writing Prompts*.

At the start of each month, we'll send you an email with at least ten prompts to get you thinking about articles, stories, press releases, blog posts, Facebook updates, letters, and other content that you could write for the following month. For example, at the start of March, you'd get writing prompts for April. That way you'll have time to think about the ideas and incorporate them into your calendar.

The idea isn't to do your editorial calendar for you or to tell you what to say to your supporters. Only you can figure that out. What we will do is give you at least ten prompts to get you thinking more creatively and strategically about what you'll write.

To learn more and sign up, go to kivilm .com/prompts.

Focusing on Results

Supporters want to hear results, and you can share them in many different ways. Here are six of my favorites.

A dramatic story. Tell your supporters the emblematic story of your nonprofit's success. Human brains are wired for narrative. We all love a good story! Tell some stories that capture the drama and excitement of your work.

Timeline or time lapse. Show big progress one step at a time. Much of the work nonprofits do day in and day out can get lost in the everyday shuffle. Take time to stop and map out just how much your nonprofit has made happen.

Before and after. Nothing works better to show change than before and after photos and stories. But you need both! If you are good at documenting the need before, make sure you build your skills in documenting the success after too. Or if you are good at capturing the conclusions of stories or projects, add capturing the beginnings to your work plan.

Behind the scenes. Using video or great storytelling, take people behind the scenes where the real action is. Much of the work nonprofits do is in places that your average donor either can't go or doesn't want to go. But you can take donors there virtually and help them understand the real impact of their gifts.

Overcoming an unusual challenge. If someone told you that it couldn't be done (whatever *it* may be), and you did it, that's interesting. Have you solved a tricky problem, developed a more efficient way to get things done, or exceeded a goal? Share your tips and get some recognition for your creativity and drive.

Client testimonials. Let the people who benefit most talk about your results. Donors love stories from the field, where they can see how their gift worked its magic through your organization to change the life of another real person. You can change clients' names or other identifying details to protect privacy if needed, but if you can use a real name and photo, all the better.

As you write stories, especially for your supporters, I urge you to think more broadly about what can be considered a successful result. That's something that Jennifer Jordan Hall, the founder of KYK9 Search and Reunite Services, is learning as she works out her communications strategy as a one-person organization. Sometime her dogs, Remy and Scout, are successful in finding people alive and unharmed. But not all the searches result in happy endings. Hall is experimenting with ways to talk about those too, as in this blog post she wrote:

> Last summer 2½ year old Christina Norris tragically drowned in the Ohio River. Nearing the one year anniversary, Christina's mother, Paige Cooper, contacted me to thank KYK9 for searching for Christina. What courage that must have taken. I asked Paige if she and her daughters, Olivia (2½), and Alix (1 month), would like to meet Remy and Scout. She bravely said yes. We met at a park where other mothers were sitting in the shade, watching their children play. Scout and Remy happily greeted Olivia and Paige with wags and licks, reaping pats and laughter.
>
> But when Scout and Remy noticed Alix, who was sleeping in the shade a few feet away, both dogs pulled to see Alix. Nobody else mattered. Paige asked why Remy and Scout were so interested in Alix. Not sure, I took one dog at a time to meet Alix. Scout approached the baby carrier cautiously, getting more and more excited. As she sniffed Alix's blanket, Scout touched the carrier with her paw, lay down and barked. Stunned, I could not believe what I saw. Scout was indicating on the baby.
>
> Paige asked why Scout was so intently focused on baby Alix. I paused before asking if Alix was sitting in Christina's carrier. No, it was not Christina's. But, Alix was wrapped in Christina's blanket. Watching Scout, Paige looked up at me and asked if Scout remembered Christina's smell. Paige said what I was afraid to—that Scout recognized Christina's scent. Eleven months had passed, but Scout had found her person.
>
> Witnessing Scout recognize Christina's scent 11 months after she drowned was overwhelmingly amazing. Moved to tears, I was afraid

to look at Paige until she said, "This may sound weird, but I feel comforted that the dogs have not forgotten Christina." No, it was not weird. Paige and I had just witnessed the life affirming miracle of memory. Just as Paige will not forget Christina's smile, Scout and Remy had not forgotten her scent. Remy and Scout's scent memories brought Paige back for one happy moment. And for that I am grateful and utterly awe struck [Hall, 2012].

Below is a note from Paige, Christina's mother:

As part of my grieving and healing, awhile back I reached out on Facebook to this person, Jennifer, part of a K9 Unit who has 2 very sweet dogs, Remy and Scout. They were the dogs that tried to rescue Christina. I wanted to thank her for trying so hard to save my baby. I was so happy when Jennifer offered for me and my girls to meet the dogs again. We met at a park and immediately both dogs went after Alix who was in her car seat wrapped in an old blanket of Christina's. The dogs remembered Christina's scent! Almost a year ago! They were trying to rescue Christina! My God, it was heartwarming. I guess you just don't realize stuff. I never even took the time to think that I wasn't the only person affected by the loss of my sweet baby girl! Not only me and my family but the people who tried to help find her and even the dogs! There are so many good people out there that just want to help and that truly do care it just amazes me. I am so grateful that I got to sit down and talk face to face with Jennifer Jordan Hall and the dogs to say thank you! I wish I could meet face to face with everyone that day and tell them all how grateful I am that they tried the best they could to save my baby! And I know Christina is safe now and that she is happy where she is. If she could be here today she would tell every one of you, "thank you so much for taking care of my mommy!"

Paige

This is obviously an incredible story, but it was one that Hall wasn't sure she should share on the blog. But with Paige's permission, she decided to share it, and it was an excellent decision. The story is dramatic, and it takes us behind the scenes. We also see the long-term impact of the work her organization is doing: it's not just about finding people, but about the hope and comfort these efforts can bring to families, even when their loved ones don't come back to them. That's a success too.

Giving Your Supporters a Role in the Story

Plenty of research shows us that stories are a very powerful way to communicate, and yet research by M + R Strategic Services with many of its clients found that stories did a terrible job in fundraising appeals compared to the more straight-forward institutional approach of presenting a need and accomplishments. In fact, in some cases the institutional approach raised four times as much as the approach with the personal story.

So what was going on?

Steve Daigneault of M+R says it boils down to this: is the donor in the story or not? (personal communication, February 2013). Personal stories of one person's situation can be very good at explaining and educating, but that doesn't mean that they will compel readers to act. For the reader to act, he has to see himself as an essential part of the story, as if something won't happen unless he acts.

In other words, in stories that compel action, the donors can change the ending of the story with their actions.

During a conference session with Daigneault, Sue Citro of The Nature Conservancy shared how her organization has shifted its approach to storytelling to be more effective. She offered these four tips (Leroux Miller, 2012):

Details matter. Details make your story credible and surprising. They are what catch people's attention.

Use the right *we*. When you use *we* or *us*, you should be referring to your organization and your supporters jointly.

Create a donor identity. Donors need to know their place in the story. Citro suggests that you frame giving as a chance "to be that special kind of person."

Make the consequences clear. Present giving as a choice that has consequences. Donors have a choice to join in as a hero—or not.

Telling a Posthole Story

What ruins many a good story about a nonprofit client, volunteer, or donor is the broad brush. It produces profiles that are way too shallow and wide. You try to cover too much about the person in too little space, and the reader ends up with an overview of this amazing individual, instead of a compelling story she can't forget.

Here's my best tip for telling a story about a single person: put down your broad brush and pick up your posthole digger.

For those of you unfamiliar with this tool, posthole diggers dig a deep but narrow hole that a fence post can sink down into. You want to do the same thing with your profile. Pick a fairly narrow aspect of this person's personality or experience, and go deep into that one aspect of the person's story.

Here are some examples, taking some typical broad brushes we see in nonprofit profiles and turning them into postholes.

Broad brush. Talking about a volunteer's family tree: for example, "Mary has been married for 36 years to Phil, and they have 4 children, and 15 grandchildren."

Posthole. Ask Mary which one member of her family most shares her passion for your cause. Explore that single relationship in your article.

Broad brush. Talking about a donor's educational background: for example, "Frank graduated from high school in Missouri, but went to college in Pennsylvania, where he received his BS in biology. He then traveled back across the country to California to work on a master's [blah blah blah]."

Posthole. Ask Frank what kind of degree he would like to get today if he went back to college. Or ask him what memory from his college days relates to his donations to your cause today.

Broad brush. Throwing in details without helping the reader to see why they matter: for example, "In her spare time, Jenny enjoys running and playing guitar."

Posthole. Pick one of those hobbies, and figure out a way to relate it to Jenny's love of the cause. Has Jenny ever run a race for charity, and how did that go? If she was going to write a song about her experience with your nonprofit, what kind of song would it be?

When you are interviewing your profile subjects, don't be afraid to go a little off track with your standard list of questions. That's how you get to the best posthole details, the ones that produce memorable, moving stories.

Stop, Think, and Discuss

Look at the last profile you wrote. How could you change that article using the posthole approach?

Dressing Up Your Dogs

You are trying really hard to focus your communications on what your participants and supporters want—to make your communications more about them, what they want to read, how they can get involved, and the good work their support has made possible.

But not everyone in your organization really understands what you are trying to do. Program staff and management expect you to write about certain events and activities because those things are important internally. Yet you know that people outside the organization will likely be bored by or, worse, annoyed by those stories.

What do you do?

You may be able to convince managers and staff that an event really is just something to celebrate internally and suggest some ways to do that, perhaps cake at lunch and a happy hour. But sometimes that just won't be enough, and you'll need to include the story, however much of a dog it is, in your communications plans.

Here are some of the stories that are most likely to be boring to outsiders, followed by some tips on how to talk about them—if you must.

- Your boss or your organization receives an award.

- The organization gets a new grant.

- The organization has redesigned its website or logo.

- The organization has released its annual report.

- The organization has added up the results of its recent fundraising campaign.

- The organization has established a new partnership.

- People from the organization attended some training.

- The organization has hired some new staff.

- Your organization is celebrating an anniversary.

It's not that these things aren't important or aren't worth celebrating, it's just a matter of whom they are important to. In all of these cases, you have to ask yourself, so what and who cares?

If you really do need to present boring stories in your newsletter or on social media, try to come up with some angles that make them more about your participants or supporters and less about your staff and board.

Try the posthole digger approach. Instead of talking about the website redesign, pick one new thing that supporters can do on the redesigned website and focus on that, mentioning later in the article that the feature is part of a larger overhaul of the site. Instead of summarizing the annual report, pick one achievement from it and lead with that.

Tell the story from someone else's perspective. Instead of talking about a new grant or a fundraising campaign results, talk about a person whose problem will be solved when the nonprofit implements the new program that the funding supports. To mark the nonprofit's anniversary, introduce readers to people who were there at the beginning and who are still involved. Or go back and interview all the past board presidents on their perspectives and then talk about the trends you observed in what they told you. When the nonprofit has a new partner, ask whom the new partnership really benefits. If it's just the organizations that benefit, skip the story.

If it's a group of people outside the organizations, talk about how their experience will be different because of the partnership.

Incorporate internal news as a factoid in a piece about something else. Instead of doing a whole story on an award your nonprofit received for one of its programs, start referring to the organization's "award-winning program" in other stories you write.

Lead with the future. Instead of talking about a training you attended, talk about how you intend to implement what you have learned in the coming weeks and months. Instead of just introducing a new staff person or board member, focus on the new or expanded services the nonprofit can offer as a result or on how this person's approach will be different from what is currently done.

Tie it to something bigger. This is what most successful anniversary celebrations do. So instead of just saying, "Woo Hoo, we are fifty years old!," you can create a special event or campaign that uses the number fifty in a special way (fifty donors or fifty dollars or fifty days).

Stop, Think, and Discuss

What potential dogs do you have on your editorial calendar now? If you can't get rid of them, can you use some of these tips to dress them up?

Writing the Headline First

Sometimes it's easier to write the headline first, and since that's the only part of the content that many people will actually read, it's not a bad idea to focus your energy there.

To get inspired to write a relevant, eye-catching headline, look at current headlines and magazine covers, especially in consumer publications. Play this game: pick a headline and swap out a word or two to make the headline about your organization.

I did this in a recent webinar, and participants turned tabloid headlines into ones they could use in their own newsletters. In *Cosmopolitan*, we found

"A Crazy-Easy Way to Stretch Your Summer Wardrobe," which Janice Selden, of Lending Hands of Michigan, suggested could be turned into "A Crazy Easy Way to Get Equipment Donations" for her medical equipment lending program. "Four Signs Your Boss Hates You," in *Men's Health*, became "Four Signs Your Child Needs Play Therapy" for Stacy Hawthorne of the Center for Children and Families, and "Four Signs Your Loved One May Benefit from Hospice Care" for Leslie Streeter of the Chaplaincy.

Here are twenty-five easy, fill-in-the-blank headlines for you:

[Number of] Miracles You've Created for _____

How Your Support Changed _____ into _____

Why We Can't _____ Without You

[Number of] Little _____ That Will _____

If I'd Only Known: Lessons from _____

Why You Should Talk About _____ with _____

How Many of These Early Warning Signs of _____ Do You Recognize?

A Simple Trick for _____

[Number of] Myths that _____ Believe

Surprising Ways to _____

Are Your _____ Dangerous? [Safe, Reliable, and so forth]

How to _____ When You Really Want to _____

What _____ Really Want to Hear from _____

[Number of] Fun Questions about _____

What's Next for _____

[Number of] Things to Do When _____

How to Find _____

How to Stop _____

Avoid the Biggest _____

Do You Have the "_____" Gene?

Small _____ with Big _____

Behind the Scenes with _____

The Best _____ to End _____

[Number of] Hottest _____ of _____

How Many of These Early Warning Signs of _____ Do You Recognize?

During the webinar, Walter Beck, of the Curtis Institute of Music, turned that last one into, "How Many of These Early Warning Signs of Opera Fanaticism Do You Recognize?"

Stop, Think, and Discuss

Fill in the blanks is a fun and useful exercise for staff meetings. Pick a handful of the examples in my list and see how many different headlines you can come up for your editorial calendar.

Why It Matters: Don't Struggle, Do What Works

Watch what your participants, supporters, and influencers respond well to, and give them more of it. Until you know what works best for you, or when you get stuck, come back to this chapter. Start with the kind of content described here. These ideas work for thousands of nonprofits every day and will work wonders for you too.

Chapter Fourteen
Foraging and Filtering
Curating Content Created by Others

> **This chapter is about . . .**
> - Finding good content created by others and sharing it with your participants and supporters
> - Learning how to add value to what others create
> - Using content created by your community members

Fresh mountain stream water, wild berries, fresh caught fish . . . enjoying the bounties that the ecosystems you hike through provide to travelers is one of the joys of backpacking. As a nonprofit, your organization lives in a rich ecosystem too, full of other groups that do the same kind of work it does or work within the same professional or geographical communities. Why not acknowledge that and enjoy it?

Unfortunately, many nonprofits see this idea as anathema.

When I sat in a room full of public relations officers for colleges and universities and suggested that, in certain situations, they might want to let their students know about events happening on a rival campus across town, they all looked at me like I was a complete idiot.

When I suggested to a Girl Scout troop leader that she might want to mention other leadership and community service activities targeting school-age girls in their city on the troop's Facebook Page, there was an uncomfortable silence on the phone, followed by throat clearing and a quick change of subject.

Why on earth, these people were thinking, would a nonprofit want to promote what another nonprofit—one competing for participants and funding—is doing? Why would we ever want to "send our people" elsewhere, is how others have phrased it.

Here's why: because people will come to know and love you as a trusted source who understands them and their needs and who puts them first, rather than as a self-absorbed and selfish organization living in some imaginary bubble world where you are the only nonprofit working in your field and the only one talking to "your people."

Reasons to Shine a Light on the Good Work of Others

Let me tell you a little story. My husband and I had been looking forward to going to one of our favorite Italian restaurants for one of our rare "date nights." When we got there, we saw a few people inside but the lights were off. It turned out that the restaurant had lost power about an hour earlier. The owners had no idea when it would come back on, and they were letting people finish but not seating anyone new.

They had three choices. First they could send us away into the night, with nothing more than an apology. But they knew we were hungry, so that wouldn't really be thinking about us, their customers.

Second, they could have referred us to another restaurant that wasn't a direct competitor—a Mexican place, for example. That would have fed us, but we really wanted Italian, which they knew we were looking forward to.

So the owners went with the third choice and recommended their favorite Italian restaurant (after their own of course), only about ten minutes away. They even called ahead for us, effectively transferring our reservation to their competition.

And we love them for it!

They salvaged our evening, and we were introduced to a new place. But the fact is we still like the first place a lot better and will return, not just for the food but for the atmosphere and the service. Had the owners turned us away entirely or sent us someplace terrible, we probably would have thought a little less highly of them. But they proved they knew what we needed and delivered.

This idea of knowing your participants, supporters, and influencers so well that you are able to sift through all the information, resources, and events out there produced by other nonprofits (and businesses for that matter), and recommend the best of it to them is, I believe, an essential part of your role as a professional marketer today. When you do that sorting, sifting, and sharing, it's called *curating content*.

When you do it well, people love you for it, because you save them time and effort. You lead them places they would have never gone themselves, and they are grateful for the passport.

It also subtly lets people know that you are so confident in your own work and in your position in your field or community, that you have no qualms about highlighting the good work of others, just as the restaurant owners did. In the course of sorting through and recommending resources, you also gain several other benefits:

- You keep up to date yourself on what's out there.

- You can easily spot gaps that you can fill.

- You can see where others are filling niches, so you don't have to do so yourself.

Of course, you don't want to spend all your time sending your supporters elsewhere. But measured doses of promoting other people's stuff are very, very good for you.

Elizabeth Benson, vice president for communications and marketing for the Greater Cincinnati Foundation (GCF), uses her organization's social media networks to highlight the work of other organizations, whether they have a connection to GCF or not. She and her staff search both social and traditional media for anything they think will interest their readers, and they welcome suggestions from other GCF staff and other nonprofits for news items or other content that might be of interest. They also encourage their followers to follow nonprofits they mention on Twitter as well (personal communication, February 2013).

"We have benefited by highlighting the work of other organizations through our social media strategy. It supports our brand equities by being a hub of all things charitable, being a tenacious community leader, and keeping donors in touch with their generosity," says Benson. "We view our Facebook presence in particular as a tool to connect with nonprofits and others in Greater Cincinnati, as well as our colleagues at other community foundations."

Stop, Think, and Discuss

Who in your field is likely to have good content that you could share with your participants or supporters? Make a list of sources to follow.

Finding Content to Curate

So where do you look for content to curate? If you are already in the habit of "listening" to social media via keyword searches or following the top organizations and thinkers in your field, odds are that you are coming across plenty of good content to share.

We do a lot of curating at Nonprofit Marketing Guide, so I thought I'd give you a backstage glimpse at how we curate content. It's not all that glamorous or sophisticated, but it works for us. The core of the strategy consists of three parts: following, tagging, and intent.

Tech Tools for Curating Content

Curating is much easier if you let technology help you. See chapter 16 for additional information on the tools mentioned in this chapter and on other technology that will help you implement your content marketing strategy.

Following

At the core of my strategy is following smart people and letting them make the first cut. Curating is all about sifting or filtering, and there's no reason why you can't use other smart people to help you do it! I follow people with a variety of specialties that all circle back around to nonprofit marketing somehow. These people sift through all the stuff they see on their issues, and share the best via their own blogs, social media, e-newsletters, and the like. I watch what they say, make my own cut on that information, and decide what to share through my own communications channels.

I follow those smart people in a few key ways:

I use a personal Alltop page to follow bloggers. You'll find people who specialize in nonprofit communications, fundraising, technology, social media, corporate marketing, creativity, and a few more random topics on my custom Alltop page. It's public, so you can use mine or, better yet, create your own. I love the way Alltop gives me the five most recent blog titles from all the people I follow, all on one page. It's easy to see at a glance not only what particular individuals are writing about but also the trends in what the broader community that I follow is writing about. I also love that I can mouse over a headline and get the first paragraph or so of the post, so I can see if it's worth clicking to read the whole thing. I do wish there was a way to import other RSS feeds into Alltop, as there are some bloggers I want to follow who aren't in the Alltop database. So I make sure I follow them in other ways—on Twitter, for example.

I keep a Must-Read List on Twitter. I've created lots of Twitter lists, including a private Must-Read List that I look at regularly via a HootSuite tab. I follow thousands of people but obviously can't read all their tweets, so I use lists to categorize these people in different ways: some by topic, some by my relationship with them. One of those relationships involves how much I trust them to be a good curator. While that particular list is private, as it contains some people I follow for personal reasons, it does contain a lot of the same people who are on my Alltop page, along with some bloggers who aren't on Alltop.

I participate in a few social media groups. I'm a member of a few groups on Facebook and LinkedIn that I find helpful, because again, smart people congregate there, answer each other's questions, and share good stuff.

Tagging

Following great people helps me find the good stuff. But I need a way to save and identify what I want to pass on to others. I also get information from other sources too, including my email inbox and random web surfing. I keep track of everything I want to keep for later curation in a couple of different ways that revolve around tagging. (I also curate instantly by retweeting and sharing on Facebook—I use tagging for the longer content.)

I use both Diigo and Evernote to save and tag content. I use Diigo primarily for my "public" bookmarks and Evernote primarily for my "private" bookmarks. In other words, when I am collecting a list of examples or additional resources that I will want to make available during a webinar, I use a tag to create that list of links in Diigo. When I am saving content that I might want to quote in a blog post or a book or incorporate into a training, I tend to save it in an Evernote notebook.

I've tried to get more consistent over time about the tags I use in both systems, but that's still definitely a work in progress. I also use some of the same tags in my Gmail account (where they are called *labels*), although I'm trying to get better about moving the stuff I really want to keep into Evernote (you can email content into an Evernote notebook directly, which is nice).

I tag everything I save with at least one topic tag (for example, "Facebook" or "fundraising"), but whenever possible, I also include a tag that reminds me of what I intend to use that content for, such as the Nonprofit Marketing Guide's *Mixed Links* roundup of blog posts—which brings me to the third part of my approach.

Intent

I find it very helpful to categorize content and ideas by how I intend to use them—or at least how I think I'll use them the first time. For me, these categories are the primary communications channels where I use longer content (email newsletter, blog, and website), types of training content (webinars, workshops, and e-books), and paperback book chapters. I've found that if I don't tag the content I save by intent that I often don't get back to it, or if I do, I don't remember exactly how I intended to use that particular piece. And that means it just sits there, saved but not really curated as content out to the Nonprofit Marketing Guide community.

Additional Tools

You may have noticed that I haven't talked about keyword searches, which is another common strategy for finding content to curate. That's because I usually get plenty of content from what I am already doing. But I do occasionally check out some custom Twitter searches on keyword phrases that I have set up in Hoot-Suite. That sometimes leads to new voices that I (and the smarties I normally rely on) would have otherwise missed.

Social media dashboards are another good tool. A dashboard is a visual way to bring lots of data together easily and automatically into an at-a-glance overview. Nonprofits can use dashboards for all sorts of purposes, including content curation. You could spend all day logging into and searching Twitter and Facebook and Google to see what's happening, but why not have all of that data sent to you automatically instead? Tools like Netvibes let you search once and then pull the RSS feed for that search into your dashboard. If you are interested in pulling content from Twitter in particular, setting up custom searches in a tool like HootSuite can also work well.

Several new tools, like Scoop.it, are coming along to help content curators even more. You pick the topic you want to curate, and these services search the web for you. You then sift through what's been suggested and post what you like to your web page to share with others.

Sharing Curated Content

You've found a bunch of great stuff. Now what do you do with it, and how do you share it?

Your first decision concerns the extent to which you want to add value to what you've found. Simply culling the best stuff from all the noise out there is a service in and of itself, and you can share your favorite links from the past week or two in a roundup post, like my *Mixed Links* posts.

But you can also add value to that collection of information in a few ways that make it even more helpful.

- Group links into categories that make sense for your supporters or participants. You might group links by topic or by experience level, for example.

- Add a little content of your own to connect the pieces you are curating so they form a more complete picture.

- Put the content in order of importance, or in a step 1, step 2, step 3 sequence so people know where to start.

Stop, Think, and Discuss
How could you go about sharing your curated content in a way that adds value to it?

Always Give Credit—You're a Curator, Not a Thief!

As you curate content, remember to always give credit to your sources. Link back to the original location where you found the information whenever possible. When it's not possible, include the attribution in your text.

It's also best to follow what are called *fair use* guidelines. For example, to be consistent with fair use, it's much better to quote a few lines or to summarize a few points in your own words and to link back to the full article than it is to reprint a full article on your own website.

If you reprint large sections or an entire article without permission, that's called *scraping* content, and you won't make any friends doing it. In many cases, you'll be violating copyright laws. When you do want to reprint a large section or the key part of something, a table or graphic, or the whole piece, always ask the author for permission. Some authors, photographers, and illustrators state very clearly what the guidelines are for using their work. If you follow the stated rules, such as complying with a particular Creative Commons license the author is using, you can use that content without directly contacting the author.

Using Conversation as the Content, Both Created and Curated

The conversations that nonprofits have with supporters, participants, and influencers are valuable in and of themselves, but they can also be used to generate original content too.

How do you create and curate conversations online and in print? It's not that different from managing face-to-face communications. You ask questions. You make a statement with a blank at the end and let your Facebook fans complete the sentence. You post with personality and express opinions that others can react to. Be a part of conversations started by others by chiming in and connecting conversations together.

Next, think about ways to take what you've heard in those conversations and turn it into new content for your website, blog, or newsletters. Pull out a few trends you see, or summarize the two sides of an argument that developed. Review conversations for questions that weren't really answered but that you could answer with a little work. Compile resources that others have mentioned into a list.

Twitter chats are a great way to turn social media conversation into content. You pick a topic and publicize that the discussion will take place live on Twitter at a certain time and with a certain hashtag. The conversation takes place, and some of it will be useful and some of it won't (it's not uncommon for some people to go off on tangents but to keep using the original hashtag).

After the chat is over, go through and pull out the best tweets from the conversation. Tools like Storify.com can help with this. You can include some screen captures of the tweets or quote the text itself in the narrative you write up to summarize the conversation.

Curating User-Generated Content

Nonprofits are using a variety of ways to collect content from their participants and supporters and then turn that into material they can use in different ways. In other words, you can actively encourage your participants or supporters to submit stories or articles to you, and then you can edit these submissions into something valuable for others.

Running Contests

The San Diego Zoo has run several contests using social media, including contests associated with the China Celebration event at its Nighttime Zoo in the summer of 2012 (San Diego Zoo, n.d.). The zoo ran concurrent Pinterest, Foursquare, and Instagram contests during the event to build excitement and awareness about the celebration. The contest concepts were simple, and the contests were easy to enter.

For the Pinterest contest, Pin for Pandas, Pinterest users just had to create a board named "Pin for Pandas" and then pin their favorite panda pictures to that board. When they were finished finding the photos, they sent the zoo a link to their board. The top three winners got a panda gift, and the grand prize winner received a backstage pass to meet the zoo's pandas close up.

The Instagram contest asked users to take a picture at the China Celebration and then post it along with two specific hashtags. If a user's Instagram profile was set to public, she was automatically entered. The zoo posted the weekly winners to its website, and a grand prize winner won backstage passes.

The Foursquare contest used Foursquare's built-in "mayor" feature, asking people to use Foursquare to check in at the zoo's panda-themed gift shop. The person who was mayor of the panda store at the end of the celebration was given a giant stuffed panda.

Keep in mind that social networks, especially Facebook, and some states have very stringent rules about the way contests must be conducted and about prize winnings.

Compiling Facebook Comments

For a fall fundraising campaign running from October through December, Children of the Nations (COTN) wanted to pair several asks meant to engage with the ongoing campaign ask for money (Leroux Miller, 2012).

The campaign was about keeping the children COTN serves, who are orphaned or destitute, in school. Donors would be asked to help with food, clean water, mosquito nets, and other items that help keep children healthy and therefore ready and able to learn. One idea I discussed with COTN was using Facebook to collect words of encouragement about staying in school from US donors and then sharing those words with COTN in-country staff to pass on to the children. It's important to COTN that donors see its work with these children as long term, and not just as crisis relief, thus the emphasis on education.

We talked about this kind of ask specifically because it was something that US donors could easily relate to, even if they had never been to the African or Caribbean countries where COTN works. While the reasons for failing to attend school in those countries (for example, malaria) may be different from the reasons for not attending school in the United States (for example, low self-esteem), US donors can still relate to the idea that kids can't get an education unless they are actually in school day in and day out.

COTN staff ran with the idea, and the results were wonderful.

On October 1, they posted the campaign launch on Facebook and asked supporters to "leave a comment encouraging a child to stay in school." Many of the comments left on the page were directed to specific sponsored children by name, while others were more general words of encouragement. To see the post, you can visit COTN's Facebook timeline at Facebook.com/Children.of.the.Nations. On the same day, COTN also sent out an email that said, "Let's overwhelm these kids with messages of encouragement and love to kick off this campaign." In addition to driving supporters to the Facebook page to post a comment, the email also provided a special email address as a participation option for those without Facebook accounts.

Over the next several days, encouraging words came pouring in on Facebook and via email. Staff at COTN headquarters in Washington emailed the responses to the in-country staff, who shared the supporters' words with the children in their care in a number of different ways.

In Uganda, Hadrine printed out the comments and read them out loud to the students. In Malawi, Chikondi printed the messages with blank space underneath where the students wrote replies. In the Dominican Republic, Reymon posted the comments outside each of COTN's schools. Older students read the comments to those who couldn't read yet.

On October 11, COTN reported all of this back to its supporters with a blog post full of pictures and stories, which was also shared on Facebook as well as through another email encouraging people to read the blog post.

Did this work? You bet.

Cassia Burke, a staff writer for COTN, shared these open and click-through rates for the original email with me: the open rate was 16.1 percent (compared to an average rate of 13.7 percent in the previous quarter), and the click-through rate was 3.0 percent (compared to an average rate of 1.33 percent previously).

On Facebook, COTN averaged 2.1 comments and 1.7 shares per post earlier in 2012. The original Facebook post where people could share words of encouragement was the single most shared update on COTN's page in 2012. It was also the third most commented-on post (after a photo album about the Run for Africa 5K and a post asking, "If you could travel to one country for free, right now, where would you go?").

While those other two posts are certainly related to COTN's work (the 5K was a fundraiser and COTN encourages country visits), this campaign post was the first post specifically about the children served to do so well.

Stop, Think, and Discuss

How might you collect content from your community and turn it into something new that you can share with others?

Lessons on Curating User-Generated Content

Give people things to do that are both easy and meaningful. For example, posting words of encouragement on Facebook is easy, and because you can envision sharing the words with a child, even if just one in your mind's eye, it's meaningful.

Make the ask something they can relate to in their own experiences. Each of us can recall words of encouragement we heard while in school—or remember the pain of not being encouraged. So it's easy for supporters to see themselves in this story.

Get your ducks in a row. COTN thought through the process of getting the words of encouragement to the in-country staff and then having those staff get stories and photos back to the US communications staff to show how they had shared the comments with the children and how the children had reacted. That kind of coordination and internal communication doesn't happen by accident.

Close the loop by sharing results. The blog post provided a huge emotional payoff to anyone who left a comment—and even to those who didn't! The children's responses are irresistible. COTN could just have said, "Trust us, we delivered your messages, and it was great." But instead, COTN proved it, providing a subtle reminder that it is trustworthy and dependable. If the organization goes through this level of effort to deliver words of encouragement, you can only imagine how responsible it must be about delivering food and other vital supplies to the children.

Get it done, fast. The messages were asked for, delivered thousands of miles away, and responded to on the blog in under two weeks.

Integrate your communications channels. COTN made this happen with a combination of email and Facebook communications with supporters, which the in-country staff then took offline to share with the children.

Why It Matters: They Are Smarter Than You Are

Curating content helps you save time, lets you share your perspective on what other voices are saying, and can position you as both a generous and thoughtful source of really good information. There are many interesting, engaging people in your field and thus a great deal of expertise that you are learning from, and your community can learn from these people too.

Chapter Fifteen
The Best Trail Mix Recipe Ever
Adding Metaphors and Humor to Your Communications

This chapter is about . . .

- Using metaphors to connect your new ideas with familiar concepts people already understand

- Adding humor to your content repertoire

After hours of hard hiking, there's nothing better than throwing a handful of trail mix into your mouth and tasting the delectable combination of the sweet chocolate and salty nuts. More than a few times after reading something a nonprofit has written on its website or an in a newsletter, I've thought, "Wow, this is good, really good." It's that awesome trail mix fix.

When I look more closely, I often find I feel that way because the writer has used one of two techniques: metaphors or humor. They both take more brain power and more trial and error—in other words, more work—than other kinds of content, but when you get them right, the payoff is huge. That's why I think of them as the secret weapons of nonprofit content.

Metaphors help you explain complex issues more clearly. If one of the goals of your content strategy is to educate, you need to put metaphors to work for you. Humor is one of the very best ways to connect on a personal, human level. It's not always easy, but when it works, there is nothing better.

Why Nonprofits Need Metaphors

Much of the work nonprofits do is either so familiar that it's easily overlooked or so technical that it's hard to understand. Nonprofit staff also frequently suffer from the "curse of knowledge"—because they know so much about their fields, they lose the ability to speak about that work in clear, simple terms.

When we use metaphors, we say that some new idea or approach is very similar to something else that people already understand. We help people to see our nonprofit from a fresh new perspective. Or we take a complicated or foreign idea and make it feel simple and familiar.

Nonprofit communicators can use metaphors in several ways.

Clarifying Your Niche

Lillian's List of North Carolina, a political action committee that raises money for progressive women candidates, uses "Feel the Power of the Purse" as a tagline, accompanied by an image of a fashionably dressed woman with a big purse. This organization also uses actual purses like the one in the image at fundraising events. This imagery nicely ties together ideas about today's women, money, and political power.

Using a metaphor as a tagline is another good way to clarify your niche.

- "Because the earth needs a good lawyer" (Earthjustice).
- "Nothing stops a bullet like a job" (Homeboy Industries).
- "Open hearts. Open minds. Open doors." (United Methodist Church).

These three winners of the 2009 Nonprofit Tagline Awards all have one thing in common: they skillfully use metaphors to convey very quickly what the organization is all about.

Making the Technical Feel More Touchy

Metaphors can also turn what might normally be perceived as something cold, scientific, or technical into something that's more touchy-feely, which can be very helpful when communicating with individual supporters.

The Nature Conservancy refers to a coral restoration project at the Mote Marine Laboratory as "The Coral Nursery." The word *nursery* conjures up images of babies that need tender care and attention, which is probably not how most people would describe rough coral on the bottom of the ocean. It's a simple metaphor that instantly changes the way we think about coral.

Overcoming Resistance

If you suspect some reluctance on the part of potential supporters to follow through on your nonprofit's calls to action, metaphors can help you overcome that resistance. Aid organizations often have trouble raising funds for projects on foreign soil because they are out of sight and thus out of mind or because donors don't feel that the plight of people in other nations is their responsibility. Beyond Borders tried to overcome that resistance with a series of animated images on its homepage. These images used travel metaphors of airplane flights and border crossings to help supporters understand why they should help Haiti.

Bringing Data to Life

Health and nutrition experts know that a diet of fresh foods—vegetables, fruit, meat, and dairy products—can help prevent many diseases and obesity. Yet the residents of large sections of many major cities don't live anywhere near a grocery store and are often forced to rely on processed foods from convenience stores and fast food for most meals.

But quoting statistics about the number of people who live a certain distance from a grocery store doesn't convey the significance of the problem. Neither do maps alone. The metaphor *food desert*, however, does. The depth of this metaphor allows advocates for better access to healthy food to talk also about thirst, starving, shifting sands, an oasis, and more.

Metaphors can also be used as presentation themes, provocative headlines and email subject lines, and more.

Replacing Worn-Out Metaphors

When you want metaphors that call up images of making connections but you want to avoid *building bridges*, you could try some of these parenting and family metaphors:

- Family meeting
- Family ties
- Family dinner
- Reconciliation
- Reunion
- Dealing with sibling rivalries
- Blending stepfamilies
- Looking into each other's eyes

When you want metaphors that suggest giving aid but you don't want to use *helping hands*, you could start with some of these travel metaphors:

- Concierge
- Flight attendant
- Bus stopping to pick people up
- Making an airplane connection
- Tow truck
- Air bag
- Roadside assistance
- Changing a flat tire
- Paving a road
- Coast Guard rescue helicopter

Coming Up with the Right Metaphor for Your Organization

Here's a five-step process for coming up with the right metaphor.

Step 1: relax! Thinking metaphorically is a creative process that's hard to force. Give yourself some time and space to think.

Step 2: understand your goal. What does the metaphor need to accomplish?

Step 3: review the list of metaphors and see what pops. Look at the list of twenty-five metaphors in the following section and see if anything jumps out at you. If not, randomly select a category and start working through the questions in step 4.

Step 4: explore your metaphor. Take a few minutes to brainstorm as many elements of your metaphor as you can. Use these questions to help you think through the possibilities for the activity or concept you want to describe.

Who does this? Who else is involved?

What do people physically do?

What things or tools do they use?

What categories are used?

What decisions do they make?

What mistakes are common?

How do they learn?

What's the timing?

What are the stages or steps in the process?

Where does it happen?

What defines success?

What defines disaster?

What are the special occasions or milestones?

What are the levels of mastery?

Who are the celebrities?

In what movies, books, or stories is this featured?

With this long list of metaphorical elements in hand, think of ways in which each one is similar to the various aspects of the programs or services you are trying to explain (for example, areas without grocery stores are food deserts and growing coral on the ocean floor is a coral nursery). Pick a handful of the best matches, and start to build your explanation or story around them.

Step 5: base your choice on your audience's experiences. As with any communications choice, your audience should be the ultimate decision maker on whether something works or not. How well will the members of your audience relate to your metaphor given their professional and personal experiences? For example, a sixty-year-old and a twenty-five-year-old would draft very different lists of iconic movies and television programs. People who have never worked in a cubicle won't understand office life metaphors in the same way as those who have.

> ## Stop, Think, and Discuss
>
> Give it a try! What's the first metaphor for your work that comes to mind? Try to flesh it out using the questions in step 4.

Twenty-Five Metaphors for Your Nonprofit

Here are twenty-five metaphors that I think can work well in the nonprofit world. This is by no means a comprehensive list, but it's long enough to get you thinking more creatively.

The metaphors are grouped into two categories: *deep metaphors* (a category based on research explained in *Marketing Metaphoria: What Deep Metaphors Reveal About the Minds of Consumers*, by Gerald Zaltman and Lindsay Zaltman, 2008) and *surface metaphors*. Deep metaphors invoke large, complex themes that work at the subconscious level. People often can't articulate these feelings directly, even though the feelings drive their decision making. Surface metaphors are those found throughout everyday language and are therefore much more easily recognized and understood.

When trying to come up with a metaphor for your work, it's often helpful to pick one deep metaphor and then explore several surface metaphors to see which ones will work within the deep metaphor (for example, you might explore how surface metaphors like weather, exercise and fitness, or fashion could be used to elaborate on the deep metaphor of balance).

Next to each metaphor, you'll find a handful of elements related to it to get you started. Remember to use the questions in step 4 to fully explore each metaphor's potential.

Deep Metaphors

Balance: equilibrium, justice, interplay

Transformation: change in substance, circumstance

Journey: meeting of past, present, future

Container: inclusion, exclusion, boundaries

Connection: relating to self and others

Resource: acquisitions and their consequences

Control: mastery, vulnerability, well-being

Surface Metaphors

Parenting: growth spurt, stage, giving birth, pregnancy, nursery, family dinner, sibling rivalry, *Brady Bunch*, discipline, adoption, empty nest, sleepless nights, divorce, packing school lunches

Travel: planes, trains, cars, delays, road trip, adventure, exploration, tickets, routes, missed flight, concierge, map, mileage, speed, tourists, airport screening, motions sickness, souvenir

Gardens, forests, and other landscapes: growth, blooms, weeds, mulch, annuals, perennials, insects, fertilizer, harvest, planting, plow, grasslands, ecosystems, mountain peaks, horizon

Sports: teams, teaming up, scoring, winning, losing, competition, practice, game face, slam dunk, heavy hitting, goal, touchdown, three strikes, penalty, take aim, best shot, marathon, sore loser

Cooking, food and beverages: recipe, cookbook, ingredients, shopping list, bar tab, chef, chopping block, culinary school, winemaking, baking, mixed drinks, burning, boiling, raw

Arts and crafts: cutting, pasting, scrapbooking, paint, color palette, texture, gallery, show, brushes, sketching, inspiration, pattern, decorating, stringing beads, finger painting, frames

Shopping: sale, bargain, price, markdown, closeout, grocery list, shopping cart, aisle, cash register, lines, secret shoppers, credit, returns, eBay, QVC, yard sale, convenience store, coupons

Banking and economics: savings, spending, budget, balance sheet, investing, overdraft, insurance, refinance, equity, sell off, fees, loans, debit card, keep the change, wealth, deposit, withdrawal

Relationships and romance: love affair, breakup, courtship, first date, reunion, anniversary, Valentine's Day, dating, marriage counseling, living together, wedding, stepparents, just friends

Science and technology: formulas, white coats, DNA, computers, wireless, programming, research, experiments, injection, immunity, data, inventions, space, labs, results, findings, cells, Bill Nye

Games: puzzle, chess board, video game, steps, solving, shell game, shuffle cards, house of cards, target, strategy, arcade, party games, players, family game night, bingo, prizes, Solitaire, patterns

Fashion: styles, trends, trendsetter, tight fit, sales, fitting room, designers, collections, catwalk, models, *Vogue*, makeup, body image, out of style, chic, shape, cut, craze, back in style

Television and movies: soap opera, blockbuster, sequel, Oscar, supporting cast, three-act play, drama, clues, black and white, reception, 3-D, *A Christmas Story*, *The Simpsons*, the big screen

Literature: fairy tale, Disney story, classics, Shakespeare, how the story unfolds, translation, mystery, autobiography, writer's retreat, hard cover, bookstore, library, better than the movie

Weather: clouds, lightning, taking cover, drought, forecasting, outlook, Katrina, soaking rains, sun shining through, storms, clear skies, temperature, floodgates, radar, TV weather forecaster, sunburn, frostbite

Superheroes: special powers, villain, X-ray vision, comic books, flying, virtue, cape, costume, idols, good versus evil, crime fighting, police dog, firefighter, save the day, daredevil, Captain _____, Doctor

_____

Faith and spirituality: revival, believe, pray, divine, worship, religion, values, soul, healing, practice, devotion, spirits, astrology, reincarnation, yoga, angels, Heaven, meditation, pagan gods, shaman, sins

Fitness, exercise, and dieting: weighing in, food diary, treadmill, pedometer, calories, sweat, personal trainer, food pyramid, 100-calorie packs, body mass index, scales, heart rate, binging, nutrition

Stop, Think, and Discuss

Which of the surface metaphors in this list could work for one of your programs or for your overall mission?

Twelve Worn-Out Metaphors Your Nonprofit Should Avoid

I'm *declaring war* on *building bridges* and *helping hands*!

While the twelve metaphors listed here may still work at some level because they are very familiar, I believe they have been used so many times and in so many different ways in the nonprofit world that they are effectively meaningless. If you are using them, it's time to get more creative and search for phrases that are both clear and truly meaningful for your supporters today.

Building bridges. This is probably the most common metaphor used by nonprofits to explain how they make connections between people or ideas. But it tells us nothing about the benefits of those connections or why nonprofits really need to make them.

Changing the world; changing lives. Change isn't always for the better. Every one of us could argue that we change someone else's life every day.

War on (fill in the blank). I don't think the military metaphors work all that well in the social service fields that most often use them. And with lagging public support for the real wars our nation is fighting, I don't think this metaphor conjures up the sense of common purpose and focus it once might have.

Making a difference. If every nonprofit on the block can use the same phrase, that's a sure sign that it won't help you stand out in your marketing and fundraising. Every nonprofit is trying to make a difference. While that idea is still relevant, this particular phrase isn't.

Helping hands. *Help* is just too generic. And much of the help that nonprofits provide isn't manual labor or even physically in person, which *hands* implies.

Cutting edge. This refers to the newest, leading research or thinking—the state of the art—but it's another worn-out cliché that says more about your lack of creativity than your approach to your work.

While I think these first six are the worst, I'd also avoid these six too:

- Strengthening community
- Creating hope
- Stand up for _____
- Brighter future
- Turning lives around
- The voice of _____

Using Humor in Nonprofit Communications

Humor is one of the fastest ways to connect with people on a human, emotional level, but many nonprofits are afraid to even give it a try. "The work we do is no laughing matter," they say. "What we do is very serious. We can't possibly make light of our work." So earnest. So sincere. So boring. And therefore so underfunded.

When I am waiting for a webinar that I am teaching to start, I'll often click over to the websites of the people who've connected early to get a better idea for who's on the line that day. That's how I ended up on the website of the Crisis Center, in Johnson County, Iowa. The Crisis Center helps people who are struggling with a range of desperate situations from hunger and thoughts of suicide to abuse and disasters. Not funny. At all.

Yet the first thing I saw on the center's website was a slider ad with a roll of toilet paper asking people to "TP the Crisis Center" for Halloween.

I can say with confidence that this is the only time I have laughed out loud while looking at a crisis center home page.

So I asked Beth Ritter Ruback, the center's communication and development director, to share the backstory with me (Leroux Miller, 2012).

One of the Crisis Center's programs is a food bank that serves over 4,000 people each month. Three-quarters of what the program distributes comes from grocery donations by Johnson County residents via food drives, individual

donations, overstock from grocers, and so on. The Crisis Center uses cash donations to purchase additional nutritionally valuable and diverse food for its clients.
But that means that other sought-after items, like toilet paper, are available only
when someone happens to donate them.

In 2010, a woman came into the Crisis Center and asked to speak to executive
director Becci Reedus about a donation. She was a former client who had visited
the food bank during a particularly difficult period in her life. She praised the
staff and volunteers who assisted her for their care and the dignity they afforded
to her when life was so hard. Fast forward and this woman was back on her feet.
She wanted to donate $1,000 to the food bank to help others—and she asked that
the money be used in part to buy toilet paper. The availability of that particular
item, one others might consider trivial, had made a huge difference to her when
she needed help.

This story touched Reedus deeply, so she suggested that the center start an
annual toilet paper drive, to call special attention to how important this item is
to people's dignity and yet how they didn't want to spend their food budget
on it. Reedus thought it made perfect sense to do it during the fall and to tie it
into the classic Halloween prank as a way to draw attention to the campaign.
"TP the Crisis Center" was born.

Ruback says the first drive, in October 2010, exceeded the center's wildest
expectations: "The response was incredible and last year, in our second year, we
had toilet paper stacked nearly to the ceiling of our storage area by the end of
the month. Simply bringing to the public's attention the need for toilet paper has
meant that for the past two years, we've always had it available when a client
requests it."

Can't you just hear the zero-fun worrywarts out there: "But what if someone
actually TP'ed the building? Then what? How awful would that be! We would
never risk something like that!"

So I asked Ruback, has anyone actually TP'ed the place?

She replied, "To be honest, we have never worried about someone actually
TP'ing the building! The community is such a huge part of our efforts and knows
how hard we work to meet need, so we haven't considered that someone would
waste the toilet paper. I really can't imagine it happening, but if it did, I'm sure

we would clean it up as quickly as possible and move on with our messaging that a simple roll of toilet paper can provide dignity for a family in need."

Sounds like a good crisis plan to me!

"TP the Crisis Center" has opened the door to other product-focused drives, says Ruback, because the community responded to the fun messaging, as opposed to messaging that "the sky is falling and it's your moral imperative to help." The center also asks people to participate in "Spread the Love," a peanut butter and jelly drive in February, and "Shower the Crisis Center," a baby products drive in April. The center is adding just one of these focused drives a year to make sure staff can manage the additional promotions required, but Ruback can envision a full twelve months of themed drives.

Ruback says, "Given that our agency has specialized in suicide prevention and intervention since its inception, we are well aware of the need for humor. Tongue in cheek has worked for us, but I think that's because we always stay within our mission and values."

Why Funny Works

Kerri Karvetski, owner of Company K Media, loves humor as a way for nonprofits to connect. "In addition to offering lots of benefits for our minds and bodies, like reducing pain and stress, and increasing relaxation, humor can really move the needle on nonprofit recruiting, advocacy and awareness initiatives, and in rare cases, fundraising too," says Karvetski.

So, why does humor work? Karvetski (2012) has identified six core reasons:

1. **It's powerful emotional engagement**. "Humor hits us somewhere deep inside," says Karvetski. Brain science tells us laughter and humor release endorphins and increase oxygen to the brain, giving us an opening for persuasive messaging. "Make someone laugh or smile and you immediately have their attention, which is a pretty hard thing to get these days," she says. Photo caption contests are a popular tool here.

2. **It breaks down walls; eases fear and tension**. Ever go toe to toe with a stubborn kid and reach that because-I-say-so moment? Make a joke (especially one at your own expense, not the kid's), and watch that

impasse melt away. How might this apply to nonprofit communications? "It gives people an easy out, or a pleasant path around your mutual obstacle—think taking action, donating, awareness, caring. Make 'em laugh, and they are more likely to get past that hump and meet you halfway," says Karvetski.

3. **It binds people together**. Laugh together and you create a positive, shared experience. "How many times have you had a conversation that went like this? Did you see that cartoon about the election? Yes, it was so funny! BOOM! Bond formed. That bond can be between you and your supporters," says Karvetski, who reminds us to never mock our supporters. Humiliate yourself instead.

4. **It's memorable**. Funny stands out and sticks with us. Recalling something humorous makes us feel good all over again.

5. **It offers freedom to say something you couldn't with a straight face**. This approach can be a bit harder to pull off, but it is the bread-and-butter of successful comedians like Stephen Colbert and of parody Twitter accounts such as @PaulRyanGosling, @DepressedDarth, @FakeAPStylebook, or @BronxZoosCobra. "In the nonprofit sphere, no one does this better than Left Action, which has built a one-million strong progressive activist empire on edgy, humorous campaigns. Left Action founder John Hlinko says, 'This approach is so much more effective it's CRAZY,'" reports Karvetski.

6. **Humor travels (dare we say it's viral?)**. Funny gets shared. Those joke emails have been, thankfully, replaced by shares on Facebook, Twitter, Google+, and Pinterest. We share funny, therefore we are funny.

Connecting with Humor

Nancy Schwartz, founder of GettingAttention.org, offers this six-step process for adding humor to your communications plan (Schwartz, 2012).

1. **Know what your organization and your base have in common, and play on that in your humor**. "That's the point of connection for all

messages, but especially for humor," says Schwartz. "The only way to find it is to know your audiences well." Humor based on common experience unites the group.

2. **Find a genuine, believable way to integrate humor into your content**. "If you're incorporating humor because you think it's the funniest thing in the world and bound to get laughs, but it has nothing to do with your core topic, then skip it," advises Schwartz. It will only distract your audience from what's really important in your outreach.

3. **Delivery is everything**. When you integrate humor into a video, e-newsletter, Facebook post, or conversation, it's crucial that you fine-tune delivery, from where the humor falls in the flow of messages to your tone and the pause before or after.

Schwartz loves the way the National Campaign to Prevent Teen Pregnancy uses humor in its outreach to teens on uncomfortable subjects where they may have little experience, like birth control. "The campaign leans heavily on humor in their print and video campaigns; and take a look at Itchy Situation, an old-style-cartoon video created to bust myths on how to know if your partner has a STD (sexually-transmitted disease)," says Schwartz. "The video uses humor to open the conversation on this squirm-inducing topic and warns 'even if you have special X-ray glasses or the observation skills of a ninja, you still can't tell if someone has an STD just by looking,'" says Schwartz.

4. **Test it first**. Take a look at comedy writers. They don't just toss a new joke out to a live audience. Instead, they try it out on colleagues and see how it rolls. If it flies, it's used. If it doesn't, it's trashed. Many, many more jokes are written than actually used on comedy programs. Although you don't have a team of humor writers to work with, you do have colleagues, families, and friends, says Schwartz. "Drip the joke or the humorous part of the post out via your organization's Facebook Page. That feedback will give you an immediate sense of whether your humor is going to generate laughs or fury."

5. **Keep it brief and use only periodically**. Humor is a less is more tactic. "The exception is when you are reaching out to a well-known and narrowly defined audience segment (or group) whom you are certain will respond positively to your humor. Then you can share laughs much more frequently," says Schwartz.

6. **Wrap it up while they're still laughing**. Don't push it. "Instead, pause, return to your more typical tone, although serious shouldn't mean deadly, and cycle in humor from time to time when the opportunity arises," says Schwartz.

Stop, Think, and Discuss

What ideas do you have for incorporating humor into your content strategy?

Which communications channel do you think would work best for adding humor? Or which segment of your community would enjoy humor the most?

Why It Matters: Creativity Pays Off with Greater Engagement

Using metaphors and humor in your communications takes much more thought and effort to pull off well than writing a straightforward description or update. But it could mean the difference between having that content ignored and having it fully embraced by your participants or supporters. Start small, but give both metaphors and humor a try.

Chapter Sixteen
High Tech on the Trail
How Technology Helps You Implement Your Content Marketing Strategy

> **This chapter is about . . .**
> - Understanding the role that technology plays in implementing your content marketing strategy
> - Learning how different pieces of software should work together
> - Sharing several of my favorite content marketing tools

High tech on the trail, like a GPS and a stove that ignites without a match, can sure make life easier. Technology can be a big help in implementing your content marketing strategy too.

The Right Technology Is Part of Your Staffing Strategy

In many nonprofits, technology budgets are seen as a luxury, especially for communications departments. After all, communicating is really mostly about writing, and you can do that on an ancient computer, right?

While that may be true in some ways, the problem is that it focuses too much on the communications product and not at all on the people whom you want to read those communications. And today, to reach the right people with the right message, you need good technology. And I am not talking about the latest version of Microsoft Office or a Facebook account.

As I was interviewing nonprofits for this book, it become clear to me that the organizations that are most successful at using content to engage their communities consider having a good combination of CRM (customer relationship management) software, website CMS (content management system), email provider, and e-commerce technology to be just as important to their success as having thoughtful and creative staff members who can write well.

It all comes back to creating content that is both relevant and valuable to your participants, supporters, and influencers. That means knowing what they think is relevant and valuable. But not everyone on your mailing list cares about the same things or has the same kind of relationship with your cause and to your organization.

That means you need to be able collect, store, retrieve, and use information about people so you can get the right message to the right people at the right time. You want to set this up in a way that is automated as much as possible, is easy to tweak as needed, and allows you to experiment with new ideas without a great investment of staff time or consulting dollars every time you need to send something out to a list.

Does This Sound Familiar?

I have conversations like the following with nonprofits all the time.

A nonprofit that serves developmentally disabled adults wants to build up more community support and engagement. I suggested that staff start with friends and family members of the one hundred–plus people the nonprofit directly serves. The problem: they have no way of knowing which individuals in their database of thousands of names are that closely connected to either current or former program participants.

A nonprofit that offers mission trips overseas as part of its programming would like to do a better job at fundraising from those participants after they return home. The problem: the names of participants are stored in a variety of different spreadsheets, and to compile a list in a format that would work for the specific kind of targeting the fundraisers want to try would require staff to spend hours, if not days, cutting and pasting data.

A nonprofit wants to start building up its email list in earnest and would like to add a newsletter signup form to its website template. But the email provider it uses doesn't integrate easily with the website CMS it uses, so it will have to pay for custom programming support just to add a simple web form. And it will have to pay again and again with each new web form staff want to add.

Here's what you should be able to do with the right combination of technology.

Collect and Store Information about People

You should be able to create simple web forms for your nonprofit's website, pretty much whenever you want, that allow people to do things like register to download a helpful e-book you created or RSVP for an event or sign a pledge or answer a few quick survey questions or donate to your organization online. This allows new people to get into the system and lets the people already in there add more information to their profiles. Staff should be able to create each form as needed and to get it live on the website in under an hour. Depending on your particular setup and what you are trying to do, that form code may come from your email provider, CRM software, or e-commerce software, and then you add it to your website content management system.

These forms then save the data about each person, usually based on their email address and usually in the CRM software. If a person fills out another web form you create later, that data gets saved in the same place as the data from the first form—or if you end up with two databases, they will be connected and can talk to each other seamlessly via a web API (application programming interface). As you start to compile more and more information about the person, it all goes in the same database or connected databases, over time. The actual mechanics of how all this works depend on which software you are using and how the databases talk to each other. The point is that they have to talk to each other and to recognize each person as the same person, which is often done through the email address.

In addition to information collected via forms, you can add other information to a person's profile based on actions they take, like opening emails or clicking links or registering for events or making an online donation. You can also add information manually or by importing data from a spreadsheet or other tracking system for events, telephone conversations, snail mail donations, or other activities that take place offline. Sometimes this information is stored with the person's individual record, and sometimes you access it dynamically. In other words, if I pull up your name and contact information in a database, it may not show me right there that you clicked a particular link in the last email I sent you. But I could do a search for people who clicked on that link, and your name would be on that list.

Retrieve That Information in All Sorts of Combinations, on the Fly

As you collect and store data, you can start to retrieve it in all sorts of ways to generate lists of people who meet various combinations of criteria. Exploring these combinations should be fairly effortless—simply a matter of thinking through the potentially useful combinations and then querying the database(s) to produce the lists of people who meet the different sets of criteria. When a set of criteria produces a list that is too small or too big for what you want to do, you can tweak the criteria to produce another list. You can do this in a matter of minutes, with the technology doing most, if not all, of the laborious compiling and sorting of records for you.

Having a system like this in place means you are no longer stuck with just one mailing list. You can have numerous specialized mailing lists, limited only by the amount and type of data you are collecting and storing and your creativity in retrieving those data and using the resulting lists.

Use It to Send the Right Communications to the Right People

Now that you can retrieve custom lists, you can use them to send out all sorts of great stuff. You can send reminder emails to people who haven't registered or donated yet, without bugging those people who have. The people who have already taken an action can get special thank-yous and follow-up information created just for them.

You can also use these lists to send customized newsletter content or fundraising appeals to people who match certain sets of criteria.

Maybe you will decide to market your nonprofit's monthly giving program to people who have donated to the organization at least once in each of the last three years (so you know they like you), have made at least one donation online (so they are comfortable with online financial transactions), and have opened emails or clicked on links about the program that the monthly giving would fund (so you know your offer is likely to align with what they care about). You see how that goes, and perhaps learn that the number of online donations was a better indicator of who would sign up for monthly giving than which links they had clicked on, so you adjust the criteria you use when you pull the list the next time. (This is just an example. Your results might point to an entirely different conclusion about your donors. So test what you are doing with your own experiments on your own lists!)

Find the Right Frequency of Communications for You and Them

How often to communicate, and to email in particular, is a huge question for nonprofits. Having this kind of system in place also helps you answer your timing and frequency questions. You undoubtedly have people on your list who would love to hear from you weekly and others who are really good with a few times a year. You can ask them directly via a web form what their preferences are, or you can watch how they interact with you online and adjust your communications to them accordingly.

This attentiveness to what people want is especially important for both advocacy organizations and nonprofits that do events. There are times of the year when you really need to be in touch with your advocates or events attendees much more often, and they welcome that more frequent communication. But sending all those emails to others on your list would likely cause them to unsubscribe, meaning you wouldn't be able to communicate with them at all anymore.

Keep Experimenting, Learning as You Go, and More Deeply Engaging Those on Your Lists

Using a combination of website, email, CRM, and e-commerce technology allows you to experiment with and tweak the content of not only your campaigns but also the lists that you send campaign content to. And as anyone who has done marketing or fundraising for very long will tell you, the quality of your list is way more important than anything you write.

It's not a matter of *whether* your nonprofit should be moving in this direction, but *when*. I'd argue the time is *now*. This is a perfect opportunity for fundraising and communications staff to collaborate and to start getting the right solutions in place. Doing this will improve the results of your work and save you an incredible amount of time in the long run. If your choice is between more staff and this kind of technology, seriously think about choosing the technology over the additional staff.

Some of My Favorite Tech Tools

This is by no means a comprehensive list of content marketing tools, but it does include most of our personal favorites at Nonprofit Marketing Guide.

For additional recommendations from others in the nonprofit sector, please visit my website for this book, at ContentMarketingforNonprofits.com.

WordPress is our website and blog CMS (content management system). WordPress lets us easily update the content on our website and blog. Various plug-ins allow us to embed video, create image sliders, add social sharing, and do just about anything else we might think of. For WordPress templates, we use Headway, Thesis, and the Aggregate theme by ElegantThemes on our family of websites and blogs.

Google Apps for Business provides our personal email and calendars. We use Google Drive for some shared documents (mostly spreadsheets). We have created several Google Calendars for our various communications channels, including one for blog posts, another for email marketing, another for social media, and another for training schedules.

Dropbox is our file-sharing and backup system. When two or more people are editing a Word document, sharing that document in Dropbox is much less confusing than emailing attachments back and forth. We also store our marketing bank—images, stock photos, logos, Photoshop files—in

Dropbox. We can access Dropbox from our desktops, browsers, and mobile devices, making it extremely versatile.

Media Temple hosts our websites.

Amazon S3 stores big files, like webinar recordings, so we don't eat up space on our web server.

Evernote Business is what we use as our Idea Bucket (the place where all the miscellaneous stuff goes) as well as for storing meeting notes, planning docs, and so on. We can write notes, record ideas, and save websites, then share them with others on the team.

Remember the Milk allows us to assign and share tasks with deadlines. We can quickly see what tasks have been done on a project and set due dates.

Diigo is the social bookmarking site we use. It lets us categorize our bookmarks and share them with others.

HootSuite is our social media scheduling and management tool. HootSuite makes scheduling updates to social networks easy; in addition it gives us the ability to create *listening dashboards* for various topics. The team option allows more than one person to update an organization's account.

Alltop shows me the headlines of the last five posts from my forty or so most favorite bloggers on my custom Alltop page. I use this when I'm curating content for my blog's weekly roundup of blog posts, articles, and reports that I think nonprofit marketers and fundraisers could use.

Why It Matters: They Expect a Good Experience

Sites like Amazon.com have spoiled people into thinking that whatever they want to do on the web should be as quick and easy as it is there. I know it doesn't seem fair, but the reality is that people do carry those expectations over to your organization, your website, and their online experience with you. Do your best with the technology you have now, and budget for better in the future.

Nonprofits have more communications channels to choose from than ever before. The eleven short and to the point chapters in this section will help you better understand what's different about each communications channel, ways to make it work for you, mistakes to avoid, and five new examples, ones I haven't shared yet, to help you see how to use each channel the right way.

These eleven chapters cover

- Websites
- Blogs
- Email
- Print newsletters
- Facebook
- Twitter
- Google+
- Video
- Images
- Pinterest
- Mobile devices

Chapter Seventeen
Websites

What's Different about This Communications Channel

When I conduct my annual nonprofit communications trends survey, one of the questions I ask nonprofit communicators is, "What are the most important communications channels for your nonprofit?" Websites have continuously ranked number one. Why? Because we live our lives online now. If we have a question or want to know about something, we pull up our favorite search engine and look it up on the Internet. You must have a website today. Nonprofits are smart and understand this—sort of.

Your website is often the first impression someone gets of your organization. With online donations increasing every year, that first impression needs to be a good one, or you could be losing potential support. Your website needs to contain information about your organization, such as what it does, and where it is. Your website and its contents also need to be designed for the visitor. Unfortunately, a lot of nonprofits throw up their web pages with little thought other than "we need to have something!" Cheesy clip art, confusing navigation, and self-congratulatory, jargon-filled text are still commonplace.

With the advent of content management systems (CMS) like WordPress and Drupal, websites can be as easy to design and update as a Word document. However, having a web designer is usually the best way to go. Having someone on call who can reset your server if the site crashes or fix issues with the back end is imperative.

Seven Ways to Make Your Content Work Here

1. **Use nice, iconic images**. The web is visual. Make sure you have at least one photo on your home page that can grab the attention of your visitor. Do not use clip art!

2. **Feature people**. People connect with people, not 501(c)s. You can let your personality shine through on your website just as you do with social media. Let us see the people behind and around the nonprofit—not just the executive director and staff but the people the organization serves.

3. **Include stories on the need and successes**. Stories make abstract mission statements real. Give us examples of the need and your nonprofit's successes through stories.

4. **Present a clear call to action**. What do you want people to do once they visit your site? Visitors may have stumbled on your site through a search, or they may have heard about your organization from friends or on the news and want to know more. Either way, you need to give them a next step once they are there. Make it clear and easy to follow.

5. **Make sure visitors can donate online easily from the home page**. Make that "Donate Now" link or button stand out so visitors can see it at first glance. Big buttons that are a different color from the rest of your site work well. Ask someone who is not in your organization to look at your website, make a donation, and report to you on the experience. While you may think it's easy because you set it up, others may not find it so intuitive.

6. **Use the best keywords for your cause**. For search engines to direct people your way, you need to use the real vocabulary on your site that people are typing into Google and other search engines. Talk in plain English, using their words.

7. **Feature endorsements or testimonials**. Let others do the talking for you. Find clients who would like to share what your organization has done for them. Get volunteers and donors to tell others how

awesome they feel after helping your cause. Also, try to get pictures from those who have given testimonials. People like to put a face with a name.

Seven Mistakes to Avoid

1. **Ignoring visitors' questions**. Your visitors are there for a reason. What are the top three answers or actions a website visitor is most likely looking for? Ensure that answers are only one click away, if not on the home page itself.

2. **Offering too many choices on the home page**. You do not need to put every single piece of information pertaining to your organization and its programs and mission on the home page.

3. **Having confusing navigation**. Make sure your visitors can easily find their way around your website. Your menu labels should be straightforward, but don't create too many of them or visitors will be overwhelmed. Use familiar labels when you can, like "contact" and "about." The *Cygnus Donor Survey 2012* (Burk, 2012) asked donors what kinds of problems they encountered on nonprofit websites. Forty-eight percent said the websites were difficult to navigate.

4. **Failing to offer offline ways to connect**. Make it easy for visitors to find you off the Internet. Visitors may be looking for a way to mail in a donation or to visit your office. You need to get your organization's physical address and phone number out there at the very least. A staff directory with clear instructions on who to call for particular questions and issues is even better.

5. **Having inconsistent design**. Your website should look pretty much the same no matter what page the visitor is on. Use the same header, font, and link colors on all your pages. You don't want visitors thinking they have accidentally gone to a different website.

6. **Keeping your blog on a separate site or platform**. If at all possible your blog should be directly on your website. Visitors to the blog will

then keep coming back to your actual site, and that will help with search rankings as well. Google likes fresh content.

7. **Filling the site with jargon**. Unless your nonprofit is a trade association and everyone visiting its website is a professional in that trade, you need to speak in plain English, not only to help with search rankings but also to speak to your visitors. Think about how outsiders would talk about your cause. Use those words on your website.

Five Great Examples to Learn From

1. **charity: water** (www.charitywater.org). This nonprofit gets your attention in just a few words. The page design draws your attention to exactly what charity: water wants you to see. You aren't overwhelmed with huge blocks of text that you have to read through to learn anything or too many options. I am not always a fan of placing the mission statement on the home page; usually these statements use confusing buzzwords or are so wordy that no one really gets the point. However, this nonprofit's mission statement is short and in plain English, so you know immediately what it does. This statement is followed by a form to sign up for email updates. And for visitors who don't want to look around the home page, there's a very simple navigation menu at the top of the page with everything a visitor could want.

2. **ASPCA** (www.aspca.org). The ASPCA updates its home page image rotation regularly, and each image is captioned with timely information, an ask, and a donate button.

3. **Greenpeace USA** (www.greenpeace.org/usa/en). Greenpeace, like all of the examples on this list, uses great visuals coupled with simple asks. It is a simple layout with a header slider and two columns. The main column features the latest blog posts and the sidebar includes the email form at the top, followed by "donate now" buttons with images. The email sign-up form is perfectly located, easy to spot, and asks for only three things. Greenpeace has done the research on why people

visit its site, and this is reflected in the simple navigation that includes "donate," "take action," "volunteer," and "what we do." The entire home page can be viewed in only a couple of scrolls.

4. **Kiva** (www.kiva.org). Kiva is a nonprofit that a lot of people have heard of, but not many know quite what it does. Its website allows visitors to quickly find answers to their questions about why they should use Kiva and how it works. The main focus of the site is the supporters (lenders) who are helping. It also includes a scrolling graphic that shares important information, such as how many people supporters have helped, how much money supporters have lent, and what percentage of money has been repaid to the lenders.

5. **The Michael J. Fox Foundation for Parkinson's Research** (www .michaeljfox.org). Transparency is key for health research organizations. People want to know how much of their money actually goes to fight the disease, and the Michael J. Fox Foundation seems to understand this. Visitors can very quickly see how it spends its money.

Chapter Eighteen
Blogs

What's Different about This Communications Channel

A blog gives you more freedom than other social networks, such as Facebook and Twitter, while also giving you a potentially bigger audience than email. Most blog posts run between 500 and 800 words, giving you the chance to fully flesh out your ideas, unlike Facebook and Twitter, which require brevity.

A blog is a great way to establish your organization's personality and tone. In addition to text, a blog post can include photos, videos, and infographics, easily making blogs one of the most versatile communications channels out there. Google loves new content, so having a blog on your website can improve your overall search rankings and allow you to gain new supporters as well.

Blogging is more of an endeavor than simply setting up a social media account. You have to select a platform and a layout, and it also requires slightly more technical skill (or easy access to a blog-savvy staffer). Blogs can also be one of the more frustrating mediums to work with. You have to have a plan to drive people to your blog, and it can sometimes feel that no one is reading. Coming up with ideas for posts on a consistent basis can also be difficult.

Seven Ways to Make Your Content Work Here

1. **Establish the type of blog you'll write**. You can mix and match blog types, but I think it's helpful to have one primary direction in mind. Think about what goals you want your nonprofit's blog to achieve.

Blog types include news, advocacy, toolbox, storytelling, and executive director–led blogs.

2. **Brainstorm ideas**. One of the hardest things about blogging is coming up with ideas for posts. What posts would help you achieve your nonprofit's goals as well as appeal to your ideal reader? Take time to jot down twenty ideas as a start. You can also ask some of your organization's more ardent supporters what they would like to read about.

3. **Have some regular features**. Come up with a few regular columns that you can create on a weekly or monthly basis. How-to or question and answer posts and news roundups relating to your organization's cause are good examples. Then you have one less post you have to get creative with and a recurring theme gives readers something to look forward to.

4. **Use repurposed content**. Since blogging gives you more freedom than social networking and sending email, it's an ideal medium in which to rework content from other channels. If you had a good response to a Facebook post, expand on it with a blog post highlighting some of the comments. Rework newsletter articles by adding more graphics that may better explain your point but would have been difficult to read in an email.

5. **Be consistent**. The best blogs offer content on a regular basis. Using an editorial calendar will help you keep track of what content you are putting where and when, so channels reinforce each other. It will also help you stay focused on your audience and your goals for the publication. Being consistent not only keeps readers coming back continually but will also help with your Google search ratings.

6. **Make it easy to share**. Allow people to share your posts with their social networks so readers can invite their friends to your blog. You also want to include ways to connect with your social networks ("like" box for Facebook, "Follow Me" for Twitter, and so forth).

7. **Allow comments**. A blog can be a great place to foster a community. Allow readers to comment on your blog posts, and make sure you

answer their questions. Encourage readers to share tips, stories, or other ideas relating to a post's topic.

Seven Mistakes to Avoid

1. **Ignoring your readers**. Whom do you want reading and commenting on your blog? Your posts should be written for those people, not your staff, executive director, or board members.

2. **Having too many voices**. While you can have more than one person writing your nonprofit's blog, switching from a corporate sounding tone to a friendly personal one (and vice versa) will confuse your readers. Guest posts can add a fresh voice to the mix, but make sure they are a good fit with your organization's personality.

3. **Not including a call to action**. As with most communications, you need to give your readers an option to do more. Ask them to post a comment, visit your nonprofit's web page, subscribe to the newsletter, RSVP for an event, and so on. Give them a next step.

4. **Using jargon**. Most people in organizations use industry-related jargon, but the fact that you and your team use these specialized words on a daily basis doesn't mean your readers will know what you're talking about. Speak in plain English, and go easy on the acronyms and abbreviations. Try to read your blog as an outsider would.

5. **Getting "cutesy" with titles**. For the most part, blog titles need to be descriptive so they will show up in web searches and get readers to click over. You can be creative but remember to include keywords.

6. **Using big walls of text**. Have you ever seen "tl;dr" on social media sites or in the comments of a blog post? It means "too long; didn't read," and that's how today's readers feel when they see big blocks of text. They won't read it. You can use long content, but break up the text by creating shorter paragraphs and using lists or bullet points.

7. **Not using any images**. People are drawn to pictures so try to include at least one image in each post. You can find royalty-free, stock photos (check whether you need to credit the source though) pretty easily on the Internet. People are also likely to immediately read any caption under a photo, so make the most of that space as well.

Five Great Examples to Learn From

1. **Feeding America** (blog.feedingamerica.org). The Feeding America blog uses a simple layout that focuses on the nonprofit's main objective—to feed the hungry. Feeding America posts on national initiatives to end hunger as well as efforts by local organizations. This blog also does a great job of featuring those affected by hunger, which makes it compelling and effective.

2. **Salvation Army** (blog.salvationarmyusa.org). The Salvation Army does a nice job of arranging its blog so visitors can easily find the specific type of information they are looking for. They can read general information in such categories as current events, disaster relief, and stories from the Salvation Army thrift stores.

3. **ReSurge** (resurge.blogs.com/resurge-blog). ReSurge International (formerly known as Interplast) uses its blog mainly to communicate with its donors. ReSurge volunteers do a lot of the writing and supply many of the photos. They do a fabulous job of sharing success stories and letting readers see behind the scenes, which are two of the best uses of blogs by nonprofits.

4. **Ottawa Humane Society** (blog.ottawahumane.ca). This blog is a good combination of behind the scenes information and asks. Although it's written mostly by the society's executive director, it's in a very friendly tone, and you get a real sense of what is going on at this organization.

5. **National Aquarium** (nationalaquarium.wordpress.com). The National Aquarium offers regular features on its blog, which makes it easier for staff to fill in the editorial calendar.

Chapter Nineteen
Email

What's Different about This Communications Channel

Email is fast, cheap, and versatile. Email allows you to personalize communications in a way that social media can't, and it is quicker and less expensive than direct mail. It provides the best way to reach a specific audience because it allows you to segment your donors, volunteers, and clients. An email can be written, sent, and received in an afternoon, whereas direct mail can take days to print and mail.

You can also better track how your readers are responding to your communications because you can check open rates and click-throughs. You can also easily test subject lines or calls to action. Sending bulk email must be done through an email service provider (ESP), as CAN-SPAM laws can be difficult to adhere to when you're sending from a personal email account. An ESP will also allow you to gather email addresses through web forms, personalize your greetings, schedule when you want to send your email, and easily design your newsletter to include logos and other branding.

But building an email list takes time so getting started can be rough. Also, it's easy to get lost in a recipient's inbox these days, and hitting the delete button takes a recipient just a second. So you have to make sure your content is interesting and relevant time after time.

Seven Ways to Make Your Content Work Here

1. **Have an intriguing subject line**. Don't sabotage a perfectly good newsletter with a boring subject line like "Summer Newsletter."

Inboxes are crowded. Your subject line needs to stand out so your email isn't deleted before it has a chance.

2. **Send the right amount of messages**. You want people to remember you and look forward to receiving your newsletter, but you don't want to drive them crazy with too much email. When in doubt or just starting out, try to send a newsletter every two to four weeks and adjust from there.

3. **Use more compelling photos**. Group photos of your board, "big check" photos, and the like waste precious space in email. Choose photos that are mission oriented and send a clear message to your reader. A close-up shot of one person will beat a group shot nine times out of ten.

4. **Segment your email list**. For example, set up your database so that you can pull a list of volunteers or donors and communicate with them without emailing everyone. Segmenting allows you to create messages that are more focused and relevant, which means they are more likely to be opened, read, and acted on.

5. **Use a personal and conversational tone**. The best emails read as personal communications from one person to another. Don't speak as a nonprofit organization; speak as a staff person working on issues your readers care about. Make sure you take advantage of your email service provider's ability to personalize greetings.

6. **Make it skimmable**. People skim email more than they read it, especially newsletters. You need to include descriptive headlines and subheadings. Before sending a newsletter by email, check that you can read only the headlines and subheads and still understand the gist of it.

7. **Make it mobile friendly**. The number of people using their smartphones to check email is growing every year. Be sure it is easy for them to read by keeping articles brief and the design simple. The majority of your email should be text, not images. Lots of email users (whether

reading on their mobiles or on bigger screens) do not automatically display the images in their emails. Be sure to have *alt text* (alternative text) for all images, so readers who do not allow pictures won't miss anything.

Seven Mistakes to Avoid

1. **Not having a clear goal in mind**. Are you using email to motivate actions like donations or volunteering? Or to educate donors about the work they have supported in the past? Or to provide services to members? Knowing what you want to achieve via email is essential to creating the right content and delivery schedule.

2. **Attaching or linking to documents**. Linking to a pdf on your website or including a pdf attachment to an email is not what people expect as an e-newsletter. Most people do not want to have to download a pdf to know what your email is about, especially when they are reading that email on their smartphone. While it's certainly fine to provide links to related resources, provide all the primary content in the email itself.

3. **Catering to staff interests**. Your newsletter should reflect your readers' interests, wants, and needs more than your staff's. Put yourself in your readers' seats. Do they really have a compelling reason to read what you are writing? Your staff may think the nonprofit's new software is awesome (and it probably is), but most of your readers don't really care.

4. **Focusing on the past**. Focus the majority of your content on today and tomorrow, rather than yesterday. People want to know what's happening now and what the next big thing is. When you do talk about past events, describe them in ways that connect to the future.

5. **Not including a call to action**. Your supporters have read your newsletter. Now what? Every email should give the reader something to do. Always provide a next step, even if it is something as simple as "Learn more," with a link to a related website page.

6. **Including a letter from your director.** Letters from the director are typically full of jargon and behind the scenes minutiae, leaving supporters feeling left out of the conversation. Effective email newsletters focus primarily on your readers, what they care about, and how they can connect to your nonprofit and its cause. Very brief director letters can work, but they must have a laser focus on the reader: plenty of "you," "you," and more "you." What if your director really loves writing that letter? Give her a blog and link to it.

7. **Listing a full calendar of events.** Instead of including a great big event calendar with boxes for each day of the week, put that elsewhere online (try Google Calendar, for example). In your newsletter, highlight a few upcoming events and include a link to the full calendar.

Five Great Examples to Learn From

1. **Wiser.org, the Social Network for Sustainability** (www.wiser.org). Wiser's email newsletter includes short and timely articles with both a headline and a subheading, which lets readers know what is in the newsletter without reading every word. The newsletter includes links for every article, so readers can learn more information if they want to, and it also includes a donate button and social media options in every issue.

2. **St. Jude Children's Research Hospital** (www.stjude.org). St. Jude's monthly *Hopeline* newsletter includes a featured story, a spotlight story, and a patient of the month, with great photos and teaser text that makes you want to click for more.

3. **Place des Arts** (www.placedesarts.ca). This nonprofit's newsletter has regular features like "What's On" and "What's New" that correspond with menu options on its website, providing continuity between the two channels. Regular features build patterns that your readers will look forward to. Readers will anticipate these features, helping your open rates.

4. **Grist.org** (www.grist.org). This organization's newsletter may appear minimalistic, but that equals a clean, fast read. It is very easy to skim, and the alt text gives you enough information so you know at a glance what you are missing if the images are not turned on. The microcontent, such as article headings, is tight and in a different style so it pops off the page making it easy and quick to read as well.

5. **National Parks Conservation Association** (www.npca.org). The *Park Lines* newsletter is packed with information but organized in a way that is easy to skim. Including lots of content in your newsletter isn't always the best choice, but NPCA does a good job with the layout, so there's no confusion about where they eye should go or where the finger should click.

Chapter Twenty
Print Newsletters

What's Different about This Communications Channel

While online communications have exploded over the last few years, nonprofits are still seeing great results with their good old fashioned print newsletters. Yes, email is cheaper and faster, but there are many reasons to keep your print newsletter.

Print newsletters are usually easier to read and look better. With email newsletters you have to worry about how they will look on different email systems and whether or not images will be seen by your readers. With print, you know exactly what your newsletter will look like to everyone who gets it.

Also print newsletters have a higher deliverability rate. Spam filters may block your email newsletter from ever being delivered, or readers may delete it before they even open it. Email list churn is also a concern—email addresses change frequently.

Seven Ways to Make Your Content Work Here

1. **Keep your target audience in mind**. If, for example, you want your newsletter to raise money, you should be writing your newsletter specifically for your donors. All the articles in your newsletter should provide benefits or interesting information to your nonprofit's donors, remind them how important they are to your nonprofit, and encourage them to continue to support its work.

2. **Keep it to four to six pages**. The length will depend on the type of communications you include in your newsletter, but anything shorter than four pages will seem as though you don't have much to say and that it isn't worth the cost, while anything more than six will usually not be read.

3. **Write great headlines**. According to Brian Clark, founder of Copyblogger, "On average, 8 out of 10 people will read headline copy, but only 2 out of 10 will read the rest." Your headline will determine whether your article is read or not.

4. **Keep it recent**. Don't summarize an event that happened three months ago. That tells me your organization doesn't have enough good stuff going on now and in the future to fill a newsletter's pages. I'm not against event summaries in newsletters, but make sure the events are very recent or that you've turned event content into some other useful form, like a how-to article. Your newsletter is not the society pages.

5. **Appeal to skimmers**. People will scan and skim your newsletter before they read it. Short paragraphs and sentences are easier to skim. Descriptive headlines and subheads with active verbs and vivid nouns will grab supporters' attention and nudge them into actually reading the text.

6. **Help readers solve problems**. To get the folks on your nonprofit's mailing list to read the organization's newsletters, you need to provide them with something of value. Include how-to articles, FAQs, and advice columns.

7. **Include a call to action**. Give your readers a next step to take, whether it's visiting your nonprofit's web page, donating, or returning an RSVP.

Seven Mistakes to Avoid

1. **Not knowing the newsletter's role in the nonprofit's strategy**. Are you using your nonprofit's newsletter to motivate action like donations

or volunteering? Or to educate donors about the work they have supported in the past? Or to provide services to members? Knowing what you want to achieve is essential to creating the right content and delivery schedule.

2. **Going crazy with fonts**. To be on the safe side, stick with two fonts: one for the body text and captions and a second one for headlines and subheads. You can use a third one as a display font for the newsletter nameplate and for other design elements, like page numbers. Use additional fonts with extreme care. Using too many fonts in the same publication is a sure sign of an amateur designer.

3. **Not speaking directly to readers**. People want to read information that is relevant to them, and the word "you" in headlines, subheads, and first sentences of paragraphs signals that the writer is talking directly to the reader. If you aren't talking to me, the reader, why should I care what you have to say?

4. **Writing articles that are too long**. People expect newsletter articles to be relatively short. If most of your feature articles have 500 to 700 words, you'll be fine. That's about the length of most columns on newspaper editorial pages, for example. It's fine to have brief articles that are shorter and maybe one or two that are longer, but in general shoot for 500 to 700 words.

5. **Using the same photo files for print and online**. You shouldn't try to use the same photo file for both print and online newsletters. Print newsletters need photos with a resolution of at least 300 dpi at the correct size. When you put a photo from an online source into a print newsletter, it will look pixelated (with the pixels visible as little squares) or blurry.

6. **Using boring photos**. Yes, readers want people photos, but those same old award ceremony and big-check photos are uninspiring and have nothing to do with your nonprofit's mission. Moreover, big-check pictures suggest to readers that the problem has been solved and there is no need to care any more about it. Also, don't use the big

group lineups—a close-up of one or two people is more engaging than a photo of thirty people lined up that is taken from so far away you can't see anyone's face.

7. **Making people look bad.** Unless you are trying to playfully tease someone or cast them as an enemy of your cause, you want to make sure that your newsletter photos make the people in them look good. When changing the size of a photo, make sure you keep the ratio of width to height constant, so people don't look stretched out or squished.

Five Great Examples to Learn From

1. **Planned Parenthood of Rhode Island** (www.aherncomm.com/ss_files/downloads/ppri_donor_news.pdf). The purpose of this nonprofit's newsletter is to fundraise and build donor retention. Communications staff use precise headlines and short articles that make the donors the stars of the organization.

2. **UNICEF New Zealand** (www.aherncomm.com/ss_files/downloads/global_parents_newsletter_opt.pdf). This nonprofit puts out a bright colorful newsletter that is written for the donor. You can tell that this newsletter is doing a good job by the number of times its uses the word "you." Also featured are personal anecdotes, photos, and drawings from those who need help.

3. **Mission India** (www.missionindia.org). Mission India gives its donors love in many ways with statements such as, "You empowered us," and, "Wow! You blew us away." Trying to connect your supporters to what is happening on the other side of the world can be a tough sell, but Mission India offers touching stories and pictures of those who are being helped and encouraged by Mission India and also relates stories about volunteers and staff back home, all the while giving its donors the credit.

4. **Virginia Beach Public Library** (www.vbgov.com/government/ departments/libraries/Pages/home.aspx). This organization's seasonal newsletter is not only sent to supporters but also placed in the libraries and used in outreach to potential customers. Because it has to appeal to a broad audience, it has to do more than give donors credit. It has to encourage supporters to donate again, while also being informative and relevant for everyone else who is interested in the library. It includes an ask that encourages people to join the library's membership program or email list, while also presenting fun tidbits and program schedules that everyone can make use of.

5. **Loveland Center** (www.lovelandcenter.com). Going through a rebranding can be tricky. Loveland Center decided to use its print newsletter to introduce its new look. Because the center was also coming up on a series of fundraisers, it thoughtfully skipped the hard ask for a donation, so donors wouldn't feel like ATMs. Instead the center highlighted the positive things that were going on at the organization and asked readers to join its email list or follow it on social media.

Chapter Twenty-One
Facebook

What's Different about This Communications Channel

Facebook is the largest social network of them all. According to the Pew Research Center survey *The Demographics of Social Media Users—2012*, a whopping 67 percent of Internet users are on Facebook. In comparison, only 16 percent of Internet users are on Twitter and 15 percent on Pinterest (Duggan and Brenner, 2013).

While most social networks are most appealing to those Internet users aged eighteen to twenty-nine, Facebook has a big number of users over the age of fifty. According to that same Pew survey, 57 percent of Internet users aged fifty to fifty-four are on Facebook, with another 35 percent of those who are sixty-five and older. Facebook is also popular with Internet users regardless of race, income, education, or urbanity. In other words, it's a big deal.

While email is more efficient in reaching your nonprofit's supporters, Facebook allows those supporters to introduce your nonprofit to their friends. For example, even if a Facebook Page only has eighty people who have "liked" it, those eighty people could have over forty thousand friends total. When the Nonprofit Marketing Guide's Facebook Page reached seven thousand "likes," friends of those fans numbered close to four million. Anytime one of your fans comments on or "likes" one of your updates, it may show up in his or her friends' news feeds, giving you greater reach.

Unfortunately, unless you purchase Facebook Ads or Sponsored Stories, your posts don't have a very long shelf life. Posting consistently is a must. Facebook also requires dedicated monitoring, so you need to have someone on staff who can check in and respond, especially if your organization is a focus of controversy. Facebook also continually changes, so what was a good idea today could be thrown out the window tomorrow.

Seven Ways to Make Your Content Work Here

1. **Post at least once a day**. Two to three times a day with at least three hours between posts is a good balance. You'll have opportunities to make it into news feeds without being obtrusive or spammy.

2. **Share photos and videos**. Photos and videos are prime real estate on Facebook now. These types of posts will get passed along the most in your supporters' news feeds.

3. **Ask questions**. Questions engage readers. Either ask in your status update or use the "Ask a question" feature. But don't make your questions too hard or deep! People should be able to answer quickly, off the tops of their heads.

4. **Mix updates that ask fans to do, think, or feel**. Engage fans with a mix of calls to action (do), interesting information (think), and emotional content (feel), such as things that are funny or touching.

5. **Keep it brief**. While you have more space to work with than on Twitter, posts should ideally be one to two lines and no longer than four lines.

6. **Make updates "like"-able**. Put a positive spin on your posts so fans can easily hit the "like" button.

7. **Respond in a timely manner**. People are on Facebook 24/7, and while you shouldn't be expected to respond at 3:00 AM on a Saturday, be sure you are checking for comments several times a day.

Seven Mistakes to Avoid

1. **Updating too many times in a short period**. Ongoing commentary on a single post is fine, but do not update your Page multiple times in a short time span. You will invade news feeds and seem spammy.

2. **Setting up a personal profile for your organization**. You need to have an official Facebook Page for your organization. Profiles are for individuals, and with an individual account you will not be able to reach as many people. Plus it's against Facebook rules, and your profile could be deleted.

3. **Scheduling updates and never checking in**. HootSuite and other social network apps are great and I highly recommend them, but you can't just schedule updates and never actually look at your Page. Pay attention when fans post something on your wall.

4. **Deleting negative comments**. Transparency and openness are vital, and deleting negative comments from your Page will come across badly. Try to address the needs of the individuals who posted the comments in a respectful way. If the situation still seems to be escalating, invite them to email or call you or your executive director to take the discussion off-line. However, when a post is abusive, offensive, or spam, then you should delete it.

5. **Autofeeding your Twitter account**. Twitter is an entirely different platform from Facebook. Hashtags and mentions have no place on Facebook (at the moment anyway), and the rapid fire nature of Twitter is a turnoff on Facebook.

6. **Asking for "likes" too often**. While you want to make your posts likeable and to encourage people to share your photos, links, and other content, constantly saying things such as "like this photo if you love animals" is annoying.

7. **Not using Facebook Insights**. Facebook has built-in metrics that will help you understand who is visiting and the potential reach of your Page. You can also see what kind of content gets the biggest response from your users.

Five Great Examples to Learn From

1. **Best Friends Animal Society** (www.facebook.com/bestfriends animalsociety). This nonprofit's Facebook Page almost resembles a

web page more than a Facebook Page. It makes great use of the boxes that Facebook lets you customize. The icons of those boxes match the color scheme of the society's logo and cover photo, giving the Page an integrated feeling. These boxes allow fans to learn more and act without ever leaving Facebook. This page also takes advantage of the "highlight" feature, which makes a post fill the entire width of the page—perfect for this nonprofit's professional-looking pictures.

2. **Lupus Foundation of America, Greater Ohio Chapter** (www.facebook .com/lupusgreaterOH). This foundation displays another perfectly integrated Facebook Page. You can easily find out how to get support for lupus or how to join the organization. The foundation also uses the Facebook Events feature to promote its classes and support groups.

3. **Children of the Nations** (www.facebook.com/Children.of.the.Nations). COTN does a great job of engaging its fans and getting them involved. It posts pictures of the children it helps and also of donors, volunteers, and staff, so visitors get a full sense of everyone involved in the organization. It is also great at using Facebook as a way to report back on what the organization is doing with donations—pictures of wells, children in school, and lots of happy faces are common on its wall.

4. **350.org** (www.facebook.com/350.org). 350.org offers a great example of a Facebook Page that curates content. It shares photos and links from other organizations or outlets that also deal with climate change. A person who wants to know the latest on the climate crisis can go to this page and find it, no matter who originally broke the news.

5. **Canadian Opera Company** (www.facebook.com/canadianopera company). The Canadian Opera Company makes great use of embedded video on its Facebook Page. These videos take you behind the scenes introducing you to the actors, directors, and others that it takes to put on an opera. They also display interviews with the audiences, which are great testimonials and may bring more people to opera. And of course there's lots of singing!

Chapter Twenty-Two
Twitter

What's Different about This Communications Channel

Twitter is the most open social media tool. It's often described as a giant cocktail party. Different groups of people are having conversations about all kinds of topics. You can chime in when you hear something that interests you or start your own conversation. And that party is happening all over the world.

Twitter is also becoming the go-to place for breaking news, whether it's coming from veteran reporters who have embraced the up-to-date action on Twitter or from regular users like you and me who just happen to be in the thick of things. You can quickly interject your nonprofit's thoughts on things like global warming, animal rescue, or medical research as news regarding those topics happens.

But Twitter, like most social media channels, moves really fast. Unless you are using relevant words that show up in Twitter searches, your tweets can easily get lost. It can also be hard to keep Twitter users focused, so you need to make sure you are putting out relevant materials consistently.

According to a Pew Research Center survey (Duggan and Brenner, 2013), Twitter is used by only 16 percent of Internet users, so you may not have a big audience there. But if you are looking to get the attention of twenty-something urban dwellers, Twitter is a good bet.

Seven Ways to Make Your Content Work Here

1. **Focus on being friendly and helpful—not fundraising**. While you can certainly add Twitter to your list of fundraising tools, that shouldn't be

your primary motivation for using it. Instead, focus on connecting with people and building rapport. That way, when you do ask for assistance later, they'll be more willing to go along. Ask and answer questions regularly.

2. **Leave space for others to retweet you**. When a message is retweeted, the letters "RT" and your Twitter username (@yourhandle) will appear in front of it and count against your 140 character limit. Try not to use all 140 characters in your tweets, so that they can be retweeted by others without truncating your original message too much.

3. **Retweet good stuff**. You aren't the only one with great ideas or thoughts related to your nonprofit's cause. Share the good stuff that others put on Twitter with your own followers by retweeting it. It's a nice way to show your appreciation for others as well.

4. **Use a Twitter management application**. Twitter.com doesn't let you get the best out of its platform. I recommend using HootSuite to manage your organization's Twitter profile. TweetDeck and Seesmic are other applications that do the same kind of thing. They allow you not only to manage what you post but also to search through and sort out what you see from others. You can also add team members, so others from your organization can post to the account as well.

5. **Tweet several times a day**. You will need to post often in order to better your chances of being noticed. Twitter moves so fast that you can post several times a day without annoying your followers. Feel free to join in conversations.

6. **Post links**. While Facebook likes photos, links get the most attention on Twitter. Link to blog posts, your nonprofit's donation page or website, helpful articles, or anything else you think your followers would find useful.

7. **Connect your blog's RSS feed**. Since links rule on Twitter, consider using a management app (like HootSuite, TweetDeck, or Seesmic) to link your RSS feed to your Twitter account. This way, all your blog posts are automatically posted to Twitter.

Seven Mistakes to Avoid

1. **Not knowing the lingo**. Like any other social media site, Twitter has its own language. Check out the Twitter Glossary to familiarize yourself with *hashtags*, *mentions*, and *retweets*.

2. **Protecting your tweets**. The goal when using Twitter is to be part of a larger conversation. By protecting tweets (hiding them where only your approved followers can see them), you are cutting out potential participants. Plus, when your tweets are protected, you can't be retweeted.

3. **Going over 140 characters**. The character limit is one of the things that makes Twitter Twitter. Learn how to condense your thoughts into less than 140 characters. Followers do not want to click to read the ends of truncated messages.

4. **Not paying attention to the conversation**. Right now there are people who don't know each other having a conversation on Twitter. What if that conversation is about your nonprofit's cause? Look for opportunities to answer questions, share tips, or link to resources. Be helpful, but not spammy.

5. **Using irrelevant hashtags**. #bieberfever may be trending on Twitter, but what does that have to do with your nonprofit's cause? Using trending keywords just to get attention is spam. You can be flagged for it and lose your account. The goal isn't just to be followed but to be followed by the right people.

6. **Not following people**. If you aren't following others, people will know you are interested only in yourself. Start off by following others in your field, then other nonprofits who are doing things the way your nonprofit would like to. You will also get your fair share of spammers who follow you, but other than those, you should consider following anyone who legitimately follows you. A quick glance at followers' profiles will let you know if they are legitimate.

7. **Having too many continuous personal conversations**. You want to interact with others on Twitter, but when you find yourself having a

long continuous conversation with one other person, move the conversation to the direct message feature. People looking at your profile won't see any useful information in your timeline and will pass on following you.

Five Great Examples to Learn From

1. **DoSomething.org** (@dosomething). Teens are the focus of DoSomething.org, and it tends to tweet a good mixture of funny and relevant content. It is a little all over the place as far as topics go, but again that fits in well with its intended audience and its brand personality.

2. **American Red Cross** (@RedCross). The Red Cross understands how valuable Twitter can be for disseminating information to a large group of people quickly. During disasters, its Twitter account is a go-to for anyone affected by the events or wanting to help. The Red Cross also uses its feed to tell supporters what it is doing to help, so they can see what their donations are being used for.

3. **Humane Society of the United States** (@HSUS). The Humane Society of the United States makes good use of hashtags and of creating events on Twitter, such as #MuttMonday and #FelineFriday. It also posts a lot of pictures and links, which engage followers.

4. **(RED)** (@joinRED). (RED) may have the added benefit of having some celebrity advocates, so its feed throws around names like Bono, but it also speaks to everyone who is interested in fighting HIV/AIDS. It posts emotional stories about people who are affected by HIV/AIDS in Africa, stories that inspire (RED) followers to help.

5. **National Wildlife Federation** (@NWF). The National Wildlife Federation offers a good mix of news, information, and helpful tips for its Twitter followers. It's a good example of how a national organization can be relevant across the country with frequent updates.

Chapter Twenty-Three
Google+

What's Different about This Communications Channel

Thanks to Google's relentless focus on weaving Google+ through all its products—Google Search, Gmail, Calendar, Maps, YouTube, and many more—it is almost inevitable that you will use it in some fashion. However, that also makes it hard to know who exactly is actively using Google+ as a social network in the traditional sense.

Google+ is the place for deep content and deep engagement. Like Facebook, Google+ features a news feed filled with content shared by your connections. But there are a few features unique to Google+ that give it an edge for content providers. Photos in posts are very large, larger than in Facebook, making Google+ enormously popular with photographers and quite effective for the visual expression of ideas. Status updates can be thousands of words long, giving your content room to stretch out. Google Hangouts, group video chat that can be recorded and viewed on YouTube, is a standout feature that is already showing enormous potential for engaging audiences and creating compelling, reusable content.

Compared to using Facebook, you may find that it's easier to build a following on Google+, that you don't need to spend as much time managing your presence, and that you attract a more internationally diverse audience.

I would like to thank Kerri Karvetski of Company K Media for providing the Google+ tips and examples.

Seven Ways to Make Your Content Work Here

1. **Remember that your priority is passion**. What are your organization's Google+ followers really into? Don't think of Google+ as just another communications channel. Experiment with different types of content and engagement (ask questions, solicit feedback) to see what resonates with your audience.

2. **Post photos**. Lots of photos. You've got the room in the news feed to post large photos, use it! Consider using text+photo to make an inspiring, provocative, and most important, enticingly sharable statement.

3. **Try a Hangout**. Attend a few Hangouts to see how they work. Then kick the tires with a friend. The possibilities are endless—volunteer meeting, Ask the Expert, panel discussion, live analysis of an event, and so forth.

4. **Use Google+ formatting options to make text scannable**. For bold, add "*" before and after the words you want to bold; for italics, add "_" before and after the words you want to italicize; for strikethrough, add "-" before and after the words you want to strike through.

5. **Add a +1 button to your blog and website**. Make it easy for people to share your content on Google+. Google+ share buttons are available on sharing platforms such as ShareThis, Shareaholic, Sharebar, Sociable, and from Google+ itself.

6. **Use hashtags to jump into worldwide conversations**. Hashtags are searchable terms you add to posts to participate in particular discussions or topics. Once solely a Twitter tool, hashtags have proliferated on Google+; start watching for them and you'll see them everywhere. Here are but a few that nonprofits can dip their toes into: #MusicMonday, #NatureMonday, #PortraitTuesday, #Music Wednesday, #HistoryThursday, #FilmFriday, #Caturday, #googleplustips, and #youtubetips.

7. **Use Ripples to discover and cultivate influencers**. A Ripple is a data visualization showing how a public post was shared, or how it ripples through Google+. Use the dropdown menu at the top of any public

post, and click "View Ripples." Add your nonprofit's influencers to a separate circle so you can engage with these special supporters in a more targeted way.

Seven Mistakes to Avoid

1. **Leaving your profile photo and cover photo blank**. Nothing screams, "nobody's home" like default images.

2. **Forgetting to follow or circle people**. This isn't Facebook. You need to follow people back—reciprocate, show the love.

3. **Shunning the posts of others**. The participation you get is equal to the participation you give: +1, comment, and share freely and often.

4. **Failing to lurk and learn**. As with any new network online, you need to put in your time and get your sea legs. Google+ is not without its quirks and tricks. Fifteen to thirty minutes a day should be sufficient to manage it in the beginning.

5. **Duplicating Facebook or Twitter feed**. A little overlap is OK. Wholesale duplication is not. Choose some unique content for Google+, or try posting content in Google+ first and making a big deal of the exclusivity or priority status available to your Google+ followers.

6. **Forgetting to cross-promote**. Use your nonprofit's website, email newsletter, and Twitter and Facebook outlets to let supporters know about your Google+ page. Do this monthly.

7. **Posting everyone else's content except yours**. By all means mix it up with other people's posts on your page, but strive for the majority of the content to be yours.

Five Great Examples to Learn From

1. **Zoo Atlanta** (plus.google.com/u/0/+ZooAtlanta/posts). Zoo Atlanta posts excellent visual content that fans love. It uses Google Hangouts as a professional networking tool, holding regularly scheduled

meetings with other small zoos and aquariums to discuss best practices and networking opportunities. You can often find Zoo Atlanta sharing the content of its colleague zoos around the country.

2. **Children's National Medical Center** (plus.google.com/ u/0/+childrensnational/posts). CNMC uses Google+ to establish itself as a thought leader and to connect with doctors and other medical professionals as well as parents and caregivers. It provides a healthy stream of unique content on Google+.

3. **Food Revolution Community** (plus.google.com/ u/0/+FoodRevolutionCommunity/about). Food Revolution Community is in the top 500 pages on Google+ with good reason. It serves up delicious photos (food photos play very well on Google+), helpful resources for advocates, plus regular Hangout opportunities to hear from experts like The Renegade Lunch Lady, Chef Ann Cooper, and policy experts from the Harvard School of Public Health.

4. **9/11 Memorial** (plus.google.com/+911Memorial/posts). This is a page that knows what its community wants—to honor and remember. The page highlight the stories of the people affected by 9/11, the visitors who come to the memorial to pay their respects, and fundraising opportunities that help 9/11 heroes and their families.

5. **KQED Science** (plus.google.com/+KQEDSCIENCE). KQED Science is the science news department of public broadcaster KQED in Northern California, and its Google+ page is a great example of how you can break a large nonprofit down by programs so you can focus on one audience and one message.

Chapter Twenty-Four
Video

What's Different about This Communications Channel

Video is probably the best online medium for storytelling. It can capture emotions in ways that still photos can't. Making videos used to involve complicated and expensive cameras and editing software, but now just about anyone can make a video. You just need access to a camera or smartphone and the Internet. Low-budget videos made with cheap video cameras have the ability to reach millions of people through video sites like YouTube and Vimeo.

Video can bring your supporters into the everyday nitty-gritty aspects of your organization, and it can also bring increased visibility for your cause. It's easy to share videos on social media and embed them in your website or blog.

You can create a video series, use videos to support a campaign, or just create a stand-alone video. Some nonprofits are even using videos for their annual reports. To further increase engagement, you can ask your supporters to submit their own videos.

While a video that you create quickly can end up being successful, more often than not, to get an engaging video that does what you want it to do, you need to invest a lot of time in planning and creating.

I would like to thank Danny Alpert, executive producer, and the rest of the team at See3 for help with these video tips and examples.

Seven Ways to Make Your Content Work Here

1. **Keep it simple**. The best stories take a complicated situation and break it down to one simple message. The story you should tell in your video should have one idea or theme, or else the viewer may miss the point. Don't confuse the viewer with too many messages.

2. **Connect to your viewer**. Most viewers won't really be interested in your nonprofit's story unless you connect your video to the things they care about. Make the viewers feel as though your nonprofit's future is connected to theirs and that it can only be achieved by the nonprofit and the viewers together.

3. **Give the viewer the next step**. Once viewers have watched your whole video, they need to know what to do next. Be sure to include a clear call to action, and then make it easy for them to follow through with that action.

4. **Make it personal**. Videos works most effectively when they create a sense of identification between the viewers and the people in the story. People connect to people, not 501(c)s. Make sure you are not talking just about your programs or policies but also about the people behind them.

5. **Be authentic**. Having a genuine story to tell is always more important than production values. A real emotion is the most powerful weapon you have. If you try to fake it, your audience members will know it instinctively, and you will lose them, however high the visual quality of the video.

6. **Let others do the talking**. Hearing from people outside your organization, whether they're volunteers or the people who benefit from your cause, is the best way for others to learn its story. Let others brag on your organization and its cause. It will have a much better effect than people inside the organization saying how awesome it is.

7. **Create a serial**. Having a series of videos on a particular topic will help you build a bigger audience and generate more buzz for your organization and its project.

Seven Mistakes to Avoid

1. **Being irrelevant**. Connect your nonprofit's story to the spirit of the times. The viewer will always encounter your story in the here and now. How does it connect? Keep an eye on politics, culture, and other current events, and find stories that connect to yours.

2. **Not appealing to the emotions of the viewer**. Feelings make people act. Avoid policy talk and intellectual language. Say something funny and make them laugh. Share something heartbreaking and make them cry.

3. **Not having a goal**. You need to understand why you are making the video and what purpose it serves. Is it to fundraise, to raise awareness, to say thanks? Is this video for donors or the board or volunteers?

4. **Saving the best for last**. Most people decide whether they are going to finish watching a video within thirty seconds of starting it. You need to make sure you are grabbing their attention within the first few seconds of the video.

5. **Not asking for help**. Do you have someone on staff who is a good videographer? Or maybe an intern or volunteer? Would a board member let you film at his business? Ask around to see if you already know someone who can help with creating, shooting, and editing your video.

6. **Having bad sound**. Even if you don't have fancy equipment, you should try to eliminate background noise as much as possible. If you are interviewing someone, don't film near an AC or heating unit, and keep everyone in the background quiet. Ask whoever is producing the video about audio adjustments that can be made during production.

7. **Not integrating the video into all communications channels**. Don't just post the video on YouTube. Embed it into your organization's website or a blog post. Share on Facebook. Link to it in emails and tweets.

Five Great Examples to Learn From

1. **Invisible People** (invisiblepeople.tv/blog). Invisible People's *vlog* (that is, a blog that revolves around videos) is a heart-wrenching, unfiltered look at what it means to be homeless. It lets the people the organization wants to help tell their own stories, taking the viewer directly into the world of the homeless.

2. **Greater Chicago Food Depository** (www.chicagosfoodbank.org/site/ PageServer?pagename=annual_report_food). The Greater Chicago Food Depository created a series of videos for its 2010–2011 annual report. The videos thank donors and tell the story of how the food bank is helping their community.

3. **Georgia Aquarium** (www.youtube.com/watch?feature=player_ embedded&v=__nE1ZZigfA#!). For World Oceans Day the Georgia Aquarium asked its visitors a few questions, about why the oceans were important and what we should do to protect them, and then posted the answers on YouTube. This video was part of a larger social media campaign the Georgia Aquarium did for World Oceans Day.

4. **Protect Our Defenders** (www.youtube.com/user/ ProtectOurDefenders). The YouTube channel of Protect Our Defenders is full of stories from people who have experienced sexual abuse while serving in the military. These firsthand accounts give a voice to those who feel they have been ignored, and let others know about this issue.

5. **San Francisco Education Fund** (www.youtube.com/watch?v=BDHcesZ GNxs&feature=plcp). This short, animated video explains exactly what the San Francisco Education Fund does and how it does it.

Chapter Twenty-Five
Images

What's Different about This Communications Channel

Being able to convey what your cause stands for visually is imperative, especially with the advent of photo-sharing social networks and websites like Instagram and Pinterest. Facebook has placed a bigger emphasis on photos and graphic images lately. Websites now feature bigger images. Big blocks of text and clip art are not going to cut it anymore.

"A picture is worth a thousand words" is a cliché for a reason. Photos, infographics, and other images can convey in one glance what a tweet, a newsletter article, or even a whole blog post cannot. A photo of a mother and child can appeal to your readers' emotions. From one photo you can learn that they need help. A well-designed "Donate Now" button can catch a visitor's eye, and an infographic containing key findings from a study can relay in seconds what could take hours to read.

Seven Ways to Make Your Content Work Here

1. **Use the right photo resolution**. As described earlier, you shouldn't try to use the same photo file for both print and online newsletters. Print newsletters need photos with a resolution of at least 300 dpi at the correct size. When you put a photo from an online source into a print newsletter, it will look pixelated (with the pixels visible as little squares) or blurry.

2. **Use the right format**. Some social networks, email newsletter templates, and blogging platforms will not let you upload certain types of image formats. The jpeg and gif formats are your best bet, with gifs being better for graphics and images with fewer colors. The gifs can also support animation. The jpegs are better for photographs and images with lots of different colors.

3. **Add a Pin It button**. Chapter 26 is devoted to Pinterest, but I need to mention here that if you are posting vibrant images or infographics on Pinterest, you need to have a "Pin It" button, just as you would have a "Tweet" button for sharing on Twitter or a "Like" button for sharing on Facebook.

4. **Pick interesting shots**. As I've emphasized previously, yes, we want people photos, but the same old award ceremony and big-check photos are uninspiring and have nothing to do with your mission.

5. **Consider hiring a professional photographer**. Or if you can't afford a professional, at least enlist a volunteer or staff member who knows how to use a good camera.

6. **Plan for search engine optimization (SEO)**. Search engine bots can't read text in infographics, so search engine rankings won't be all that affected by the image itself. Make sure your title and alt text include keywords and that you supply a few sentences explaining the image.

7. **Include a call to action**. You've gotten attention with a beautiful photograph or helpful infographic. Now what? Make sure you have given viewers an opportunity to follow up on the image, even if it's just a link to your nonprofit's website.

Seven Mistakes to Avoid

1. **Making people look bad**. I'll remind you again that, unless you are trying to playfully poke fun at someone or genuinely make them look bad because they are an adversary of some kind, you want to make sure that any photos you use make the people in them look

good. When changing the size of a photo, make sure you keep the ratio of width to height constant so people don't look stretched out or squished.

2. **Focusing on a big-check donation**. Big-check pictures indicate to readers that the problem has been solved and there is no need to care any more about it.

3. **Not having relevant data**. Infographics are popular for a reason, but you need to make sure the data you offer in your visualization are telling a story people will want to hear.

4. **Lining everyone up**. Don't use the big group lineups for photographs—a close-up of one or two people is more engaging than a photo of thirty people lined up that is taken from so far away you can't see anyone's face.

5. **Not linking on Facebook to the full infographic**. Infographics need to be big enough that you can read all the information on them. Facebook will shrink them down automatically. Make sure you put a link to the full graphic (either on your website or a photo-sharing site like Flickr) in your description.

6. **Ignoring alt text**. Most email clients do not automatically display images in emails. So you may have beautiful graphics, but your readers may not be seeing them. When the images are turned off, the *alt text* (alternative text) is displayed instead, so make sure you include language that explains what the images are.

7. **Using cheesy clip art**. With so many options available, there is no reason to include those horrible clip art images in your newsletter or on your website. They look cheap and unprofessional.

Five Great Examples to Learn From

1. **Girlstart** (www.girlstart.org/about-us/by-the-numbers). I am big fan of alternative forms of annual reports, and Girlstart's 2012 annual report infographic, "By the Numbers," displays the highlights of the

year as easy-to-read graphics and pie charts. Supporters can see at a glance how many girls were helped, without sifting through pages and pages of a traditional nonprofit annual report. Infographics are also easy to share via email or social networking, making it more likely that supporters will share the results with others.

2. **Monterey Bay Aquarium** (www.facebook.com/montereybayaquarium). The Monterey Bay Aquarium posts a lot of images on Facebook, along with caption contests and other ways to engage viewers. In 2012, it released Valentine's Day e-cards featuring animals from the aquarium and encouraged people to share these images with their Valentines on Facebook.

3. **Operation Smile** (www.operationsmile.org). From its before and after board on Pinterest to *The Smile Blog*, Operation Smile is all about photographs. Operation Smile can convey what it does in simple before and after images. It also chronicles through photographs what its staff and volunteers are doing around the world for children with cleft lips and palates. While the before and after pictures of the children would be powerful on their own, seeing the work that must be done by the doctors, nurses, and other volunteers helps supporters get a better sense of all that is involved with these operations.

4. **Epic Change** (www.flickr.com/photos/epicchange/6198868204/in/set-72157627691593573). I got an awesome thank-you email from Epic Change that did everything right. It was personable and positive, it reported results, and it made me, the donor, feel like a hero. One of the best things was the class graduation photo. Instead of the usual lineup of kids, it showed one child. He was wearing his graduation cap, and you can see other children with their caps on in the background, so you know what's going on in the picture. But by focusing tightly on his smiling face, this photo made you feel instant joy for what these children had accomplished. This nonprofit also posts its photos to its Flickr photostream, and yes, it had lineup shots available, but it wisely went with the close-up for this email.

5. **WithinReach** (www.youtube.com/watch?v=3CBXeWYjx6o). You don't always need to hire a photographer to get great photos. Just ask! For its ParentHelp123 website, which connects families with health and food resources, WithinReach began the Washington Cute Baby Campaign, asking for videos and photos of babies from the state of Washington growing and developing throughout their first two years. This great example of supporter-generated content curation culminated in a video that was eventually used for a TV spot that got attention (cute babies!) and that showed families where they could find the services they need.

Chapter Twenty-Six
Pinterest

What's Different about This Communications Channel

I'll admit I still have mixed feelings about Pinterest, mostly because it's still fairly new, and if you are going to invest time in social media, I think Facebook and Twitter are better options. Nevertheless, there is tremendous excitement about Pinterest, and lots of people I respect believe it has enormous power—if you do it right.

Pinterest is quickly catching up to Twitter among Internet users. According to the Pew Research Center's Internet & American Life Project survey *The Demographics of Social Media Users—2012*, 15 percent of Internet users are on Pinterest, compared to 16 percent on Twitter (Duggan and Brenner, 2013). The big demographic takeaway is its appeal to women. Yes, there are men on Pinterest, but the overwhelming majority of users are women.

The fact that Pinterest is so visually oriented has huge potential. But you need to have the right kind of visual content either to share yourself or to curate from others. The stock photographs you might be using for blog posts or photographs taken at an event really aren't going to cut it here. The images on Pinterest need to be either captivating or informative. You can also pin videos to Pinterest. Animal rescue organizations are likely to thrive on Pinterest, with their never-ending stock of cute animal pictures, but any nonprofit can create compelling imagery, whether in the form of photographs, videos, or infographics (or through *pinning* other people's stuff!). You just need a little creativity.

Seven Ways to Make Your Content Work Here

1. **Create a business account for your nonprofit**. While there isn't too much difference on Pinterest between a personal account and a business one at this time, Pinterest may be developing different options for those accounts. If you have a business account, followers will have an easier time finding you, and you'll be notified of any added features.

2. **Repin others' pins**. Much like retweeting, repinning allows you to share other users' content within Pinterest. Repinning, as opposed to pinning straight from a web source, helps build the Pinterest community at large and establishes you as curator of interesting content.

3. **Craft a good description**. The description of a pin is featured prominently on the Pinterest home page so it needs to be well thought out but not too long. A sentence or two will suffice. Explain what the pin has to do with your cause if it isn't from your website.

4. **Feature do-it-yourself boards**. Pinterest gained traction as a great place to find arts and crafts projects and yummy recipes. Find a way to relate your nonprofit's cause to a fun project. You don't need to think up the project yourself—just repin someone else's idea or photograph.

5. **Highlight other nonprofits**. Even if they aren't in your industry, find some nonprofits doing good things on Pinterest and add their content to a separate board.

6. **Add a Pin It button**. I mentioned in the chapter on images that you need to give folks the ability to add your content to Pinterest. Pinterest is great for SEO, as all pins link back to their original source, creating important backlinks to your site. Adding a "Pin It" button will make it easier for your blog readers or website visitors to pin your images.

7. **Add text or your logo to your images**. Consider discreetly adding, through Photoshop or another visual editor, your nonprofit's logo or name so it will be seen on the image itself. If you think it will detract too much from the image, use a translucent font color so it blends in

better. Just your nonprofit's name or logo in a bottom corner of the image should work and will also help you get proper credit if the image is posted elsewhere.

Seven Mistakes to Avoid

1. **Having only one board**. Boards on Pinterest are sort of like tags or categories on blogs. Think of how you can organize your content, and create as many different boards as you need.

2. **Using a pdf for your infographics**. Make sure your infographic or anything else you want shared on Pinterest is in a picture file format, such as jpeg. Pinterest looks for photo or video files and won't see a pdf.

3. **Pinning only your stuff**. Pinterest specifically says in its best practices section to pin from various sources. Just as in all social media, the idea is to interact with others, not stand off to the side screaming at others about your cause. Pinning other content makes it a lot easier for you to round out your page as well.

4. **Not paying attention to repin sources**. While Pinterest does encourage you to repin other content, check out the website that content links back to, just to make sure it isn't offensive or doesn't undermine everything your cause stands for.

5. **Ignoring keywords**. You can boost your search results by using keywords in the names of your boards and your pin and in board descriptions.

6. **Sticking to your very narrow field**. Since you can create a variety of boards, you can easily add a board that has a little broader topic. For example, if your organization is an environmental agency, create a board that features recipes with sustainable ingredients. Have a board with things that make people laugh. Be creative!

7. **Posting pins too close together**. As on other social media platforms, your pins will easily be swept aside throughout the day as more

pins are added by others. Space your posts out, just as you would on Twitter or Facebook, to get the biggest audience. However, you can pin many times a day.

Five Great Examples to Learn From

1. **PETA** (pinterest.com/officialpeta). PETA sticks to Pinterest's roots by posting vegan recipes and do-it-yourself projects that aren't harmful to animals. It offers relevant seasonal boards with ideas and recipes for holidays and events like the Super Bowl. It also has boards of celebrities who endorse PETA's cause, of animal-friendly fashions and beauty supplies, and of PETA merchandise for sale.

2. **Trees, Water & People** (pinterest.com/treeswater). This nonprofit has a board each for trees, water, and people, with relevant infographics, photos, and quotes. It also has boards dedicated to environmental issues, pinning what other groups are doing in those areas, and a board that allows others to pin ideas or news on renewable energy.

3. **Heifer International** (pinterest.com/heiferint). Heifer International breaks its boards down into such expected categories as animals, videos, people, giving, and infographics, but it also has a board where Heifer International staff can pin content they find interesting. This board has a disclaimer stating that its pins are from staff and may not reflect the views of Heifer International; at the same time, this staff involvement gives the organization's profile more personality and an element of fun.

4. **National Committee to Preserve Social Security and Medicare** (pinterest.com/ncpssm). NCPSSM mixes serious politics with humorous images and stories on its Pinterest page, which is geared toward seniors. Activism and nostalgia are perfectly melded here.

5. **BookEnds** (pinterest.com/bookendsla). BookEnds works with students to collect children's books to give to the less fortunate. It does a good job of posting thank-you notes from the kids who have benefitted and

posting recommendations about kids' books, but its People Reading board is a particularly good example of what you can do with Pinterest. This great board is made up solely of pictures of famous people reading. Most of them are artistically posed and photographed, but they're really just people reading. A simple idea for sure, and one that can easily be adapted for other nonprofits' communications.

Chapter Twenty-Seven
Mobile Devices

What's Different about This Communications Channel

Smartphones and tablets put the world at our fingertips wherever we are. We can check our email and the weather, pay bills, find the best restaurant nearby, and connect with our friends and family through texts and social networking apps.

Nonprofits know that texts, emails, and apps are all popular ways for people to communicate using their smartphones, but mobile marketing seems to be one frontier most nonprofits don't want to explore. It seems too hard, too techy, too overwhelming. But there are some relatively easy things your organization can do to benefit from the popularity of mobile devices.

At the very least you need to make sure your email and web content will work on smartphones. You can also take advantage of these devices with apps created specifically for your organization and with text fundraising campaigns.

Seven Ways to Make Your Content Work Here

1. **Know what you want to do on mobile devices**. Are you going to start texting donors with news and updates? Start a text-to-donate campaign? Or do you just want your nonprofit's website to work on smartphones and tablets? Brainstorm with your staff about ways you could use mobile marketing and fundraising.

2. **Collect numbers now**. Even if you are just considering the possibility of connecting with your supporters via text, you need to start asking for their cell phone numbers now. Add a mobile sign-up form to your website, or add a mobile number field to your regular contact information sheets.

3. **Optimize your website**. Talk to your web designer about responsive web design. You want to be sure your website will be able to recognize the type of device it's being viewed on and able to adjust its format accordingly. If you created your organization's website yourself, chances are you can find a plug-in that will adjust your site automatically when a smartphone is detected.

4. **Ensure that your donation page works**. If you will be directing people to your organization's donation page via texts alerts or QR codes, then you may need to create a separate donation page that is mobile friendly. Test the page on different types of phones and tablets to make sure it works on all operating systems.

5. **Think ahead about text fundraising**. If you want to start a text-to-donate campaign, do some research and strategizing first. Know why you want to run this type of campaign, how your donors will respond, and how you will promote it. Also look into the different services you can hire to run your campaign. Most charge setup fees, monthly fees, or processing fees. Some charge all of them. Do the math, and make sure you won't pay more than you take in. You will also need to deal with wireless carriers, and some won't work with smaller nonprofits.

6. **Watch your character count**. Just as with tweets, you have only a certain number of characters to work with when texting your supporters; 140 characters should work. If you go over that limit, your texts may be split into two messages. This is annoying and could cost your supporters money.

7. **Go easy on the textspeak**. Yes, those who are receiving your texts are more than likely text savvy and will know what BTW (by the way),

and FWIW (for what it's worth) mean, but you still don't want to come across like a thirteen-year-old in your messages (unless your audience members are in fact teens and young adults).

Seven Mistakes to Avoid

1. **Not testing on a variety of mobile devices**. You need to look at every aspect of your nonprofit's website on all different kinds of mobile devices. Open the website on your smartphone, and make sure it is mobile friendly. Then, find coworkers or friends with different types of smartphones, and check it out on those as well. Then look at the website on an iPad and other tablets. Different phones and tablets run on different operating systems. Text and images can look drastically different from device to device.

2. **Not testing in different browsers**. Smartphones used to connect you to whatever browser your phone's maker had installed. Now you can install Chrome, Safari, Firefox, and other browsers on smartphones and tablets, and these browsers work in different ways. Look at your organization's website in all browsers, and make sure it's looking good.

3. **Having landing pages that aren't mobile friendly**. If you use QR codes or other linking methods for supporters to connect with you on the go, make sure the page they are sent to is designed for smartphone and tablet use. Make sure any web form on that page looks normal and that users don't have to scroll and pan to see everything.

4. **Thinking you have to have an app**. Not every cause needs an app. If you don't have helpful information that people will need to access regularly then you probably don't need an app—your mobile site will suffice.

5. **Not giving enough information about your app**. The description of your app that appears in Google Play and the Apple store and other app sources needs to let readers know why they need to install your

app. Just saying what your nonprofit does to help the world isn't enough. They don't need an app for that. What does your app do that will help them specifically?

6. **Not getting permission to text**. Your organization should never send a text message to someone who hasn't opted in to receiving these messages, even if you have been given the supporter's cell number. Texts can cost the receiver money, depending on her wireless plan.

7. **Texting too often**. Even when you do have permission to text supporters, texting too often can be annoying and can cause people to opt out. Again, depending on a supporter's plan, he might have only a limited number of texts before he is charged for them.

Five Great Examples to Learn From

1. **Museum of London** (www.museumoflondon.org.uk/Resources/app/you-are-here-app/home.html). The Museum of London offers a mobile app that facilitates a trip through time. Its Streetmuseum app allows users to go through the streets of London and see what present-day scenes and locations looked like long ago, offering a window through time. The user can then continue this journey by checking out related historical objects in the museum.

2. **WNYC** (www.wnyc.org/articles/features/2011/may/05/your-favorite-bird-watching-spots-nyc). A radio station in New York City, WNYC, asked listeners and readers to text in the word "bird" and the location of their favorite bird-watching site in the city. From that information the station created a live Google Map that lets others know where to spot certain birds.

3. **Children's Museum of Pittsburgh** (pittsburghkids.org). The website of the Children's Museum of Pittsburgh is a great example of responsive web design. Depending on whether you visit this website on your desktop, tablet, or smartphone, you will get the version that's formatted to look and work its best on your device.

4. **Capital Area Food Bank of Texas in Austin** (www.austinfoodbank
   .org/ipheedaneed). This Austin food bank has created a fun app for
   iPhones that not only allows supporters to stay updated on upcoming events, volunteer, and donate but that also includes recipes and a
   fun game called "Catch the Can." The game allows you to stock your
   virtual pantry with healthy options to earn appliances for your virtual
   kitchen.

5. **Franciscan Friars of the Holy Name Province** (www.hnp.org/
   publications/hnp_today_view.cfm?iid=218&aid=4423). The Franciscan
   Friars of the Holy Name Province have initiated a "Text a Friar"
   program that allows people to text in prayer requests. They received
   more than 4,000 prayer requests in the program's first week alone.

Conclusion: Don't Go If You Won't Have Fun

Nonprofit communications in general and content marketing in particular are hard work. There is always more to do. You always wish you had more time to make the piece you just published even better. You have so much to learn, and you feel you are on shaky ground more often than solid. You don't have the support or resources to really do the best job possible for your good cause.

And yet, here you are, reading the conclusion to this book. Even if you are reading this before starting the book, the message is the same: don't jump into this profession unless you see all of these struggles as part of the fun, at least most of the time.

I love nonprofit marketing. I love creating content. I love nonprofits. I suspect you do too. We're the ones who can make really good things happen, and we have a great time while we do it. It's OK to get frustrated, and you will definitely get stressed out. But take a deep breath, and put one foot in front of the other. The view at the top is spectacular. It's worth it, I promise.

Nonprofits Included in This Book

The lessons learned in this book come from the collective wisdom of people working at literally thousands of nonprofits who have interacted with me directly via webinars, workshops, comments on blog posts, conversations via social media, and more. The following 118 nonprofits are the ones I have included in the book by name, as examples for you to learn from. Individuals from many of them have shared details and stories with me directly via surveys and interviews. I have highlighted some additional nonprofits because I admire their work and want you to learn from them as well.

350.org

9/11 Memorial

Almost Home

American Diabetes Association

American Red Cross

The Arc of Atlantic County

Archie Bray Foundation for the Ceramic Arts

ASPCA

Bergstrom-Mahler Museum

Best Friends Animal Society

Beyond Borders

Black River Action Team

BookEnds

California Genealogical Society

Canadian Opera Company

Capital Area Food Bank of Texas in Austin

Case Foundation

Center for Children and Families

Chaplaincy

Charity: Water

Chemung ARC

Children of the Nations

Children's Museum of Pittsburgh

Children's National Medical Center

Coalition for Sonoran Desert Protection

Community Neighborhood Housing Services

Community Thread

CompassPoint Nonprofit Services

Conservation Trust for North Carolina

Crisis Center, Johnson County, Iowa

Cross-Lines Community Outreach, Inc.

Curtis Institute of Music

Dana-Farber Cancer Institute

DePaul Industries

DoSomething.org

Earthjustice

Epic Change

Extreme Response International

Feeding America

Firelight Foundation

Food Revolution Community

Foundation Center

Franciscan Friars of the Holy Name Province

Gaston Day School

Georgia Aquarium

Girlstart

Greater Chicago Food Depository

Greater Cincinnati Foundation

Greenpeace USA

Grist

Groundwire

Gyalwa Gyatso Buddhist Center

Hebrew University

Heifer International

Homeboy Industries

HOPE *worldwide*

Humane Society of United States

Invisible Children

Invisible People

Kiva

KQED Science

KYK9 Search and Reunite Services

Land Trust Alliance

Legal Aid of Western Missouri

Legal Information for Families Today

Lending Hands of Michigan

Lillian's List

London Fire Brigade

Longview

Loveland Center

Lupus Foundation of America, Greater Ohio Chapter

Mentoring Partnership of Southwestern Pennsylvania

Michael J. Fox Foundation for Parkinson's Research

Mission India

Monterey Bay Aquarium

Museum of London

National Aquarium

National Campaign to Prevent Teen Pregnancy

National Committee to Preserve Social Security and Medicare

National Parks Conservation Association

National WIC Association

National Wildlife Federation

Nonprofit Technology Network

The Nature Conservancy

Ohio Environmental Council

Operation Smile

Ottawa Humane Society

PETA

Place des Arts

Planned Parenthood of Rhode Island

Policy Matters Ohio

PRAESA (Project for the Study of Alternative Education in South Africa)/Nal'ibali

Protect Our Defenders

Public Advocate Inc.

Pulmonary Hypertension Association

Queens Council on the Arts

(RED)

ReSurge International

Salvation Army

San Diego Zoo

San Francisco Education Fund

Save the Redwoods League

Scholarship America

St. Jude Children's Hospital

Trees, Water & People

UNICEF New Zealand

The United Methodist Church

United Nations Population Fund

Virginia Beach Public Library

VolunteerMatch

Washington Humane Society

We Are Visible

WEAVE

Wiser.org

WithinReach

WNYC

Youth Education in the Arts

Zoo Atlanta

References

Chapter One

Association of Fundraising Professionals and The Urban Institute. (2012). *2012 Fundraising Effectiveness Survey Report.* www.afpnet.org/files/ContentDocuments/FEP2012Report.pdf.

Blackbaud. (2012, October). *2012 State of the Nonprofit Industry, Survey Summary Report.* www.blackbaud.com/files/resources/soni_final_2012.pdf.

Brenner, Joanna. (2013, January). *Pew Internet: Mobile.* pewinternet.org/Commentary/2012/February/Pew-Internet-Mobile.aspx.

Burk, Penelope. (2003). *Donor Centered Fundraising: How to Hold on to Your Donors and Raise Much More Money.* Chicago: Cynus Applied Research, Inc.

Burk, Penelope. (2012, June). *The Cygnus Donor Survey 2012: Where Philanthropy Is Headed in 2012.* Cygnus Applied Research. www.cygresearch.com.

Ericsson ConsumerLab. (2011, May). *Consumers Take Their Lives into the Cloud.* www.ericsson.com/news/110512_cloud_244188810_c.

Flannery, Helen, and Harris, Rob. (2011, July). *2011 donorCentrics Internet and Multi-channel Giving Benchmarking Report.* www.blackbaud.com/targetananalytics/multi-channel-report.

MarketingCharts. (2012, September). *Younger Boomers Outspend Older Boomers, Seniors on CPG.* www.marketingcharts.com/wp/topics/demographics/younger-boomers-outspend-older-boomers-seniors-on-cpg-23454.

Pew Internet & American Life Project. (2012, December). *Demographics of Internet Users.* www.pewinternet.org/Trend-Data-(Adults)/Whos-Online.aspx.

Rainie, Lee. (2012, October). *25% of American Adults Own Tablet Computers.* www.pewinternet.org/Reports/2012/Tablet-Ownership-August-2012.aspx.

Wolfe, Ira. (2012, July). "A Digital Divide Grows Between Baby Boomers . . . and Other Boomers?" *Huffington Post*. www.huffingtonpost.com/ira-wolfe/baby-boomers-technology_b_1663751.html.

Chapter Two

Bhagat, Vinay, Loeb, Pam, and Rovner, Mark. (2010, March). *The Next Generation of American Giving*. www.convio.com/signup/next-generation/next-generation-resources.html.

Charity Dynamics and Nonprofit Technology Network. (2012, September). *Nonprofit Donor Engagement Benchmark Study: Insights into Donor Engagement Behavior and Preferences*. www.nonprofitdonorengagement.com.

DonorVoice. (2011, September). *What Is Your Relationship Status with Your Donors?* thedonorvoice.com.

Leroux Miller, Kivi. (2013, January). *2013 Nonprofit Communications Trends Report*. nonprofitmarketingguide.com/2013.

Chapter Three

Bhagat, Vinay, Loeb, Pam, and Rovner, Mark. (2010, March). *The Next Generation of American Giving*. www.convio.com/signup/next-generation/next-generation-resources.html.

Blackbaud. (2012, November). *Donor Perspectives: An Investigation into What Drives Your Donors to Give*. www.blackbaud.com/files/resources/downloads/10.12_DonorProfile_whitepaper_FINAL2.pdf.

Charity Dynamics and Nonprofit Technology Network. (2012, September). *Nonprofit Donor Engagement Benchmark Study: Insights into Donor Engagement Behavior and Preferences*. www.nonprofitdonorengagement.com.

Charney, Jennifer. (2012, December). "What Would Your Supporters Say about Your Publications?" *Kivi's Nonprofit Communications Blog*. www.nonprofitmarketingguide.com/blog/2012/12/10/what-would-your-supporters-say-about-your-publications.

Corporation for National and Community Service. (2011, August). *Volunteering in America: 2011 Research Highlights*. www.aarp.org/content/dam/aarp/livable-communities/learn/civic/volunteering-in-america-research-highlights-2011-aarp.pdf.

Daigneault, Steve, Davis, Mark, and Sybrant, Milo. (2011, June). *Connecting Online Advocacy and Fundraising.* www.blackbaud.com/files/resources/downloads/WhitePaper_ConnectingOnlineAdvocacyAndFundraising.pdf.

Fowler, James, and Christakis, Nicholas. (2010, March 23). "Cooperative Behavior Cascades in Human Social Networks." *Proceedings of the National Academy of Sciences of the United States of America.* www.ncbi.nlm.nih.gov/pmc/articles/PMC2851803/?report=abstract).

Kanter, Beth, and Pain, Katie. (2012). *Measuring the Networked Nonprofit: Using Data to Change the World.* San Francisco: Jossey-Bass.

Leroux Miller, Kivi. (2013, January). *2013 Nonprofit Communications Trends Report.* nonprofitmarketingguide.com/2013.

Salant, Jonathan. (2011, September). "Bachmann Following Obama Lead in Wooing Small Donors for 2012." *Bloomberg.* www.bloomberg.com/news/2011–09–12/bachmann-following-obama-lead-in-wooing-small-donors-to-show-2012-momentum.html.

US Bureau of Labor Statistics. (2011, September). "Table 1: Volunteers by Selected Characteristics." Economic News Release. www.bls.gov/news.release/volun.t01.htm.

Van Wyk, Jon, and Brooks, Jeff. (2010, July). "How Many People Are Likely to Give Now and in the Future." *Future Fundraising Now* (blog). www.futurefundraisingnow.com/future-fundraising/2010/07/how-many-people-are-likely-to-give-now-and-in-the-future.html.

Chapter Four

American Diabetes Association. (2012). Advocates in Action Calendar. www.diabetes.org/assets/pdfs/advocacy/2012-advocate-in-action-calendar.pdf.

Brooks, Raven. (2012, March). "The Anatomy of Kony 2012." *Case Studies.* www.netrootsfoundation.org/2012/03/the-anatomy-of-kony-2012.

Burk, Penelope. (2012, June). *The Cygnus Donor Survey 2012: Where Philanthropy Is Headed in 2012.* Cygnus Applied Research. www.cygresearch.com.

Charity Dynamics and Nonprofit Technology Network. (2012, September). *Nonprofit Donor Engagement Benchmark Study: Insights into Donor Engagement Behavior and Preferences.* www.nonprofitdonorengagement.com.

Dixon, Julie, and Keyes, Denise. (2013, Winter). "The Permanent Disruption of Social Media." *Stanford Social Innovation Review.* www.ssireview.org/articles/entry/the_permanent_disruption_of_social_media.

DonorVoice. (2011, September). *What Is Your Relationship Status with Your Donors?* thedonorvoice.com.

Eglin, Shayna, and Hankin, Stefan. (2012). *The Advocacy Gap: Research for Better Advocacy.* dl.dropbox.com/u/2336449/AdvocacyGap-ResearchReport.pdf.

Ellis, Susan J. (2000, August). *If Not Your Home Page, Then Where?* www.energizeinc.com/hot/aug00.html.

Ellis, Susan. (n.d.). *Q &A with Faculty: Volunteer Management.* University of Wisconsin-Extension. www.uwex.edu/ces/cced/nonprofits/management/q-a7.cfm.

Greater Good Science Center, University of California, Berkeley. (2013). *What Is Altruism?* greatergood.berkeley.edu/topic/altruism/definition#why_practice.

Groundwire. (n.d.). *Groundwire Engagement Pyramid.* blogs.salesforcefoundation.org/2012/09/13/groundwires-10-rules-of-engagement.

Hope Consulting and GuideStar. (2011). *Money for Good II: Driving Dollars to the Highest Performing Nonprofits.* www.guidestar.org/ViewCmsFile.aspx?ContentID=4040.

Leroux Miller, Kivi. (2010). *The Nonprofit Marketing Guide: High-Impact, Low-Cost Ways to Build Support for Your Good Cause.* San Francisco: Jossey-Bass.

Leroux Miller, Kivi. (2012a, April). *Fundraising Stories That Don't Work—and What's Different about the Ones That Do.* www.nonprofitmarketingguide.com/resources/fundraising/fundraising-stories-that-dont-work-and-whats-different-about-the-ones-that-do/#.

Leroux Miller, Kivi. (2012b, November). "Website Content for Homeless People?" *Kivi's Nonprofit Communications Blog.* www.nonprofitmarketingguide.com/blog/2012/11/15/website-content-for-homeless-people.

Leroux Miller, Kivi. (2013, January). *2013 Nonprofit Communications Trends Report.* nonprofitmarketingguide.com/2013.

Lyubomirsky, Sonja. (2008, December). *The How of Happiness: A New Approach to Getting the Life You Want.* New York: Penguin Books. thehowofhappiness.com.

MAP for Nonprofits. (2012, March). *Unleashing Innovation: Using Everyday Technology to Improve Nonprofit Services.* www.mapfornonprofits.org/index.asp?Type=B_BASIC&SEC={78DB52F5–40A1–4BFE-9ABC-311F165BFB74}.

National Coalition for the Homeless. (2009, July). *Employment and Homelessness.* www.nationalhomeless.org/factsheets/employment.html.

Ogilvy Public Relations Worldwide and The Center for Social Impact Communication at Georgetown University. (2011, November). *Dynamics of Cause Engagement.* www.slideshare.net/georgetowncsic/dynamics-of-cause-engagement-final-report.

"Kony 2012 in Numbers." (2012, April). *The Guardian*. www.guardian.co.uk/news/datablog/2012/apr/20/kony-2012-facts-numbers.

Theory of Change Community. (2013). *How Does the Theory of Change Work?* www.theoryofchange.org/about/how-does-theory-of-change-work.

University of Southern California. (2011, December). "Homeless Teens Consider Smart Phone as Important as Food." News release. www.usc.edu/uscnews/newsroom/news_release.php?id=2571.

Wallis, David. (2012, November 8). "Getting into a Benefactor's Head." *New York Times*.

Chapter Five

Harrison, Scott. (2006). "Scott's Story."charitywater.org/about/scotts_story.php.

McDermott, Clare. (2013, January). "How Nonprofits Can Sidestep Content Marketing Pitfalls." contentmarketinginstitute.com/2013/01/nonprofits-content-marketing-pitfalls.

Chapter Six

Greenhalgh, Diane. (2012, November). "6 Tips for Managing Project Requests from Staff without Losing Your Own Priorities." www.nten.org/articles/2012/6-tips-for-managing-project-requests-from-staff-without-losing-your-own-priorities.

Leroux Miller, Kivi. (2012, August). "6 Tips for Nonprofit Board Retreats on Marketing." www.nonprofitmarketingguide.com/resources/professional-development/6-tips-for-board-retreats-on-marketing-your-nonprofit.

Monnell, Allison. (2011, July). "Storytelling Works: Capturing Success Stories and Sharing Them." *Kivi's Nonprofit Communications Blog*. www.nonprofitmarketingguide.com/blog/2011/07/26/storytelling-works-capturing-success-stories-and-sharing-them.

Spiegel, Beth Ann. (2012, June). "Creating a Culture Where Everyone Is a Marketer." *Kivi's Nonprofit Communications Blog*. www.nonprofitmarketingguide.com/blog/2012/06/06/creating-a-culture-where-everyone-is-a-marketer.

Chapter Seven

Jones, Eddie. (2011). *Plotting Simplified: Story Structure Tips for the Break-Out Novelist*. Raleigh, NC: Lighthouse Publishing of the Carolinas.

Chapter Nine

Burk, Penelope. (2012, June). *The Cygnus Donor Survey 2012: Where Philanthropy Is Headed in 2012.* Cygnus Applied Research. www.cygresearch.com.

Leroux Miller, Kivi. (2013, January). *2013 Nonprofit Communications Trends Report.* nonprofitmarketingguide.com/2013.

Chapter Ten

Charney, Jennifer. (2012, December). "What Would Your Supporters Say about Your Publications?" *Kivi's Nonprofit Communications Blog.* www.nonprofitmarketingguide.com/blog/2012/12/10/what-would-your-supporters-say-about-your-publications.

Chapter Eleven

Barnes, Kerry A. (2011, November). "Seniors and Social Media? Longview Says Yes!" *Kivi's Nonprofit Communications Blog.* www.nonprofitmarketingguide.com/blog/2011/11/10/seniors-and-social-media-longview-says-yes.

Dixon, Robin. (2012, June). "It Worked Because We Were Ready for It." *Kivi's Nonprofit Communications Blog.* www.nonprofitmarketingguide.com/blog/2012/06/18/it-worked-because-we-were-ready-for-it.

Scott, David Meerman. (2011). *Newsjacking: How to Inject Your Ideas into a Breaking News Story and Generate Tons of Media Coverage.* E-book. New York: Wiley.

Sims, Peter. (2011). *Little Bets: How Breakthrough Ideas Emerge from Small Discoveries.* New York: Free Press.

Chapter Twelve

Burk, Penelope. (2012, June). *The Cygnus Donor Survey 2012: Where Philanthropy Is Headed in 2012.* Cygnus Applied Research. www.cygresearch.com.

Daigneault, Steve, Davis, Mark, and Sybrant, Milo. (2011, June). *Connecting Online Advocacy and Fundraising.* www.blackbaud.com/files/resources/downloads/WhitePaper_ConnectingOnlineAdvocacyAndFundraising.pdf.

Leroux Miller, Kivi. (2012a, February). "Making Progress on Thanking Donors." *Kivi's Nonprofit Communications Blog.* www.nonprofitmarketingguide.com/blog/2012/02/15/making-progress-on-thanking-donors.

Leroux Miller, Kivi. (2012b, November). "My Favorite Post-Sandy Email." *Kivi's Nonprofit Communications Blog.* www.nonprofitmarketingguide.com/blog/2012/11/16/my-favorite-post-sandy-email.

Leroux Miller, Kivi. (2012c, January). "Success Story: A Shift in Communications Worked." *Kivi's Nonprofit Communications Blog.* www.nonprofitmarketingguide.com/blog/2012/01/26/success-story-a-shift-in-communications-worked.

Spiegel, Beth Ann. (2011, November). "The Rabbit Hole and Community Engagement." *Kivi's Nonprofit Communications Blog.* www.nonprofitmarketingguide.com/blog/2011/11/21/the-rabbit-hole-and-community-engagement.

Chapter Thirteen

Hall, Jennifer Jordan. (2012, July). "Baby Christina, Part II." *KYK9 Blog.* www.kyk9.org/blog/baby-christina-part-ii.html.

Leroux Miller, Kivi. (2012, April). *Fundraising Stories That Don't Work and What's Different about the Ones That Do.* www.nonprofitmarketingguide.com/resources/fundraising/fundraising-stories-that-dont-work-and-whats-different-about-the-ones-that-do.

Chapter Fourteen

Leroux Miller, Kivi. (2012, October). "Fabulous Example of Facebook Engagement from COTN." *Kivi's Nonprofit Communications Blog.* www.nonprofitmarketingguide.com/blog/2012/10/26/fabulous-example-of-facebook-engagement-from-cotn.

San Diego Zoo. (n.d.). *Nighttime Zoo: China Celebration.* www.sandiegozoo.org/nighttimezoo.

Chapter Fifteen

Karvetski, Kerri. (2012, November). "Using Humor: Six Reasons Why It Works." *Company K Media Blog.* www.companykmedia.com/2012/11/29/using-humor-6-reasons-why-it-works.

Leroux Miller, Kivi. (2012, October). "The Crisis Center with a Sense of Humor." *Kivi's Nonprofit Communications Blog.* www.nonprofitmarketingguide.com/blog/2012/10/25/the-crisis-center-with-a-sense-of-humor.

Schwartz, Nancy. (2012, November). *Humor Them: Sharing a Laugh Always Connects (Part One)*. gettingattention.org/articles/3373/message-development/humor-nonprofit-marketing.html.

Zaltman, Gerald, and Zaltman, Lindsay. (2008). *Marketing Metaphoria: What Deep Metaphors Reveal About the Minds of Consumers*. Boston: Harvard Business School Press.

Chapter Seventeen

Burk, Penelope. (2012, June). *The Cygnus Donor Survey 2012: Where Philanthropy Is Headed in 2012*. Cygnus Applied Research. www.cygresearch.com.

Chapter Twenty

Clark, Brian. (2006). "Writing Headlines That Get Results." www.copyblogger.com/writing-headlines-that-get-results.

Chapter Twenty-One

Duggan, Maeve, and Brenner, Joanna. (2013). *The Demographics of Social Media Users—2012*. www.pewinternet.org/Reports/2013/Social-media-users.aspx.

Chapter Twenty-Two

Duggan, Maeve, and Brenner, Joanna. (2013). *The Demographics of Social Media Users—2012*. www.pewinternet.org/Reports/2013/Social-media-users.aspx.

Chapter Twenty-Six

Duggan, Maeve, and Brenner, Joanna. (2013). *The Demographics of Social Media Users—2012*. www.pewinternet.org/Reports/2013/Social-media-users.aspx.

Index

content to evoke positive response by, 266. *See also* Influencers; Participants; Supporters

Public Advocate Inc., 217–218

Public officials, tips on working with, 87–88

Pulmonary Hypertension Association, 134–136

Q

Queens Council on the Arts, 88

R

Rainie, Lee, 11

(RED), 336

Reedus, Becci, 291

Reich, Julia, 245–246

Relevant content, 235–251; example of, 248–251; importance of, 51, 235–236; as realistic, 239–240; as refreshing, 246–248; as responsive, 242–244; as revealing, 245–246; as rewarding, 236–239; timeliness of, 241–242

Reliable performer, as voice, 106

Remember the Milk, 303

Repurposed content, 203–218; examples of value of, 203–204, 215–216; material appropriate to become, 206–207; professionals using, 204–206; recommended amount of, 140, 200, 204; time saved with, 217–218; using technology to

create, 217; ways to produce, 207–215

Research, by donors before giving, 8

Resistance: dealing with, within organization, 136–137; using metaphors to overcome, 283

Results, content focusing on, 257–260

ReSurge International, 316

Rosenthal, Robert, 28–30

Rovner, Mark, 33, 52

Royal, Sarah, 108

Ruback, Beth Ritter, 290, 291–292

S

Salant, Jonathan, 55

Salvation Army, 316

San Diego Zoo, 276

San Francisco Education Fund, 344

Sauber, Jenna, 223

Save the Redwoods League, 64–65, 208

Scholarship America, 104–105

Schulman, Kevin, 32–33, 35–36, 81

Schwartz, Nancy, 293–295

Scott, David Meerman, 225–227

Search engine optimization (SEO), 28, 104, 165, 346

Second Mile, 229

Segmenting a list, 4–5, 209

Selden, Janice, 265

Senioritis, 13

Shang, Jen, 77–78

Sidebars, 212, 216